# CRISSCROSSING PATHS

## through

## Sorry, Joy, Departure, Reunion

*William Hawke*

GYAN

ISBN 9788121219662

Published, 2019

*Published by*

GYAN

Gyan Publishing House
5, Ansari Road
Daryaganj, New Delhi-110002
Phone: 011-47034999, 9811692060
www.gyanbooks.com
E-mail: books@gyanbooks.com

Printed at: G. Print Process, Delhi.

## *Dedication*

The last line of the first three verses of the Naval Hymn of the United Kingdom, her Dominions and the United States of America end with the words ***'For those in Peril on the Sea'.*** This book, however, contains elements of Army, Navy and Air Force combat. I have therefore altered the words of the Naval Hymn to the following:

***For those in Peril on the Ground,***
***in the Sky, and on the Sea,***

and for

***Cheryl, Barbara, Brenda and Wayne***

# Contents

# Foreword

Crisscrossing Paths is an intriguing title for a book; any book. Straightaway the thought comes to mind: "Who is headed Where" or "What is happening Where". On both counts the author provides fascinating outcomes. It is a strange book. It is an intriguing book. It is an amazing book. On all counts the author holds the reader's attention to the very end on a journey that begins in the trenches of France and Flanders in World War I and from there builds on the saga of several generations of Canadians and Englishmen through World War II and the Cold War across four continents and ends again in a final journey by Capt. Elliot's descendants to Dharamsala. The Himachal town as it was between the two wars under the British Raj in a quiet and reposeful pastoral milieu where Captain Elliot retires to nurse his mind that was scarred during the First Great War of the century. It was idyllic. That was before the Dalai Lama fleeing from Tibet in 1959 chose McLeod Ganj as their abode in what would turn out to be a prolonged exile from their homeland occupied by the Chinese invaders in 1950. The chapters based on Capt. Elliot's self-imposed retreat from England and return on a ship sailing from Bombay (now Mumbai) after a prolonged stay are easily two of the most absorbing chapters of the book.

It is a book that will enthral English speaking people everywhere in the erstwhile British territories and dominions. Above it all it will hold in thrall soldiers, sailors and airmen as the story rides across the waves and finds our hero through many ups and downs as a seaman on several ships after having refused to join the successful middle class professions that were available to wards of well-off parents. His father – the son of Capt. Elliot – puts him through his paces in tough construction jobs during school breaks. It is where fact and fiction again move in and out of the narrative till young Herbie goes to sea on a Royal Canadian Navy ship. Thereafter the narrative moves through the sea domain following the hero's shenanigans in various ports. A girl in every port is a phrase common to all seamen. But Herbie and his mates' escapades are funny, fraught with danger and boisterous in the extreme. Sailors when on shore invariably get embroiled in fights in bars and brothels. That is the norm. But Herbie manages to keep his virginity intact or so William will have us believe till he gets married to his sweetheart in Canada in the city of Dartmouth across the harbour from his home port of Halifax, Nova Scotia. If memory serves me right that was where in 1917 the Norwegian ship *SS Imo* collided with the French ship *SS Mont-Blanc* which was laden with explosives. The ensuing fire caused an explosion that wiped out a large portion of the north-ends of both cities.

William Hawke has written about himself in the Epilogue of the book. It comes as no surprise. After reading the story of his life or rather William's adventures in the most interesting and often dangerous climes in the world one begins to understand where he comes from: solider, sailor, tinker but not spy. He has done it all. He has been through it all. Between the book and its author hangs a fascinating tale.

*Maj. Gen. (Retd)*
**Vinod Saighal**
Author: Third Millennium Equipoise
www.vinodsaighal.com
New Delhi, Saturday
December 1, 2018

# PREFACE

> *Love your art, poor as it may be, which you have learned and be content with it; and pass through the rest of life as one who has been entrusted to the gods with his whole soul and all that he has, making yourself neither the tyrant nor the slave of any man.*
>
> — ***Marcus Aurelius***
> *AD 121 to 180*

The words of Roman Emperor Marcus Aurelius's first line *'Love your art, as poor as it may be'* inspire me. That's because I have been an artist from almost as long as I remember. I started by drawing with crayons as a preschooler, and my Mama always laid on the accolades as though my artwork should be hung on the walls of the Hermitage in Leningrad (St. Petersburg nowadays). In public school I worked my way up from crayon to watercolour according to the curriculum. I always received high marks in the subject of Art on my report cards, but the remaining subjects were ranked as average or below.

That was due to the fact that I have always been a daydreamer. In school I looked out of the window and dreamt of far off places I had seen in the pictures of National Geographic Magazine (I never read the stories; only looked at the pictures), and far-fetched things I wished to see or do. At age 73 as I wrote these words I was still a daydreamer. While writing the book signs of possible prostate cancer started to appear. I had a biopsy and it turned out to be positive; I had an operation and survived while all the time dreaming of finishing the book before the Good Lord called me to his flock beyond the stars. When these dreams crept in however, I remembered the famous words of Napoleon Hill – *What the mind can conceive and believe; the mind can achieve.* I *believed* I *WOULD* finish it. And now, here it is.

I had to abandon my visual artwork in my first occupation after I left school; there just wasn't enough space to store my paint, canvases and brushes in a 6.5 X 2.5 sq. ft. aluminium locker, or in the boot locker below my bunk.

But in the past ten years I have picked up my paint brushes again; now I use enamel utility paint and do my artwork on medium-sized fragmented marble scraps I find on the road outside houses under construction. I paint pretty flowers with butterflies on their petals, animals, birds, wooden sailing ships, and hang them on the walls of our office. I also paint designs on clay pottery I purchase dirt-cheap from roadside vendors.

I have also developed the art of storytelling; both oral and written. As folks age however they tend to become forgetful. For example, just the other day I asked a young fellow staying with us if I had ever told him the one about the time I received a wink from the late Nelson Mandela. He said, "Yes Bill, twice now."

Emperor Aurelius says, '*... poor as it may be*'. My first attempt at commercial writing was a semi-autobiography titled, *'My Life after the Navy in a Conch Shell'*. I thought it would be a big success, especially since I had moved to India, but it was a financial disaster – probably because I set the price too high. I printed 500 copies in Canada and sold about 100; most of which were at the 2005 book release in the Chiefs and Petty Officer's Mess at Canadian Forces Base, Halifax.

But I didn't give up. I now write short stories; mostly 'Salty Dips' about my Navy days and travel stories about my visits to the sub-Saharan Dark Continent.

This is my first attempt at factual fiction writing.

'What's factual fiction,' one may ask? If that's the case; in brief, factual fiction is a story with fictional characters and circumstances based around actual events which have taken place in the past, such as wars, politics, natural disasters, amongst many others. I found that factual fiction writing is not an easy task. The author must ensure all the circumstances which he portrays have taken place at the proper time in history. And also he cannot have products or services which were not invented or provided at the time of the circumstance; for instance, 'The first thing the soldier did, after being rescued from Dunkirk was to head for MacDonald's for a Big Mac'. Ok, that was an extreme example, but I hope it drives home my point.

I was motivated to make an attempt at this craft after being totally engrossed while reading the '*Ibis Trilogy*' by Amitav Ghosh and the '*Clifton Chronicles*' by Jeffrey Archer (both of which I highly recommend.) After reading these classic examples of factional fiction, I started saying affirmations to myself: *Hey; I am going to do this; I have an imaginative mind; I do have a story to tell; I am an excellent storyteller; my book will sell thousands of copies and win me a Nobel Prize.*

This book, 'CRISSCROSSING PATHS through Sorrow, Joy, Departure, Reunion' is factual fiction. It starts in 1916 on the first day of the World War I 'Battle of the Somme' and follows the crossing paths of four families or people as they grieve, rejoice, say good bye and reunite over the course of approximately one hundred years.

This Preface wouldn't be complete if I didn't thank the following: Mrs. Juhi Saighal the editor; Ruth Macdonald – Acting Archivist, The Salvation Army International Heritage Centre, London, England; Will Austin, Mrs. Jo Teasdale, Tracey O'Farrell, and Samantha Bevan of the Barnstaple Town Council located in North Devon, England, for their inputs on their beautiful mediaeval town centre which I have visited; and, Maj. Gen. (Retd) Vinod Saighal for his valuable advice on the heritage of India and for writing the Foreword. So, have a happy or sad (or both) read depending upon where the paths take your mind.

I will leave you with that, except for the fact that I'll let you know by social media or email when it's ready for purchase. Oops. I just remembered: you won't be reading these words until after purchase. Forgetfulness doesn't describe me anymore; bone-headed might work.

**William Hawke**
New Delhi

# Part - I

# One

BOOM; BOOM; RATTA-TAT-TAT. Machine guns, rifles and grenades were scything across 'No Man's Land', with murderous effect. A combined four divisions of the Sheffield City Battalion and the Accrington Pals, under the command of Lt. Colonel Andrew Snelgrove continued to move forward. It was 7:45 am on 1st July 1916, fifteen minutes after the start of the Battle of the Somme.

Cannons boomed, grenades exploded, machine guns rattled. Sergeant Major Irving Hall forged ahead one hundred yards to the north of Lt. Colonel Andrew Snelgrove. Soldiers fell. Soldiers cried out in pain. Whistles blew. Soldiers kept forging ahead toward an enemy determined to hold ground. The fields behind the advancing British troops were strewn with dead and wounded.

By the end of the day, little gain had been made. In fact, the British had been driven back almost to the point where they had started. While on the retreat Hall observed two of his soldiers, who he knew to be brothers, lying in the dirt while hugging ... both were dead.[1]

A hush fell over the battlefield. Not a bullet was fired as soldiers on both sides watched in disbelief while an unarmed British Major marched into 'no man's land' as though he was on parade. And in fact he was. Once he reached the halfway point he bent down, picked up an injured soldier, held him in his arms and carried him back to safety. Soldiers on both sides of the lines, who only minutes before had been firing upon each other, cheered.[2] After such a display of bravery, compassion and mutual respect, German and British stretcher bearers advanced to recover their wounded.

Hall looked all around. He could not see Lt. Colonel Snelgrove. *'How could we have become separated? Had he been wounded?'* He dared not ask himself the obvious next question. He was, nevertheless, worried. He walked up and down the line looking at each stretcher as the bearers passed.

That was when he saw his colonel; he was on one. He walked alongside it and when the bearers placed their cargo onto the ground and went back to retrieve more, he knelt down beside him. The Lt. Colonel was breathing weakly with two red blood stains on his battledress, one on the left chest and the other on the midriff. Hall took his hand, and knowing his colonel was dying said, "We have taken our objective Sir. Your men are in good hands. I will look over them."

Strangely for an army man, the colonel's last words resembled those of Admiral Lord Nelson who had died in the 1805 Battle of Trafalgar.[3] He said, "Take care of my wife Wilma, Hall ... take care of Wilma." After a pause of roughly ten seconds he faintly whispered, "Thank God I have done my duty," and faded away into darkness. Corporals and privates had gathered around. Not wanting to show weakness at this point, Hall wiped his welling up eyes with his soiled index finger.

Although Hall was slightly older than Andrew Snelgrove, he loved him as though he was his own father. Snelgrove was the best officer he had ever served under – firm, fair and friendly, and a stickler for discipline, virtues which any good officer should possess.

The two had advanced through the ranks together in the Boer War, when they had been stationed together with their regiment in India and the last two months of the current war when they had been called up as reinforcements. He had never met Mrs Wilma Snelgrove, but knew she must be a good woman. He swore to himself if he ever got home alive he would carry out his fallen colonel's final orders.

❄❄❄❄

JOSEPH BENNING SAT with his head bowed in silent prayer in the back row of Barnstaple Baptist Church. It was Sunday morning 2nd July. Dr. Allan Butler a prominent senior citizen of the town delivered the first reading of the gospel: *"For God so loved the world... He gave His only begotten Son...whomsoever believeth in Him shall not perish...but have everlasting life; John 3 Verse 16."*

After the readings, Pastor Mr. Willis-Wilks conducted the sermon. Earlier, during the announcements, as was the practice in all churches of Barnstaple, he would inform the congregation of any grieving families in the community due to the Great War. Thankfully there were none on this day.

Joseph's family owned a cattle farm eight miles outside of town. It was a prosperous business as North Devon ruby red cattle beef was considered superb and thus highly sought after in the London market. Beef sales had slowed down during the war years, but the family was surviving on earnings from more prosperous years. His parents, both in their mid-to-late fifties, lived on the farm. Joseph lived in the family townhouse on Kiln Lane. He was employed by his father to supervise the loading of cattle onto trains destined for London.

But any of the farmhands could do this work; most lived in town anyway. Joseph desperately wanted to serve his king and country by fighting in the Great War. He had volunteered, but was rejected due to flat feet. This caused disdain among villagers. Most didn't give him so much as a nod as they passed him on the street; they didn't accept he couldn't fight. They just imagined he wouldn't.

The only ones who showed any compassion or understanding were Mrs. Wilma Snelgrove, wife of a lieutenant colonel who was serving in France, and his church Pastor. Joseph was depressed.

When the service ended, Joseph was the first to leave the church; he didn't want to mix with the scrum that would gather outside after the service. He shook hands with Pastor Willis-Wilks who smiled, patted him on the back and said, "Keep the faith Joseph, keep the faith." Joseph returned a weak smile and slowly walked towards home.

Joseph Benning was twenty-four, of husky build and five feet eleven inches in height. His legs, back and arms were muscular and he was an excellent cricket player; a sport he played in grammar school and university. He enjoyed playing chess, reading history and biographies, and he read verses of the Holy Bible several times a week.

❄❄❄❄

WILMA SNELGROVE SAT in an armchair knitting in front of the fireplace of her Barnstaple home. She was in her eighth month of pregnancy and was knitting baby clothing for the expected newborn. She chose blue because she hoped for a boy who she'd name Andrew after the man she loved. At age 38, she was almost beyond child-bearing age and she and Andrew had prayed for pregnancy for a long time. The Good Lord had answered their prayers.

Andrew, her husband, was in France somewhere fighting in the Great War. He was in the British Fourth Army and she'd read in the *Western Morning News* that his regiment was engaged in the Battle of the Somme which commenced the day before. It was Sunday; she had prayed for Andrew's safety at ten o'clock Mass at 'St. Mary Immaculate Mother of God' as she always did. Her live-in maid-servant Jessie, an Anglo-Indian, had accompanied her.

Wilma was also an Anglo-Indian. Her father had been British and was the manager of a branch office of an India shipping company in northern India. He had married Winifred Sinclair an Anglo-Indian from the foothills town of Dharamsala. So Wilma was blessed with a partial brown complexion. Both her mother and father had died of malaria when Wilma was 18 and she had moved to her mother's hometown and volunteered at the mission school. She fell in love with and married Andrew Snelgrove at age 28, when he served in the cantonment of the British Army in McLeod Ganj. Andrew and his Sergeant Major, and hundreds of lower rank soldiers were transferred to England in late 1915 as reinforcements in the war against Germany.

Wilma along with many other army wives travelled on the same ship as their husbands. She and Andrew set up home in the town of Barnstaple in North Devon, north of the naval port of Plymouth, and a couple of miles from the village of Goodleigh where Andrew was born. Andrew was only with her for a week before his home leave expired. Most of their time together was spent purchasing furniture and setting up the house.

Barnstaple is possibly the oldest borough in England. It is a former river-port, located at the lowest crossing-point of the River Taw, flowing into the Bristol Channel. From the 14th century, it was licensed to export wool, since the merchants claimed the town had been declared a free borough in Saxon times. This brought great wealth to the town, whose Centre still preserved a mediaeval layout and character. Later the town became an importer of Irish wool. When its harbour silted up, it developed other industries, such as shipbuilding, foundries and sawmills. Its Victorian market, with its high glass and timber roof on iron columns, survived. Barnstaple railway station was the terminus of a branch line from Exeter, known as the Tarka Line.

The Snelgroves residence was a two story house situated on Queen Street, about a ten minute walk from the Strand on the banks of the River Taw. Wilma enjoyed walking down to the Strand in the evenings to sit on a bench, and watch passing boats and smile at passersby.

No one smiled back. She found the residents to be rather snooty, and imagined it was her mixed race that caused their discourtesy.

Later, in the afternoon, she and Jessie walked down to Butcher's Row market to fetch the weekly provisions. Several older women and army wives, clad in full-length dresses and wearing fancy hats were also shopping. Most were accompanied by a servant in a plain dress and white bonnet. Much of the talk in the market was of the war. And although news of casualties hadn't come in yet, everyone knew from the newspaper that the Fourth Army was currently engaged in the Battle of the Somme. North Devon was home to many soldiers of the Fourth Army.

Wilma encountered Joseph Benning sitting on a bench beside a vegetable cart. He appeared to be depressed. Wilma knew the reason. She sat down beside him and placed her palm on his forearm. They often sat and conversed as she also experienced occasional depression due to the bigoted townsfolk. She said, "Move away Mr. Benning. Go to Canada... Australia ... New Zealand ... even India."

He replied, "I have been considering that Mrs Snelgrove. My elder sister lives in Toronto and has been urging me to pack up and move there, but I just haven't decided if that is a viable option. Should I run away and hide, or should I stay and prove myself as a worthwhile human being and not a mangy street dog?" Joseph was a staunch Baptist. He said, "The Good Lord will tell me which path to take when He's ready."

Just then a servant carrying a piece of paper that appeared to be a telegram ran past them and turned into a side lane. The woman had tears running down her cheeks. Wilma excused herself, told Jessie to follow, and ran down the same lane where fresh fish were displayed on rough carts. They came to a sudden halt. A fashionably dressed woman was screaming. The one who had run past Wilma and Joseph stood in front of the woman with bowed head. Other shoppers ran to the grieving woman and embraced her. *"My son, My son!"* she wailed.

Wilma dropped her shopping bags on the cobblestones and despite her pregnancy, darted off towards the house.

Upon arrival she walked up the three stone steps and opened the mail box. There was a sealed envelope inside. She took it out and immediately knew it wasn't a telegram; it didn't have the same shape. It was a letter from Andrew. She breathed a sigh of relief as she stepped inside the house. Jessie arrived shortly after, carrying the empty grocery bags. She had a distressed look on her face. Wilma said, "No telegram Jessie; only a letter from Sir." She then settled into an easy chair, opened the letter and started reading.

*My Dearest Wilma,*

*All is well at the moment. The generals have briefed us saying this wretched war is far from won. It looks as though we will be away from 'Jolly Old England' and those we love for quite some time to come. I do hope it is not true. Too many men on both sides of the line have died; too many once-beautiful cities and villages now lie in ruin; too many dreams have been shattered; enough of the doom and gloom.*

*My stay in Barnstaple was so short there was no time to introduce you to the few townsfolk I know before I had to depart. I do hope you have fit in well with the community. I have written a letter to my sister-in-law Norma in Goodleigh and requested her to visit you occasionally. She is a good person. And as you know my younger brother Alan is also in France. He holds the rank of Captain, unless he has been promoted since I last heard of him.*

*I suppose our child will be born sometime in August. I do hope she's born healthy. Yes Wilma; I'm hoping for a girl. I know your heart is set on a boy, but I would rather have my little nephew Donald carry Father's name down in history as a famous scientist who discovered a cure for leprosy, a renowned musician, or the highest-selling author of the 20th century, than have my own son fight in another war.*

*Nevertheless, we should start thinking of our future Wilma. There are a few questions which require answers. For instance: should I remain in the army after the war or not; if I were to relinquish my commission and retire what would I do in civilian life; should we return to your beloved India? Think about these questions Wilma.*

*I must sleep now my Dear. It will be a heavy day tomorrow and it's getting late. This letter should go out in the mail bag tomorrow morning.*

*With all my love,*

*Andrew*

WILMA RESTED HER HEAD against the back of the arm chair and dozed off. She dreamt, and when Jessie shook her gently and hour later she knew she had been dreaming a pleasant dream but couldn't remember it. "Mr. Benning is at the door Madam," said Jessie.

Wilma wiped the sleep from her eyes and said, "Show him in Jessie. Show him in."

Jessie escorted Joseph to the living room and departed to the kitchen. Wilma started to rise, but he said, "Please Mrs. Snelgrove don't get up; I saw you hustling home after you witnessed that episode in the market, so I dropped by to see if you needed someone with you at the moment. I can tell though there was no bad news waiting in your mail box."

"Oh Mr. Benning, how good of you. How thoughtful of you. Thank you, there was no telegram, but there *was* a letter from Andrew... And now that you are here, I insist that you remain for dinner."

"I would be most honoured Mrs Snelgrove."

Wilma said, "Mr. Benning would it by alright with you if we reverted to a first name basis whilst in private?"

Benning smiled and said, "That's fine with me Wilma. My name is Joseph."

Dinner was a spread of roast of pork, dumplings, baked potatoes and vegetables. Dessert was apple pie. Wilma normally ate alone; the accepted custom in any mistress-servant household. She was happy to have Joseph's company on this evening, as loneliness often crept in from the shadows.

During the meal she said, "You know Joseph, I have read that the Salvation Army provides motor ambulances and drivers, refreshment huts in military camps, and parcels of food and clothing for combatants. Some officers also serve as chaplains...I don't imagine a person would especially require arched feet to serve in *that* Army ... If you were to join them and serve your countrymen in Europe instead of running away as I earlier suggested, when it's over you could return to Barnstaple with your head held high." She waited for his reaction.

Joseph took his time before responding, "That is indeed an interesting proposition Wilma. I *could* do that. It *would* be a very worthwhile thing to do, and I don't mean to save face with my neighbours; I mean as a man who wants to serve his country; as a man who cares ... truly cares."

FOUR DAYS LATER there was a sealed letter in the Snelgrove mail box with no stamp. She opened it and read.

*Dear Wilma,*

*I have departed for London to join the Salvation Army. I shall visit you and the Colonel upon return.*

*Farewell,*

*Joseph*

Wilma smiled with a sense of satisfaction ... she was happy.

❄❄❄❄

JOSEPH INFORMED his father of his decision, and after arrangements to replace his vacant job had been made, he boarded a train destined for Exeter and arrived at Central Station on Queen Street two hours later. There he purchased another railway ticket for one destined for London. It was an overnight trip with one transfer at Southampton. He arrived at London Bridge Station in the late afternoon the following day. The farthest away from Barnstaple he'd ever been was Cambridge, located in the central part of southern England, so this was his first visit to England's capital city.

He was a little confused when he walked out of the station through the ticket booth exit. He saw a sign indicating he was on London Bridge Street, but couldn't see the bridge. He walked along it for a while and then at an intersection he saw it. He was anxious to see the Thames so he moved in that direction. And then, there it was – the River Thames which had been written about for centuries. He stood in the middle for half an hour watching the small boats pass below his feet. Downstream was Tower Bridge with its two Gothic towers. Remembering that at one point in time London Bridge had been crumbling he hummed the children's song *'London Bridge is Falling Down'*.

Then he realized that dusk was falling and remembered he had been forewarned that the city would be blacked out after dark due to bombings by massive German Zeppelins. He hurried into the city, found a reasonably priced hotel and lay his head down for a full night of uninterrupted sleep; the previous night had been sleepless with clackity-clack-clackity-clack-clackity- clack ringing in his ears.

In the morning he rose from his bed, washed and shaved in cold water, and climbed down the stairway to the lobby. He entered the small dining room and sat by the window. There was a hustle bustle outside as people walked to their places of employment; some men wearing top hats. When the elderly waitress arrived he asked her what they had on the menu that day. She answered with a smile, "Lamb, ram, sheep or mutton as usual," and laughed at Joseph's strange look. Then she said, "Can't you tell when someone's pulling your pisser? We've got about anything you'd imagine there'd be for breakfast in a small London hotel. Except steamed lobsters and fried jelly fish of course."

Joseph smiled up at her and said, "I'll have bangers, red lead and poached eggs."

The waitress replied, "P-p-p-p".

Joseph said, "Oh! Excuse me; please." As she walked way, she again said something that sounded like, 'Atta boy'.

After breakfast he asked for the bill. The waitress pulled out a small pad and pencil, and started scribbling digits. When the lead broke she said, "An attempt to use a pencil with a broken lead is pointless. I'll be right back."

Once the bill was paid Joseph went back up to the room to retrieve his small suitcase. He then walked down to the lobby again to check out. A stern-looking reception woman did the essentials and then said, "What's a strong looking lad like you doing on this side of the Channel? Why aren't you on the other side fighting for your country like other young men your age?"

Joseph realized the stigma would follow him everywhere, and said, "I volunteered to fight but they rejected me due to flat feet. Now I'm on my way to join the Salvation Army. They service the needs of soldiers of our country in Europe. Do you happen to know the address of the headquarters?"

The woman warmed up a bit and said, "They're located not far from here at 101 Queen Victoria Street. Here, I'll draw you a simple map; you can walk there in half an hour; that is if your flat feet allow it." The woman who had been so cold-hearted at first now chuckled. He smiled, thanked her and departed.

Joseph walked through the headquarters entrance, travel bag in hand. A pretty young 'Doughnut Lassie' greeted him at the entrance. The Lassie said, "Good morning Sir; how can I assist you?"

Joseph proudly said, "I'm here to volunteer to be a Salvation Army soldier."

"Normally a soldier volunteers at the corps nearest his home. What is your hometown?"

"Barnstaple, but please don't tell me I must return to join; there isn't even a corps there; although there is one in Exeter, but I passed through that town yesterday on my journey to London."

"Don't despair Sir; since you are here, you can join at a local corps in London. Here is a little map to the closest one." She was well prepared. She took out a small map from her pocket which looked as though it was hand-drawn and passed it to Joseph and continued. "It's only about a 30 minute walk." He thanked her and departed.

When he walked into that corps building he was greeted by another 'Doughnut Lassie' who smiled and said, "Good morning Sir, I'm here to welcome volunteers who want to become a doughnut lassie like me. I don't suppose you are interested in joining us?"

Joseph smiled and said, "I've been called many things lately including a coward, but not a transvestite...But actually I *am* here to volunteer as a male member; a soldier."

"Good Sir. Follow me please." Joseph already admired the respect he had experienced while in Salvation Army premises.

She took Joseph's hand and escorted him to the waiting room of the recruitment office. Three other hopefuls sat on chairs against the wall. Joseph joined them and engaged in their conversation. They were from other parts of England and were not in Europe for various reasons other than flat feet. Interestingly, their names were Mark, Luke and John. Appropriate names, thought Joseph, for the army they wanted to join. They were individually called into the recruitment officer's office.

Joseph and John watched as Mark and Luke walked out at ten-minute intervals with defeated looks on their faces, not saying a word. John got to his feet looking a little apprehensive and walked into the recruitment officer's room. After seeing two rejects walk past, Joseph was feeling a little apprehensive as well. But John walked out with a smile on his face and stopped at Joseph to say, "My last name is Wilson. If you are also successful we will most likely meet in a few days when they conduct the medical examinations."

Joseph replied, "Wonderful John Wilson. My last name is Benning. I hope to see you there." He shook John's hand before walking into the other room.

When Joseph entered there was a middle-age uniformed gentleman standing behind a desk. They shook hands over the desk and the gentleman said, "Welcome; my name is Captain Scott."

Joseph replied with his name and added "I'm pleased to meet you Captain."

The Captain said, "You are here Mr. Benning because you obviously want to join *our* Army. May I ask why you didn't join the *British* Army instead?"

Joseph replied, "I volunteered Sir, but was rejected due to flat feet."

The Captain looked him in the eyes and said, "Mr. Benning do you realize the risk you took by telling me you were rejected due to your feet problem?"

"Yes Sir, I ran the risk of having you reject me as well. But I *will not* perjure myself."

"I admire you for that Mr. Benning; too many men of your age will say anything these days simply to get that which they desire. Flat feet will not pose a problem. What is your age?"

"Twenty-four Sir."

"Excellent. Please take a seat ... Now let us begin with a few questions about our faith, and before I ask them I must remind you that although we are a Christian Army we serve the needs of humans of all religions."

Joseph nodded approval and added, "I would expect so Sir."

"Now, the first question: Why was the Apostle Thomas called 'Doubting Thomas?"

"It was due to the fact that at one point he expressed doubt that the ascension of Our Saviour occurred. Little is it known however, that in 70 AD St. Thomas introduced Christianity to the Indian sub-continent. In fact, when the Portuguese navigator Vasco da Gama landed in India in 1498, he was astonished to learn that Christianity had been there for many generations; although how many he did not know.

"You are a learned man Mr. Benning. Even I did not know that fact. To what level were you educated?"

"I earned a Bachelor of Science in Animal Husbandry at Cambridge Sir, as my family are cattle breeders in North Devon. But I have always been fascinated with history, even in my elementary school years."

"With an university education, you qualify to be a chaplain, but all chaplains must serve as soldiers first ... I don't think there's a need to ask you any more questions about our faith, so let us move on to how we have been contributing to the war effort. Do you know anything about that aspect Mr. Benning?"

"Yes Sir; the Salvation Army serves at the frontlines by offering comfort and pastoral support to members of the armed forces. There are the famous Salvation Army 'Doughnut Lassies; one escorted me to your waiting room this morning. During major engagements, Salvation Army soldiers drive ambulances, set up; and work at field hospitals and rest centres for soldiers to write home to loved ones. They go to daily burial services and pray over the graves of our own soldiers and those of our enemies ... I can't serve as a 'Doughnut Lassie' due to my gender, but I can indeed lend my hands and faith in field hospitals or other such services that your soldiers conduct."

"Mr. Benning, if you are selected, you will have to sign a document called *'The Articles of War'*. That can wait until you pass the medical examination. Further, there are two British Armies in desperate need of our soldiers; the Second and the Fourth. Which one would you choose if all goes well?"

Joseph rapidly replied, "The Fourth Sir."

The Captain look at him with some scepticism in his eyes, "That was a rather rapid reply; even a little too rapid for my liking. Can you explain?"

"Many men from Barnstaple are in the Fourth Army Sir; some have already died, and I want to be *seen* there."

Again, the Captain seemed sceptical saying, "*Seen* there? Is being *seen* there more important than serving the needs of our fighting men?"

Joseph replied, "Sir, the people from my town do not except my flat feet as a reason for not fighting. To them it is an excuse. Some spit on the sidewalk as I walk past; old family friends don't even make eye contact if we come face-to-face on the street. They sneer. I want soldiers from my village to see me at the frontlines and mention my name in letters to loved ones, so that when I return I will be able to walk down the cobblestones with my head held high. That said Sir; the more I hear and read about the services the Salvation Army renders, the more excited I have become about the prospect of serving. So, in a nutshell, being *seen* is important to me for reasons mentioned, but no more important than serving.

"If you are turned down for Europe deployment due to medical reasons, but are fit enough to serve us on the home front will you still consider joining our ranks?"

"I will serve until the war has ended and after that I cannot say for sure."

"We can wait for that Mr. Benning. You have passed the first milestone. Please report to the examination centre at 10 o'clock on Wednesday morning. Miss Sullivan outside will give you the address. Good luck and God be with you." Captain Scott shook Joseph's hand, smiled and dismissed him.

Joseph was elated.

❄❄❄❄

AT 11 O'CLOCK on Friday morning on 11th July 1916 there was a knock on the door of 20 Queen Street in Barnstaple. Jessie opened the door and a few seconds later walked into the dining room carrying a piece of paper. Wilma rose from her breakfast table, glanced at the paper for a moment and fainted into Jessie's arms.

When she felt a cool cloth being stroked across her forehead she woke to find herself in the living room armchair with Jessie sitting on a footstool beside her, tears rolling down her cheeks. Wilma was confused at first, but then the gravity of what had happened sank in. She began to sob ... "My beloved Andrew ... Oh God! Please tell me it is not so," but she knew it was. The Army didn't send such telegrams by error. She wept again, and continued for over an hour.

Finally, Jessie placed a hand on Wilma's forearm and asked, "Shall I go to Goodleigh and inform your sister-in-law Mrs. Snelgrove?"

Wilma looked up at her; "Oh yes Jessie, please do."

Jessie picked up the fateful telegram and left the house. She arrived at the other Snelgrove residence in forty-five minutes. Three and a half year old Donald was rocking on a hobby horse when she walked across the wide veranda, and knocked on the door. Donald said, "Good morning Miss Jessie."

"Good morning Donald. I've come to talk to your Mama for a minute." When Donald started to disembark she added, "Please wait for a few moments to be called Dear; it won't be long." She was relieved to see him get back onto his hobby horse.

Norma Snelgrove answered the door. "What brings you here alone Jessie?"

Jessie lowered her gaze and almost whispered, "Madam is mourning," and passed Norma the telegram.

Norma didn't have to read the telegram in order to know the content. Women didn't mourn when their husband or son was maimed; they almost sighed in relief knowing at least he would be coming home alive. They only mourned the finality of death.

Jessie led Norma to an armchair where the latter placed her hands to her face, rested her elbows on her knees and wept silently. Andrew Snelgrove was her husband's only sibling, and she remembered how he, as a youth, had watched over him like a guardian angel when he was a child. Yes, Norma and Alan had been friends since they were infants.

Little Donald had grown tired of waiting outside and entered the room. He saw his mother crying and stood beside Jessie with concern in his eyes. He knew he had a father, but didn't understand why he had never seen him. All he had been told was "Your father is away serving his country," whatever that meant.

When Norma recovered she saw the concern on young Donald's face and said, "Papa is fine Dear." She then looked at Jessie, "I must go to Wilma." She took Donald's hand and the three of them set out in the direction of Barnstaple. When they arrived at the house, Jessie led Norma and Donald into the living room where they found Wilma. She was not weeping. She was moaning ... She was in labour.

## Notes

1. Eye-witness account from letters reported on BBC on the 100th anniversary of the first day of the battle.
2. Same as above
3. Admiral Nelson said to Captain Hardy – captain of HMS Victory – "Take care of Lady Hamilton Hardy; take care of Lady Hamilton." Source: The Phrase Finder - www.phrases.org.uk/

# Two

**JOSEPH BENNING HAD PASSED** his medical examination in London and had gone through an intensive four month training period. While the training was carried out at Camp Borden not far north of the English Channel, the barracks were located at Camp Aldershot thus requiring a 20 mile march in the morning and evening. Needless to say, by the end of the training period Joseph and the fifty or so other Salvation Army volunteers were physically fit when they landed in France.

Joseph and six others transported supplies to the position of the Fourth Army, catching up with them on 6th January 1917. Their first major engagement was tagging along behind British troops as they chased the Germans retreating to the Hindenburg Line between March and April. During that episode of the war they carried out the disciplines they had been taught before landing in France.

While with the Fourth Army he met several soldiers he knew from Barnstable. Instead of asking them to tell their parents they had *seen* him he said, "Say a hello to your parents from me in your next letter home". He thought that would be a better way of conveying the message that he was there.

❄❄❄❄

CANNONS ROARED AGAIN, machine guns rattled again, boots slogged through thick mud and fog again; men cried out in agony again. This was on 9th August 1918 – the close of the second day of the two-day Battle of Amiens. General Henry Rawlinson's Fourth British Army was at the spearhead of this push that historians would later describe as the *'Hundred Days Offensive'*. This two-day battle was the first stage of the offensive which was believed to be the one that would eventually bring the enemy to its knees and end the death, destruction and grieving.

But the end of the war had already come for Sergeant Major Irving Hall. He lay on his back in the mud; bone fragments projecting from several gashes on the lower portion of his left leg. He was semi-conscious as an army medic applied a tourniquet to arrest bleeding. Hall didn't know about his leg; it was numb – he was dumbfounded.

When daylight arrived, the frontline was far enough to the east to allow field ambulances to arrive on the scene. These were designed to carry between eight and ten patients, and there were only three of them; alas, more than a hundred wounded needed to be transported that day.

The most-seriously injured would go first; the ambulances would return. Hall was amongst the first batch to go. He, along with fifteen others, was bundled into an ambulance and taken to a field hospital set up temporarily in a nearby abandoned schoolhouse. Large bold words on the side of the ambulance said **'Gift of The Children of Nova Scotia',** but Hall didn't see them. He was unconscious.

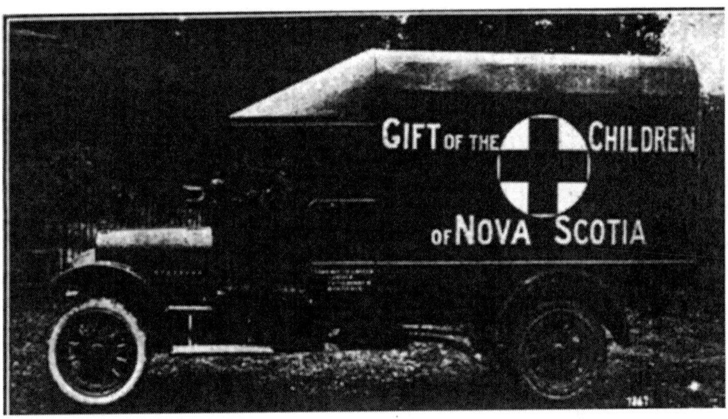


Upon arrival at the hospital he was laid on a camp cot. One of the two doctors assessed that Hall had lost a great deal of blood and carried out a transfusion. He regained consciousness within an hour, but his flexed facial muscles indicated severe pain. The doctor injected morphine. It worked; the pain was eased. It was only then that he noticed his heavily bandaged left leg elevated by a sling at the end of the cot. He now had no doubt; his war was over. He laid his head on the cot and dozed off to sleep.

He woke up two hours later, rubbed his eyes and stared at his bandaged leg. *'How severe is the wound? Will I ever walk again? Will they chop it off? Will I have to wear one of those dreadful steel braces? Will I ...*

"Good day Sergeant Major. My name is Joseph Benning."

Hall replied, "Good day Benning. I see you're in the Salvation Army. Are you about to bring me tea and doughnuts?"

"No Sir. I'm not a Doughnut Lassie. The Red Cross is suffering a temporary shortage of nurses, so between driving ambulances and setting up hospitals like this, field-trained Salvation Army soldiers are lending assistance until more come our way. But before you asked, I was about to say, 'I trust you are feeling as well as can be expected given the present circumstances'."

Hall said, "I don't feel pain due to morphine, but my heart aches ..."

Joseph darted away. Thirty seconds later when he arrived with a doctor in tow, Hall was laughing. Eventually he roared, "You dough-head! I'm not having a heart attack! I was saying 'my heart aches because I won't be in the fight to the end' but you, you numbskull, ran off in panic before I finished." He continued his laughing spell and added, "Victory was so close we could almost smell it." Joseph and the doctor smiled.

"We must leave you now," said the doctor as he took Joseph's arm and they hastened off.

Joseph called back over his shoulder, "I'll summon a Doughnut Lassie for you," and they were gone.

A WEEK LATER HALL, along with three hundred other wounded warriors, was transported across the Channel in 'X' Lighters, commonly known to soldiers as *'Beetles'*. He was delivered to Royal Sussex County Hospital in Brighton, which had been treating wounded soldiers since the war began. Brighton was located on the Channel, 55 miles south of London and 40 miles east of Portsmouth, his home town.

An Armistice was signed in Paris on the 11th hour of the 11th day of the 11th month 1918. The total number of military and civilian casualties of the Great War was more than 37 million – 17 million deaths and 20 million wounded.

❄❄❄❄

AT 12 NOON ON 16th April 1919 Joseph Benning stepped off a train in Barnstaple wearing his Salvation Army uniform. He walked across the road and by coincidence saw one of the horse-drawn wagons owned by his father approaching. He hailed the driver down, hopped onto the seat beside him and said, "Good morning; my name is Joseph Benning. I don't believe we've met."

The driver flicked the reins and replied, "My name is Sam Rankin. We haven't actually met, but I worked as a field hand, while you were the town man when you left. I have been promoted since then and now do transport."

"Nice meeting you Sam. I assume you are going back to the farm."

"Yes Sir." They chatted idly until they arrived in front of the house.

Joseph disembarked, walked up the garden path, crossed the veranda and slowly opened the front door. He crept inside to surprise his mother. She wasn't in the living room or the kitchen. Then he spotted her through the kitchen window hanging out the wash on the back porch. He opened the door quietly, sneaked up behind her and whispered, "Hello Mother" in her left ear.

She turned, dropped a pillow case in the dust and threw her arms around him and shrieked "Joseph! Joseph! Thank God you are home! You are safe!" With tears rolling down her cheeks and her arms still around her only son; in a calmer voice asked, "The war ended almost six months ago, what kept you so long?"

"So many graves on both sides to pray over; so many wounded to be transported to the Channel; so much useable equipment to be salvaged from the field hospitals." He continued, "It took us ages, and further, the mail was secondary. All postal personnel were pressed into the effort. Therefore, I couldn't even write to let you know when I'd be home; besides the fact that I didn't even know. All I did know was that had I perished, you would have been informed by telegram."

"But now here you *are* my dear, and that is the main thing."

"Yes it is Mother."

"Where and when did they land you on this side?"

"The ship I was onboard docked in Southampton before dawn yesterday morning. Upon arrival, I took an overnight train to Exeter and from there the other train. And here I am."

"You must be exhausted. I'll run you a bath and afterwards you can sleep for two or three hours before your father returns. He'll also be happy to see you. Not a day passes when he doesn't mention your name. I'll let you surprise him the way you did me."

"Thank you Mother."

Three hours later Joseph was awakened from the deepest sleep he had experienced in three years by something wet and cold touching his arm. When he opened his eyes to investigate the source he saw two large eyes peering into his own. For a moment he thought he was having a nightmare, but when he felt warm licking on that arm he realised it was Rusty the family golden retriever. The coldness had been his wet nose. He reached down and ruffled the dog's furry head and ears; something he knew Rusty liked. The dog wagged his tail begging for more.

Joseph put on a fresh set of undergarments and made his way to the end of the hallway still wearing his uniform. He climbed down the stairs as quietly as he could and walked into the living room, the tail-wagging Rusty at his heels. He found Mr. Benning Senior sitting in an armchair leafing through the *North Devon Journal*. Joseph leaned over and said, "What's the price of beef in the market today Mr. Benning?"

"Normal," he said as he looked around to see who the interrogator was. When he saw it was Joseph, he rose quickly and clasped his hand. While shaking it he threw his left arm around his son and drew him into a one-armed arm hug. After he released the hug he took the other hand and held Joseph at arm's length, while he looked him over. "Thank God you're still in one piece."

"I've been thanking God I'm still alive every day since I arrived close to the lines Father. And indeed there were some close calls, especially when the enemy regrouped and drove our forces back to where we started."

"You must have experienced a mixture of the dreadful and the wonderful."

"There were elements of 'wonder' Father, but hundreds more of 'dread' – mostly the human cost on both sides. When will mankind realise war is not the answer?"

"Well said Son. Now tell me ... What are your future plans? Of course you know the farm will always be here, but I think you are destined for higher plains than a cattle breeder.

You can be anything you believe you can."

"Thank you for your encouraging words Father. Too many men in your position attempt to throw out a cloud of doubt and guilt by saying, '... but who will take care of the farm when I'm no longer capable?' but you didn't. You encouraged me. And I thank you for it."

"Did you have any chances to play chess while you were away Joseph?"

"Not once Father. Were you about to challenge me?"

"Let us start a game now Son, and if I haven't whipped you by dinner, we'll continue afterwards."

"I accept your challenge, but I must forewarn you; over the past couple of years I've become as *sharp* as that whip!"

TWO DAYS AFTER his homecoming, Joseph and his mother and father rode to town in the family carriage. Their destination was Barnstaple Baptist Church. Joseph wore his Salvation Army uniform. A new minister Mr. D.J. Llewellyn welcomed the family at the entrance as he did all members of the congregation each Sunday morning. He shook Joseph's hand enthusiastically and said, "Welcome home Joseph Benning. Thank you for your effort on the other side of the Channel over the past couple of years."

Joseph gave the pastor a warm smile without saying a word.

Mr. Llewellyn's practice was to welcome home individual soldiers from the congregation during the service. This day was no exception. Before the sermon he rose and said, "Dear friends, please join me in welcoming Mr. Joseph Benning home from France. As you can see by his uniform which he wears with dignity, he served the war effort without having to fire a bullet or canon ball. He drove ambulances; he set up field hospitals; he prayed over graves; and at times helped the Red Cross in patching up or comforting our wounded soldiers. Thank you Mr. Benning."

Several young men who had survived the horror walked over to Joseph and shook his hand. Although he tried to hide it, he relished the recognition. The dark shadow which had followed him before he left would now vanish.

After the service many attendees gathered around him to welcome him home. Joseph simply acknowledged their welcome with a handshake, while his mother beamed with pride. When everyone had dispersed he told his parents he'd walk over to St Mary Church to see Mrs. Wilma Snelgrove, and that he'd be home for dinner.

JOSEPH WALKED into St Mary Immaculate Mother of God Church as the mass was about to start. Wilma Snelgrove was sitting in the choir benches. When she saw Joseph, she smiled, got up and whispered something into the choir leader's ear. He also smiled and then nodded. When Father Carl entered from the side door, the choir leader said something to him.

During the mass when the first hymn was about to be sung Father Carl said, "Dear Friends, I would like to welcome home our Baptist friend Mr. Joseph Benning. He has returned from the

Great War where he served Our Lord, our country and our soldiers during his tenure in the Salvation Army ... And it is therefore only appropriate that we have changed our first hymn today; please open your hymn books to page 256."

The organist started playing the first chords, and the congregation stood and broke out in song *'Onward Christian soldiers; Marching as to war; With the Cross of Jesus; Going on before'*. Parishioners turned their heads towards Joseph while singing and gave him warm smiles. He returned their smiles. On completion of the hymn the congregation clapped; a gesture rarely done during a Mass. When the clapping ended, Joseph remained standing for a few seconds. He put his hands together in front of his chest, looked skyward and said a silent prayer; "Thank you Lord."

After the Mass, Joseph waited outside for his friend Mrs Wilma Snelgrove. People approached and welcomed him home. One young man limped towards him. Joseph shortened the distance by advancing toward the crippled man. When they met they shook hands. Joseph noticed that he was concealing a hair lip under his thick moustache. The soldier who introduced himself as Samuel Sewell said, "One of your brothers named John Wilson took good care of me."

"I met John Wilson in the recruitment office almost three years ago, but haven't seen him since. We also lost men. Do you know if he survived?"

"He took good care of me on a ship on the way back across the Channel. Unless he slipped and broke his neck while walking down the gangplank when we arrived I assume he did survive." After a short chuckle by both men Sewell continued. "If you ever see him again, please pass on my thanks."

"Thank you Mr. Sewell. If I ever cross paths with him I'll convey your message. Now if you don't mind, my friend Mrs Wilma Snelgrove is standing by patiently waiting for our conversation to end."

"Of course Mr. Benning, and thank you once again."

*"MR. BENNING; MR BENNING!"* cried Wilma. "It's so nice to see you. I'm so glad you are home at last." She clasped his hand, brought it to her lips and kissed it.

"Mrs Snelgrove it is indeed wonderful to be home again. And I saw you whisper to the choir leader; thank you for your thoughtfulness."

"You can thank my sister-in-law Norma. She has been feeding short articles about the work of the Salvation Army in France to the local press. Many have been published."

"That was good of her Mrs. Snelgrove; I assume with a little persuasion from you."

"It didn't take much persuasion. Her husband Allen was also in France. Thankfully, he survived ... Now you must walk me home. We have a great deal of catching up to do."

"But the colonel; is he with you today? ... Don't tell me ..."

Wilma bowed her head slightly and whispered, "Yes Joseph, we lost him at Somme. I learned about it after you departed. Thankfully, little Annie arrived on the day I received the sad news. Andrew lives on in Annie's blood." Then a surprised look came to her eyes, "Oh, Annie!" She turned towards Jessie who was standing behind her. "Jessie, please bring Annie to meet Mr. Benning."

Joseph smiled, "Hello Annie Snelgrove. I hope you enjoyed the Mass."

The shy child stationed herself behind Jessie and peeked around her upper leg. All three adults laughed in delight.

After their walk back from St. Mary's, Wilma and Joseph sat in her living room and continued the conversation they had started along the way.

"So Joseph, all in all, besides witnessing unimaginable suffering, your tenure in France was personally rewarding?"

"Yes Wilma, it certainly was. I would have willingly gone to the trenches if my feet weren't flat, but I was there on my chosen path serving Our Lord, our King and our soldiers just the same. It brought me great satisfaction and indeed pride,"..."and then when I arrived home to be accepted by the community was an added bonus."

"Now, let's change the subject" ... "What is your age Joseph?"

"Twenty-six, but where is this leading?"

"Wait for it" ... "There is a young woman named Mabel Arthur who moved to Barnstaple from Exeter just after you departed. She was one of the few people who visited me to offer condolences after the death of dear Andrew was announced in your church. Since then, she has continued to visit occasionally."

"Now I see where it's leading, you old scallywag!" He laughed while saying it.

"Hear me out Joseph" ... "She's beautiful, she's intelligent, she's well educated, she's compassionate, she comes from an upright family; and the best part is she's also a Baptist just like you." ... "Being your first Sunday home I assume you will be having Sunday dinner with your parents this evening, so if you agree, I'll invite both of you to dinner next Sunday."

ON SUNDAY 29th April 1919 Jessie, with little Anne at her heels, answered the door. Joseph Benning, clad in a suit and tie, stood on the threshold. It was around five o'clock. He said, "Good evening Jessie," and bent over to say, "Good evening Annie." This time the child showed no shyness, she smiled up at Joseph.

Jessie and the child escorted Joseph to the living room where Wilma was sitting. They chatted until half an hour later there was another knock on the door. Jessie and Annie emerged from the kitchen and welcomed Miss Arthur.

"Good evening Miss Arthur. We've been expecting you; please follow us." Jessie and Annie escorted Mabel to the living room, where Wilma and Joseph were already on their feet.

Wilma was the first to speak saying, "Welcome Miss Arthur."

Mabel offered a perfect curtsy, "Thank you Mrs Snel-grove."

"Miss Arthur, this is my friend Mr. Joseph Benning."

Again Mabel curtsied and said, "It's a pleasure to make your acquaintance Mr. Benning."

Joseph bowed and said, "It's my pleasure Miss Arthur; Mrs Snelgrove tells me your family moved north from Exeter about two years ago. Exeter is a nice town. I pass through it quite frequently. In fact I passed through just last week on my journey home."

"Yes Mr Benning I know, I was in the congregation last week when you were welcomed home. And I noticed you again this morning, but I didn't know it was you Mrs Snelgrove was referring to when she told me there was someone she'd like me to meet. In fact, I didn't even know it was a gentleman."

"She's a sly one Miss Arthur, but a wonderful sly one."

Wilma was laughing at this point. Mabel said, "I don't know about 'sly', but she is indeed a wonderful woman."

Half an hour later they all sat at the dining room table. Wilma sat at the head and the two young folks sat facing each other on two sides. Little Annie sat beside Joseph in a high chair.

A chair was placed beside her so that Jessie could assist her in eating. Jessie would eat alone later.

During the meal Wilma said, "Shall we revert to a first name basis while in private?"

Both Joseph and Mabel gave their approval.

Wilma continued, "Good ... Joseph, what are your plans for the future? Do you intend to remain in the Salvation Army?"

"No Mrs ... whoops, I mean Wilma, that's not in my plan. Father has a close friend who is the manager of a company called Cassidy's located in Toronto, Canada. They import fine china from Britain and sell it at wholesale prices to hotels and high-end restaurants; and at retail prices to the general public in their stores. He told me he'd give me a reference letter and was absolutely certain the gentleman would give me a good career opportunity. Our family had assisted that family back in the late '90s when they were poverty stricken due to two years of crop failure. Father also offered to lend me the money for passage and living expenses until I get financially secure."

Mabel stepped in, "I've heard that Canada is a wonderful country; wide open spaces, lots of forests, and plenty of lakes and wildlife. I've also read about the sacrifices their soldiers made in the war ... Do you plan to take advantage of the offer?"

"I think I mentioned to Wilma a few years ago that I have an elder sister who married a man of Swedish origin named Herman Stensson and emigrated from Barnstaple to Canada. They moved to Toronto in 1910 and established Sheridan Nurseries. They live in Sheridan, which is just west of Toronto ... The business is flourishing and my sister has been urging me to move to Canada." He paused for thought, "I just haven't decided yet."

After dinner Wilma said, "I normally walk my elderly neighbour's dog at this time in the evening. I'm sure you folks will find things to talk about for half an hour or so." After getting positive responses from both of her guests she said, "Come Jessie, come Annie, it's time to walk Joe-Joe."

Joseph noticed the quizzical expression on Jessie's face and suspected why.

While Wilma and entourage were out walking Joe-Joe, Mabel and Joseph sat in the living room and chatted. Joseph was the first to speak, "Going by the look on Jessie's face, I'm not convinced there *is* a Joe-Joe. I think Mrs Snelgrove just wanted to give us time to get acquainted, and if that is the case I'm grateful."

While the troop was away they spoke about common interests: favourite Shakespearian sayings and plays; favourite motion picture actors; books; childhood nursery rhymes; and other such likes and dislikes. They discovered they had a great deal in common. Towards the end, Wilma and gang re-entered as Joseph was saying, "I am seriously considering taking over the 'Baptist Boys Brigade'. They lost Mr. Scott their last mentor in the war and Mother tells me nobody has stepped in to fill the void."

"Did you say 'Baptist Boys Brigade' Joseph?"

"Yes Wilma I am considering volunteering. The mentor sits with a group of ten to twelve year old boys once a week and they discuss all sorts of worthwhile topics, such as the Bible of course, but other things like respect for others, manners, etiquette and the changes they can expect when evolving from boyhood to manhood. This was very helpful for me as a boy."

"That's a wonderful idea. What do you think Mabel?"

"I only wish they had a 'Baptist Girls Brigade' when I was young. I don't even think they do yet."

Joseph walked Mabel home when the evening ended.

❄❄❄❄

A HUSKY MAN with prosthesis and crutch stood at the door of 20 Queen Street when Jessie answered the knock. "Good morning Sir," she said, "How may I help you?"

"Good morning, my name is Irving Hall. I believe this is the home of Mrs. Wilma Snelgrove."

"Yes that is correct Sir, I will inform Madam that you are here?" Hall nodded and smiled. "One moment please Sir."

She was back in a flash, "Please come in Mr. Hall." Jessie escorted the hobbling Irving to the living room. Wilma was on her feet when they entered. Little Annie was standing beside her.

"Good morning Mr. Hall. Are you the 'Hall' Andrew wrote so highly of in letters I received?"

Well Mam, I never saw his letters, but I was beside him as his Sergeant Major until Somme.

"Were you nearby when he fell?"

"We were separated in the confusion, but afterwards I found him on a stretcher. He was hit but still semi-conscious. Although we had lost ground that day, I could see that he was about to die so I told him we had taken our objective. I held his hand and he looked me in the eyes and said, 'Tell Wilma I'll wait for her on the other side Hall' ... 'Tell Wilma I'll wait,' and after a pause he whispered, 'Thank God I have done my duty', and faded away." He bowed his head. The room went silent and remained so for a full minute. Wilma wiped tears from her eyes.

Hall wasn't ashamed he had altered the colonel's last words. He didn't want Wilma to know he said, 'Take care of Wilma,' for fear she'd think that was the only reason he was there. The fact was, he was there because he wanted to be. He had loved his colonel – Lt. Colonel Andrew Snelgrove.

Wilma broke the silence saying, "Jessie was just frying crumpets for afternoon tea Mr. Hall. Would you like tea and crumpets?

"Yes please Mrs Snelgrove."

Jessie's voice came from the kitchen, "I heard Mam. I'll have tea ready shortly. The crumpets require about seven more minutes."

Wilma felt a gentle tapping on her wrist. She looked down to see inquisitive eyes looking up at her. She exclaimed, "Oh! Mr. Hall; this is my little 'bundle of joy' Annie Snelgrove. She was born on 21st July 1916; the same day I received that fateful telegram." She continued, "Annie dear, this is Mr. Hall."

The little girl gave Hall a curtsy.

Hall bowed as best he could and said, "It's a pleasure to meet you Miss Annie Snelgrove." Annie beamed at him. Wilma, full of pride, smiled.

"Are you able to manage an easy chair Mr. Hall or shall we bring one from the dining room?"

"A dining room chair would be better Mam. I'm afraid I may require an overhead winch to get up should I sit in an easy chair."

When Jessie appeared with a chair from the dining room before being told, Wilma said, "I would swear you have elephant ears Jessie. Did any of your ancestors hail from Jaipur?"

After Jessie recovered from a fit of laughter she replied, "I don't think so Mam, but I must admit sometimes I wake from a nightmare wherein a Maharaja is riding on my back up the ramparts of Amer Fort. Is Amer Fort in Jaipur?"

Wilma replied, "Is London Bridge in London?" Even little Annie laughed this time.

After the room had settled to normal Wilma asked, "Are you up to telling me when the war ended for *you* Sir."

"Yes Mrs Snelgrove; it was difficult to tell people for about a year, but now I am comfortable talking about it" ... "I was downed at Amiens only a few months before it all ended. I was brought back to England and convalesced in Royal Brighton Hospital not far from my hometown of Portsmouth. While there they tried their best to save my lower leg, but it was too mutilated. They had no choice but to amputate. A recovery period followed and then came the getting used to moving around with the assistance of a crutch. They told me I will eventually be able to put the crutch into retirement and adopt a cane, and possibly even to cope without one in due course."

"And when were you released from the hospital?"

"When I was released in July 1919, I went home and stayed with Mother for about six months. As I was her only son she was so happy I survived. She told me she was relieved I had joined the army and not the navy."

"Why was that? The army certainly was dangerous ... the total number of losses is still rising"

"As you know Mrs Snelgrove, Portsmouth is a naval port. So many boys from the city now rest in the deep after the horror of Jutland."

"Will you live in Portsmouth now?"

"Well, it will depend on where a crippled man like me can gain employment. I'm disabled in one leg from the knee down, but not in my brain, or my strong back and arms. I am semi-skilled in carpentry, as I worked in that trade for about five years before I joined the army halfway through the Boer War. And I have many contacts in Portsmouth – elderly businessmen – who are looking for men. But I've always liked the west-country Mrs Snelgrove. My family used to vacation on this side when I was a youngster, and Barnstaple seems to be a nice town."

Wilma thought for a moment then said, "There is an elderly gentleman, I'd estimate to be around sixty years of age who single-handedly runs a carpentry business not far from here. He has a good patronage and could very well use an extra hand. He recently did some cabinet work for me and I can introduce you to him if you wish."

"I accept your kind offer Mrs Snelgrove. There is no harm in talking to him, although I'm not quite sure if I am ready to commit at the moment. But we'll see."

"It's 3:30 pm and I don't suppose you have booked a hotel room yet. So, if not, I insist you stay the night in our guest room. We can relax all morning and then we'll walk down and talk to Mr. Crawford the carpenter in the afternoon."

"Thank you Mrs. Snelgrove. Again, I accept your kind offer."

AT TEN MINUTES to three the next afternoon Wilma Snelgrove and Irving Hall walked into 'Barnstaple Carpentry'. Mr. Crawford approached. "Good afternoon Mrs Snelgrove; good afternoon Sir. It's a brisk one today isn't it?"

"It certainly is Sir" ... "Mr. Crawford, this is Mr. Irving Hall. He was injured at Amiens in 1918 and was at Somme when Colonel Snelgrove fell. He was Andrew's Sergeant Major at the time and committed his last words to memory. He recited them to me last evening. He's a little disabled at present, but the doctors have told him he may be able to walk on his own in time".

"It is an honour to meet you Mr. Hall. Thank you for your sacrifice."

"My honour Mr. Crawford."

Mr. Crawford turned to Wilma. "I trust your kitchen cabinets are still working well Mrs Snelgrove."

"Yes Sir, perfectly well; but we aren't here about work at my home. We're here because we were wondering if you could use another carpenter to help you in the business. Mr. Hall was trained in carpentry before he joined the army and went to the Transvaal in '97. I can vouch for his integrity."

"A recommendation is not necessary Mrs. Snelgrove. I have a knack for judging character by sight alone ... and to answer your question, yes, I certainly could use another man, and especially a veteran. I had an apprentice before the war, but he also fell at Somme. Now that the boys who survived have all come back to England, those from Barnstaple have returned to their original places of employment or to their family cattle, sheep or vegetable farms."

Wilma turned to Irving. "It sounds as though Mr. Crawford is offering you a position Mr. Hall. After the old fellow nodded, Wilma continued, "What do you say?"

"I accept on one condition."

Crawford looked at him, cocked his head and said, "A condition? What condition?"

"That you drop the 'Mr.' from my name Sir. My name is simply Irving Hall and that is how I would like to be identified when being introduced to people. You Sir, please simply call me Irving."

Crawford smiled, "Only if you agree to drop the Sir and simply call me by my first name, Stephen."

"That's a deal Stephen."

Wilma, who had been standing on the sidelines while the two men got familiar piped in, "If you don't have pressing work to do Mr. Crawford why don't the two of you go down to the local for a pint or two while I go home and assist Jessie in preparing the dinner? And of course you're invited Mr. Crawford."

"Thank you Mrs Snelgrove. I've been cooking my own meals since my wife Susan passed away last year, and I'm a far cry from the type of cook she was. Shall we proceed to the 'Pig & Whistle' Irving?"

After dinner Jessie served tea in the drawing room. Upon completion, Mr. Crawford excused himself and departed. Wilma and Irving reached for their books and started reading.

A MONTH LATER Jessie escorted Joseph Benning and Mabel Arthur into the living room. Wilma let out a short squeal of delight and cried, "Joseph, Mabel, I see you have struck up a friendship. It's so nice of you to drop by after so long." She turned to Irving and back to the couple then said, "Joseph and Mabel, this is Mr. Irving Hall. Mr. Hall, it's my pleasure to introduce this young couple, Joseph Benning and Mabel Arthur."

"I'm pleased to meet both of you," said Hall.

"It's not only a pleasure for us Sir, it's an honour. The word is out that Mrs. Snelgrove has taken in a boarder; a veteran soldier who was injured in the war no less. Where were you injured Sir?"

"On the leg, can't you see?" he laughed.

"No, no, Sir: which battle?"

"Amiens."

"Oh! I was there serving in the Salvation Army."

"Yes, I know," replied Hall with a smile on his face. After a puzzled look from Joseph Irving said, "Do the words, 'I'm alright given the circumstances but my heart aches' ring a bell?"

Joseph contemplated the words for a moment before the lights came on. Then he burst out laughing, as did Hall. Everyone laughed including Annie although none knew the reason for the merriment. Wilma exclaimed, "What are we laughing at! What's so funny?"

When Irving told the story, with interjections from Joseph, the laughing exploded again.

Then Joseph said, "Wilma, when we entered you said, 'I see you've become friends,' but I'm happy to inform you we're now engaged. The wedding will be held at our church in July just before the Barnstaple Fair. We request you to be the soloist at the wedding."

Wilma was ecstatic. "Congratulations to both of you,' she exclaimed, "and after only knowing each other for such a short period of time. It's wonderful. I'm so proud of you! And yes, I will be the soloist."

"And that's not the end of the story Wilma; we plan to sail to Canada shortly after the wedding. That will be our honeymoon. I've decided to take that position if it's available. Father has already mailed a letter to his friend in Toronto."

THE WEDDING of Joseph Benning and Mabel Arthur took place on Saturday 9th July 1921, the weekend before the annual Barnstaple Fair. A photographer from the studio of 'J.D. Vickery, Victoria House, The Bridge', was hired to take pictures. A friend of Mabel, Cheryl Stewart was the bridesmaid and Joseph's friend, Roger Hunt was the best man. Annie Snelgrove was the flower girl. The whole Arthur family, relatives and friends from Exeter arrived for the occasion. Mr. Arthur proudly walked his daughter Mabel down the aisle and Pastor Mr. Llewellyn performed the ceremony. And as promised, Wilma Snelgrove was the soloist; she sang *'The Lord is my Shepherd'*.

Afterward, the whole congregation walked down Boutport Street, onto Maiden Street and then down to a dance hall on the Strand beside the banks of River Taw for a reception. It was a joyous occasion.

During the celebration Joseph and Mabel stood on the podium where a small group of violinists were playing and called for everyone's attention. When silence came over the assembly Joseph announced, "Dear friends, I'd like to announce that Mabel and I have taken the decision to move to Canada. I've been offered employment in Toronto and I've accepted. We will sail on the White Star Line's RMS Olympic from Southampton to New York in September and upon arrival travel by train to Toronto. We're both quite excited about the prospect."

DURING THE SHORT period since Wilma Snelgrove and Irving Hall had met each other they too had fallen in love. They were married on 4th September 1920, before Joseph and Mabel were due to depart. Since Wilma still didn't have many female friends, Norma Robb, her sister-in-law, acted as the maid of honour and Stephen Crawford the carpenter walked her down the aisle. A man named Norman Powell who Irving had befriended at the local served as his best man. Little Annie Snelgrove again performed the duties of flower girl.

# Three

**"WHO'S THAT!?"** He woke with a start. He had seen the silhouette of something or someone staring at him through the mosquito mesh entrance of his tent. The figure disappeared. He scrambled to his knees, swung the mesh open enough to stick his head out for a look – nothing, nobody, only silence.

He was reminded of the old Scottish prayer his granddad taught him; '*From goulies and ghosties and long-legged beasties, and things that go bump in the night, Good Lord deliver us*'. But he was certain he hadn't been dreaming a childish nursery rhyme. He was absolutely certain he saw something. But what was it, man or beast?

Walter Elliot was accepted by the locals as a meat eating sahib when he strolled through the village of Dharamsala, bamboo lathi in hand, and clad in a kurta. No one had ever harassed him. The snow leopards had enough to eat as deer were plentiful high in the foothills. The deer would be too timid to venture that close. It had to have been a human, and perhaps the motive was simply curiosity. Regardless, whatever it was had departed.

The sun was about to rise from behind the glacier-tipped peaks of the Himalayas far to the east. It was time to start his day. He emerged from the tent, soap, towel, toothbrush in hand. He sat at the crude camp table to wait for enough light for a walk to the mountain brook in the forest.

Walter's campsite was located at the edge of an approximately five hundred square yard grassy field where he often saw a shepherd boy tending sheep. The brook was situated not far away at the foot of a slope at the end of a path, well beaten due to his daily treks.

He enjoyed his daily walks to the brook. It was currently the second week of September and the leaves of the few hardwood trees had started their annual change from green to gold. There were, however, more pine trees than hardwood. The mountain air was clean, much different from the dusty plains far below. Sometimes when he started out before the sun actually broke the horizon he'd see the tails of deer disappear into the forest; there were none on this day, but of course, it had already become light.

The water of the brook was cool and clear. Sadly, it would run down the mountain side and eventually join one of the many tributaries of the Yamuna, the second most holy river in India for Hindus. By the time it merged with the Ganga and passed the holy city of Varanasi – a city as old as the long gone Babylon – waters of the once-clear mountain brook would be polluted. This was due to the sludge of animal gut dumped in the water by leather tanneries of Kanpur and garbage of other industrial areas. *'A crying shame',* he thought; especially since the largest importer of that leather was his homeland, where shoes, belts, saddles and such were manufactured.

After Walter brushed his teeth and bathed he slowly walked back to his tent.

But prior to opening the mosquito mesh, a glitter in the grass by his right foot caught his eye. He bent over and picked up the source. It was an oval locket. The colour was shiny white, not yellow. Due to this he was certain it was platinum. On the front was an embossed lotus flower. He opened the locket to discover a crucifix engraved in an inset golden oval. He closed it and inspected the back. This had what appeared to be engraved initials, but there were only fragments of letters. He couldn't make them out.

The locket must have been dropped by ...

WALTER ELLIOT WAS a 28 year old former British soldier with a height of 6 feet and a muscular build. He had auburn hair and hazel eyes. His arms and face were tanned, but white strips revealed a few light scars here and there; evidence of what appeared to be deep scratches inflicted earlier.

He decided to walk down to the village, do a little shopping and perhaps stop at 'St John's in the Wilderness Church' and talk to the minister Mr. Whitaker as he often did. He would not mention the locket, only the mysterious visitor. He had learned through experience that secrets in this remote village remained as such until you had departed, even if the confidant was a man of the cloth. He smiled as he imagined the shepherd boy running up to him upon his return and asking to see the locket.

His tent was located at an equidistance from Dharamsala, Forsyth Ganj and McLeodganj in a triangular shape. St. John's was in the former. He dared not leave the locket in the tent so he slipped it into his pocket and set out in that direction; the distance was only 2 miles over abandoned fields and through a pine forest. Again, he marvelled at the beauty.

Dharamsala was a town in the upper reaches of the Kangra Valley surrounded by dense coniferous forest consisting mainly of stately deodar cedar trees. Besides McLeod Ganj and Forsyth Ganj, other close by villages included Bhagsunath, Dharamkot, Naddi and Kotwali Bazaar. One of the main delights of Dharamsala was Triund Hill, the Jewel of Dharamsala. Triund was a one day trek to the upper reaches of McLeod Ganj, about 5.5 miles higher up. Walter did that trek during the first spring of his stay in the hills. From there he got a spectacular view of the majestic Himalayas.

Upon arrival at the church he encountered Reverend Whitaker inside polishing the benches. By mid-September all the senior British government bureaucrats who came north to escape the seething heat of Delhi had returned. While they were in town, the weekly collections of 200 rupees totalled enough to maintain the lives of Mrs Whitaker and the pastor, and to employ a Christian working-class man to do chores, but not after the plainsdwellers departed. The helper was let go until the following summer.

The reverend saw Walter walk slowly inside and said, "Hello Walter, nice seeing you old chap. What's been happening in your dull life these days?" Walter just smiled. The reverend carried on, "You seem to have a puzzled look on your mug."

Walter replied, "I didn't think it would be so obvious, but I *am* somewhat puzzled," and went on to describe his strange encounter at daybreak.

Whitaker said, "That is a strange story. There were no clues left behind?"

Walter was tempted but stuck to his guns saying, "Nothing, nothing at all; only darkness and silence."

Whitaker thought for a few seconds and said, "I suggest you walk down to the village temple and talk to the pandit. He's a jolly fellow and very learned, having studied at Oxford. There's not a single thing, whether it be incident or person that he doesn't know everything about in Dharamsala. In times of crises people run to this one man and that includes Christians, and even Muslims because the Imam down at the Jama Masjid is, in my personal opinion, a grumpy old sod. And by the way, everyone including foreigners addresses the pandit as 'Panditji'."

The reverend then changed the topic. "Walter, I know why you live the way you do. A soldier from the cantonment told me...But

Walter, you have nothing to be ashamed of;...you bravely did your duty...You can't remain in virtual solitude the rest of your days, away from family and other people of your own kind...Look at your clothing for Heaven's sake...You've become a classic example of the comparison linking phrase Brits use nowadays; that's *'colonisation of the coloniser'* ...Go back to England for Heaven's sake."

Walter just sat silently, his eyes closed, his head turned towards the plastered ceiling. He saw the terror in five sets of eyeballs. He saw smoke and fire spurting from the barrel of his Lee-Enfield rifle ... He saw them fall ... He heard them cry out. He knew it was a case of kill or be killed ... but he suffered guilt nonetheless. He also knew that others had suffered guilt from similar circumstances in earlier Anglo Wars; for instance, the Boer War and the more recent Anglo-Afghan War, but this was no consolation; it only reinforced his sense of guilt.

He finally rose, excused himself and departed.

*Captain Walter Elliot had served in the Second British Army under the command of General Sir Herbert Plumer. Elliot had served in France earlier in the war, and had been trained in the art of reconnaissance, as had his righthand man, a corporal. 6th June 1917 was the day before his division was about to commence the Battle of Messines.*

*Late that afternoon Elliot and his corporal were summoned to the tent of their Major. They were instructed to go behind enemy lines after nightfall and determine the location of the command-post of the German regiment that was put up in a nearby village.*

*That evening after darkness had fallen they slithered across 'No Man's Land' between the two forces with their bellies as low as snakes. They snipped enough barbed wire to allow access to the enemy side. After passing under the wire, they were in complete darkness; the only light being from the explosions in the night from other engagements around them. There were many. They employed more stealth than lizards to proceed as they squirmed past breaks between trenches.*

*Once inside the village, they used a small periscope to peer around corners before advancing. Their rifles were always at the ready. It was pitchdark except for those explosions. They were halfway down a short alleyway when five unsuspecting German soldiers walked around the corner ahead.*

*Being on their own side of the wire, they were much too confident as they approached. Rifles were not at the ready.*

*Walter was surprised that they seemed to be astonished to see two British soldiers standing in front of them with rifles blazing. The surprised looks in their eyes turned to horror as bullets began piercing their bodies. They all fell…dead. None had returned fire; it had happened too rapidly.*

*Walter Elliot and his corporal stole away into the darkness.*

*Walter had fired more rounds from his rifle during the war than he could count; he had probably killed many times before, but from a distance. And in those cases men were returning fire. He had never before been engaged in close combat and killed a man point blank while at a distance of only ten feet.*

*When he arrived back to report to his Major, his senior shouted; "You're back too soon! You fucked up didn't you?! I chose you for this job because I thought you were reliable! More of our men will die tomorrow because we don't know the whereabouts of the enemy commanders! I hope you are one of them, ya worthless hunk of dog shit! Get out of my sight!*

*The next day the Major died along with many others; Walter Elliot lived on …*

Upon arrival in Dharamsala Walter stopped at the paan wallah to pick up some paan and a newspaper. The paan wallah said, "Hello Saab. Who are you?"

Walter answered, "I am well thank you." The first time the man had used those words Walter had given him a strange look, so the man came out from behind his stall and said, "Who are you Saab?" So Walter had just answered, "I am me." The man then said, "No; no Saab. You are Tee Kay," while rubbing his stomach. Then Walter got it. He replied, "Ohhhh. *How* are you?" The man smiled, "Ya, ya Saab, who are you?" From then on, Walter simply answered, "I am well thank you".

The date on the three week old newspaper was 9th September 1921. The headline blared, 'Charlie Chaplin Welcomed to London by Thousands'. Walter continued walking. As he bit into his paan, he was reminded of the reverend's remark about *'colonisation of the coloniser'*. Many Indian men chewed paan.

While walking along, he moved to the opposite side of the roadway to avoid the stench as the untouchable pulled his cart towards the next outhouse to scoop up the waste for deposit outside the village. Indian pariah street dogs followed him. The fumes from the blacksmith's furnace caused him to cover his nose with a cloth, but it still stung his eyes.

He passed the village carpenter who was sawing a plank of wood on a sawhorse. He stopped to observe the village potters making decorative flower pots. He was also impressed by the coordination of the dhobis as they worked together washing, rinsing, hanging cloths to dry and ironing. It was a family business – man, wife and children.

Upon reaching the village temple Walter spat the last of the paan residue from his mouth, removed his sandals, propped his lathi against the wall and walked through the door. He encountered panditji dozing cross-legged on the floor with his back against the wall. He was clad in a white dhoti with an orange cotton scarf and turban. He turned to leave, but the pandit woke up and with a chuckle said, "Sleeping comes so naturally to me, I could do it with my eyes closed." He paused and added, "So what brings a heathen dressed in Indian garb to a Hindu temple?" He chuckled again.

Walter smiled and said, "Good day Panditji. It's nice to find someone with a sense of humour for a change."

"Surely you haven't come to convert to a religion where one goes through a cycle of birth and death before he is liberated, when a Christian – if he's a true believer – can ascend to heaven after only one lifespan on this troubled planet. I welcome you anyway. There must, however, be a reason to explain why you have graced my presence. Tell me my friend."

Walter told the story of the encounter, again leaving out the final details.

The pandit thought for a few minutes and said, "That *is* unusual. I can understand why you want to solve the mystery. I know there are a shepherd mother and boy living in a hut not far from your humble abode. The father is in Amritsar working as a casual labourer and sends money back to help support them whenever he can. Maybe the mother was just curious enough to want to lay her eyes on the white man her son had reported. The boy told me about you once when he came here for puja." He paused thoughtfully then said, "An apparition of the Virgin Mary was reported in Portugal four years ago, but I don't imagine she would appear here in Hindustan. And apparitions of Hindu gods have never been recorded. You may not know it, but Hinduism predates the beginning of recorded time ... It must only have been a curious shepherd woman."

Walter thanked him and said, "May I take my leave Panditji?"

"Yes Walter. In my evening puja I will ask Lord Shiva to watch over you."

Walter smiled and said, "I didn't even know you knew my name. It must be the powers of Hinduism." The pandit smiled and gave that Indian affirmative left-right gesture of his head. Walter continued, "And thank you for thinking of me in your evening puja. If I were a Hindu I would hope my caste fell under the purview of Lord Shiva."

Walter knew that Lord Shiva – the protector or warrior god – was one of the three main gods in the Hindu Holy Triad along with Lord Brahma, the priestly one, and Lord Vishnu the preserver, and that Lord Hanuman the so-called 'Monkey God' to whom this temple was dedicated fell under the umbrella of Lord Shiva. The Gurkhas – those fierce and especially loyal soldiers of eastern Nepal and northern Bengal who fought so gallantly for the British for over 100 years worship Lord Shiva. Their motto is 'It's better to die than to be a coward'.

He had encountered a few Gurkhas in England preparing for the forthcoming war in Europe. Most only spoke in a language that was foreign to him, but one day he sat with an English speaking Gurkha who told him about his home in the foothills. He also mentioned Dharamsala, where the cantonment of his last tenure in South Asia was situated. Walter was fascinated.

Walter thanked the pandit again, walked out of the temple after dropping a token offering in a shiny metal pot near the door. He put his sandals back on and commenced the walk back to his tent.

He hadn't gained much from the village visit. The parson was as boring as ever. The talk with the pandit was at least entertaining if nothing else. He thought he may pay him a visit in the future just for intelligent conversation.

He spent the remainder of the day whittling a six-inch deer from a block of soft wood. Once finished, a young soldier he knew from the cantonment would send it by post to his sister who would give it to his son when he was old enough to understand what it was and from where it came.

❄❄❄❄

SMACK! SMACK! In far off Toronto a baby cried. A mother lay in agony mixed with relief, after easing her womb of an eight and a half pound baby boy. The doctor held the baby in his hands while showing him to the mother, twenty-five year old Rebecca Cunningham. "It's a boy," he said.

"May I hold him?"

The doctor saw the longing in Rebecca's eyes and said, "... but just for a moment. I must take him for cleaning up and conduct a bit of surgery."

Rebecca took her son into her arms and kissed him. "Welcome to the world William Cunningham. I've been awaiting you for a long time." She kissed him again and passed him back to the waiting arms of the doctor who smiled. He passed the baby to a nurse and walked away in the direction of the waiting room.

The doctor reappeared in two minutes saying, "I assumed that Mr. Cunningham would be in the waiting room and I was going to tell him the good news. No gentlemen were there, only a couple of women sitting on opposite sides of the room."

Rebecca replied, "There is no Mr. Cunningham doctor. One of those women would be Winifred Dawson my sister. Please return and tell her."

The doctor knew enough not to ask questions in cases such as this and replied, "Thank you, I'll do that now," and walked off again.

Two weeks after the birth of her baby, Rebecca bundled him up and went to the office of the Registry of Births in downtown Toronto. Rebecca lived in the village of Leaside just north east of the city. The office was thus quite a distance away.

She left with a birth certificate with the pertinent information being:

| | |
|---|---|
| Last Name: | Cunningham |
| First Name(s): | William |
| Date of Birth: | 10 May 1921 |

❄❄❄❄

"AREN'T THEY BEAUTIFUL," said Mabel as she and Joseph had bundled up in their winter coats after dinner on 13th September 1921 and climbed the ladder in order to lean against the guardrail on the starboard weather deck of the RMS Olympic to see the icebergs the ship was passing. The setting sun in the west cast a slight orange hue to these massive blocks of ice. The ship was approximately 300 miles north east of Halifax, Nova Scotia where the so-called '*unsinkable*' Titanic had met its fate on 15th April 1912.

Passengers had been informed that extra lookouts would be deployed at night while passing through the ice fields. This was conveyed in thin leaflets containing safety and emergency procedures that were placed in all cabins prior to departing Southampton. In three days they would be berthed at one of the Chelsea Piers on the West Side of Manhattan in New York City. Eventually they returned below decks to their cabin and made love for the second time that day.

Upon reaching New York the couple loaded their huge trunk and suitcases into the baggage compartment of a Buffalo NY-bound train. They disembarked at Niagara Falls NY with plans to stay two nights at the LaFayette Hotel, named in honour of French General, the Marquis de LaFayette, who helped the Americans in the American Revolution. It was reported to have an excellent view of the magnificent Niagara Falls. While at Niagara they walked hand-in-hand across the Honeymoon Bridge[1]. They both agreed that the view from the Canadian side of the Niagara gorge was better than that on the American side. Two days later they boarded a bus of the Clifton Incline Bus Line bound for Toronto, arriving on 10th October.

They booked a room at the King Edward Hotel located at 37 King Street East. After breakfast on the morning of 11th October Joseph asked the receptionist if he had ever heard of the Cassidy's store in the downtown, and if so, could he please give them directions.

The receptionist said, "Cassidy's Limited is an importer of fine china from Britain and supplies it to most of the high-end restaurants and hotels in Toronto. They also have a retail store on Young Street. Give me a moment and I'll check the address in the telephone directory."

Joseph said "Thank you," then smiled at Mabel who had been standing next to him. The couple stood silently for two minutes until the receptionist answered.

He replied, "When you go out to the street, just turn to your right and walk to Young Street. Take a street car on Young and tell the driver you want to get off at Gerard. The store is situated at 356 Young, just this side of Gerard."

The couple thanked him and followed his instructions. Mabel was impressed by the sight of all the tall buildings; they had boarded the train in New York as soon as they left the ship and it was dark as they passed through the city. They walked into the Cassidy's store about 45 minutes after leaving the hotel. Joseph told a clerk his name and asked if he could speak to Mr. Richardson the manager.

"Do you have an appointment Mr. Benning? asked the clerk.

"My name will be all that'll be required; once again, my first name is Joseph."

The clerk noticed the same British west-country accent as that of her boss and said, "Please follow me."

Upon reaching Mr. Richardson's door the clerk knocked and entered. He reappeared in ten seconds and said, "Please enter."

Mr Richardson was a greying man who appeared to be in his late fifties. "Well I'll be a monkey's uncle, if it's not Joseph Benning from Barnstaple," he said, "and who's this pretty lady with you?"

"This is my wife Mabel Benning, Mr Richardson ... Mabel, I'm pleased to introduce Mr. John Richardson, the gentleman I had spoken of before we left home."

Mabel curtsied and said, "It's a pleasure making your acquaintance Mr. Richardson. Joseph's family spoke so highly of you and your family before we left home."

"Thank you Mrs Benning." Richardson turned to Joseph and said, "Your father tells me you're looking for a career opportunity Joseph."

"That is correct Sir. Do you have room for a hard working young man?"

"Well Joseph, there's something you must understand. Everybody who starts at Cassidy's comes in on the 'ground floor' so to speak. When I was recruited from another company to be the manager about ten years ago I was required to work one month in every department. That means I worked in backroom shipping and receiving, sales clerk, accounts and administration, and finally became the manager – the position for which I was recruited. This was to ensure that I knew the workings of the organization before managing it. Do you understand so far?"

"Yes Sir."

"Then I'll continue. You, on the other hand, will come in as a member of the backroom shipping and receiving department. But there will be nothing blocking you from working your way up through the ranks by merit to the top of the heap, for instance, manager some day in the years to come. I'll be retiring in about eight years and who knows who'll replace me?"

"Your salary will be thirty cents an hour and our store is open from Monday to Saturday. Employees are compensated for working on Saturdays by one of the other days of the week off." He paused for a few seconds, "Now, where do you intend to live?"

"We have no idea Sir. We only arrived yesterday and are currently putting up in the King Edward Hotel on King Street."

"Well, there is a two-room bungalow located in the town of Leaside just north-east of here. Knowing you were coming I checked it out and in my opinion, it'll be perfect. The best part is that I live in the same town and will be able to drive you to and from work."

He continued, "We close at 6 pm, so why don't both of you explore the city. Walk down to the waterfront and see the fresh water of Lake Ontario. Take a ferry ride to Toronto Island and walk around. Come back at six and we'll drive up to see that house. You can stay for supper at our place and I'll drive you back to your hotel afterwards."

"That's most kind of you Sir. We'll be back at six o'clock. Thank you."

Once out on the street Joseph said to Mabel, "Did you notice his use of the word 'supper' rather than 'dinner'?"

"Yes I did," she said, "I think there will be other such differences word-wise that we'll have to get used to."

"The American influence I suppose."

They viewed Toronto Island in the morning and returned to the hotel at noon for lunch and an afternoon nap."

❄❄❄❄

ONE MORNING about two months after his first encounter with Panditji, Walter thought he may just pay him another visit on one of his frequent visits to town.

Again as he entered the temple barefooted the pandit was sitting on the floor, but this time twiddling his thumbs with his eyes closed. Assuming he was meditating Walter sat down beside him on a mat and waited.

A moment later, and with his eyes still closed, Panditji uttered, "Good day Walter. I trust you have had no further strange visitors."

"No strange visits Panditji, but how did you know it was me with your eyes closed." He was more impressed with the answer, "I sensed your presence."

So they spoke on various topics for ten or fifteen minutes until Panditji used the phrase *'this troubled planet'*.

"Panditji, during our first meeting you described the planet as being troubled. Why do you reckon the planet is *troubled*?"

"How many hours can you spare Walter?"

"Thirty-six if need be."

"Alright, you've been forewarned so here I go...I'll just lay the groundwork and you can take the evolution forward using your own intelligence...Let us start with the scriptures of the Christians, Muslims and Jews which describe the creation of the World. Your Bible says something to the effect of 'In the beginning God created the Heavens and the Earth. He placed Adam and Eve in the Garden of Eden, and told them not to eat the fruit of a certain tree."

"Now, all of these things are symbolic: Adam and Eve represent 'mankind'; the 'Garden of Eden' represents a glorious unspoilt environment He created; and telling them not to eat fruit from a certain tree represents the fact that He introduced 'temptation'. But Adam succumbed to 'temptation' by eating the forbidden fruit. As punishment he was condemned to a life of work. That, Walter, was the first step towards the emergence of what I call 'this troubled planet'."

"Are you with me so far Walter?" After receiving a nod he continued. "So being condemned to a life of labour, Adam – I'll just call him 'Man' henceforth – began felling trees to clear land for cultivation. He sharpened sticks with stones and created points on straight branches to make weapons. He used those weapons to kill animals...We often hear tales of the unicorn. Was he mythical or real? Nobody knows. If he was real did man's hunger for flesh or his greed for his precious horn cause the unicorn's extinction? Nobody knows for sure except God ... Then man rubbed two sticks together and created fire. He cooked his meat over fires. As the millennia advanced he discovered coal and found it would burn. Smoke then emerged into the skies, blackening them. He dumped coal ash into rivers and streams polluting the waters that common people needed for survival."

In this part of the world we believe Chanakya, born in the first millennium BC, is the 'father of statecraft'; other parts of the world may have their own 'father of statecraft'. Regardless, what element of the essence of statecraft was applied when man waged war? Your Moses brought 'The Ten Commandments' down from Mount Sinai; what commandment was mankind obeying when he coveted or turned to dacoity?"[2]

**Chanakya**

**Moses**

"For instance, mankind formed clans and boundaries to territories. Others coveted those territories and invaded. Wars erupted. People died. The current world population is estimated at approximately 1.7 billion. I would make an estimate that the number of deaths from war since the beginning of recorded time doubles that figure; but mind you Walter, that was stated by a pessimist on such matters."

"Stepping back into more recent centuries, Europeans began coveting far off lands and colonization began in Asia, Africa and the Americas. Muslims from Persia and Afghanistan colonised the northern part of South Asia for around seven hundred years. Your own country, Walter, eventually overran all of South Asia, plus North America and the better part of sub-Saharan Africa."

"In India alone the British East India Company stationed itself in Calcutta. At first they were welcomed as friendly trading partners, but then they changed. What commandment were they obeying when they coerced landless peasants from the villages, plains and city streets, and transported them to East Africa in the stinking holds of ships? The agents got them to place their marks on contracts, but they were illiterate. Agents told them they'd be labourers, but they became *indentured* labours Walter ... *slaves!*"

"And what commandment were they obeying when the Company formed an army and dragged boys out of orphanages. These boys became pipers and marched ahead of troops into battle. They were 'cannon fodder' – *expendable*!"

"Further, the Company exploited farmers in the vicinity of the Holy Ganga on the eastern plains. They forced them to cultivate poppies rather than crops. When the farmers were hungry they had no choice but to purchase victuals from Company stores."

"Poppies were transported to factories in Calcutta where opium was manufactured for transport to China. They experienced no guilt in the fact that opium was banned in their own country... *Your England!* They described the Chinese as being uncivilized, not realizing that China had been civilized long before Christianity even landed in the British Isles, and quite possibly a thousand years before Mary and Joseph hastened into the desert to prevent the wicked King Herod from killing the Christ Child."

"After the Indian Sepoy mutiny of 1857 Queen Victoria disbanded the East India Company and our colonizers became known as the British Raj. They imposed taxes on farmers that were constant – *fixed* – and not based on income; for instance the same taxes regardless of times of plenty or scarcity. They are now using those taxes to build a railway network to all the major seaports to transport our natural resources, cultivated crops and manufactured goods back to Britain."

Walter interjected, "Panditji a moment ago you mentioned King Herod and Jesus. You know a great deal about history and religion. Where did you learn so much?"

"History interests me and I know a great deal about most world religions Walter. Take Islam for instance, the divisions of the two major sects commenced upon the Prophet's death. The Prophet declared that Abu Bakr, the father of his wife Aisha, would be his successor, but his cousin and son-in-law Ali Ibn Abi Talib, the father of his grandsons Hasan ibn Ali and Hussein ibn Ali, thought he deserved the honour. Hence the division; Sunnis follow the teachings of Abu Bakr – the Prophet's preference – and Shias follow those of Ali Ibn Abi Talib. Sunnis are by far the majority worldwide."

He carried on, "My degree at Oxford was 'Theology'. In fact, sometimes before a lecture while in the Hinduism phase, my professor would take me aside in order to clarify certain points. I give the curriculum credit though, there were few."

"Oxford is a costly university. Do you come from a family of wealth Panditji?"

"My erstwhile father was a lumberman based in Lahore. He bought cheap and sold high, exploiting those on both ends of the supply chain. The British were his major buyers and that did not bother me as much as the exploitation of the poor suppliers from these hills and those of Kashmir. I deplored that aspect. He also used unethical tactics such as bribery to outdo his competitors. As his only offspring, I inherited the business when he passed away, I sold it and paid for my own education. And upon graduation I came to Dharamsala and built this small temple with the remainder. It's a Lord Hanuman temple due to all the Gurkhas in the cantonment."

"Was your mother still alive when you did?"

"No, she expired before father...but Walter, tell me a little about your background."

"There is nothing spectacular about it Panditji. I was born into a middle class family in Bedford located not far north of Southampton. My father owns a small hardware store and my mother is a housewife. I have a sister two years younger than me. Father sacrificed a great deal so he could afford to send me to university where I earned a Bachelor of Arts degree...I'd like to carry on a bit with my background if I may."

"Please feel free to do so Walter."

"I married in early 1914. Unbeknownst to my wife Brenda and me, she was pregnant when war broke out and signs of the pregnancy showed after I joined the army to serve. Sadly, Betty died during delivery of our little boy while I was in France. My son survived and was cared for by my sister Joan, who named him Charles.

"Anyway, when the war ended I returned to my hometown of Bedford, but things I saw and did during the war tormented me. Those things were dreadful. I couldn't face people of my own kind. I thus made a life-altering decision to sail away on a ship to those foothills a friendly Gurkha had spoken of as my final destination. My sister loved my son and agreed to keep him as long as her brother wished ... Now here I am in Dharamsala high in the Himalayan foothills of British India."

"Thank you Walter, and I think we have drifted from our original topic, but I'm certain you know where it was destined. I have a few things to attend to now if you don't mind dropping it."

"That's fine with me Panditji. Thank you for your time."

"You are always welcome Walter. Let me know when you are ready to convert to Hinduism."

"Don't hold your breath while waiting Panditji ... Good day."

AFTER TALKING TO PANDITJI the shepherd boy ran up to Walter while he was walking across a field on the way to his homestead.

There was a distressed look on the boy's face. He cried, *"Meri mummy ko kutch pareshani ho rahi hai kripaya meri madad karein."* The only word Walter could decipher was 'mommy'. Due to the boy's horrified cry though, he knew something was amiss with his mother.

The boy took Walter's hand and they both ran in the direction of the family hut. He then led Walter through the door of his shelter. His mother was clad in a red and yellow sari and was lying on a straw-filled mattress. She was moaning and was shaking with severe chills. He put his hand on her forehead and she was definitely feverish. She was sweating profusely; a puddle of vomit partially sullied the ground and mattress; some had dribbled down her cheek and merged with her dark hair. He was no doctor, but knew she was suffering from malaria or something else just as bad. He had seen the symptoms before.

The boy helped him drag his mother out of the shelter. There was nothing Walter could do, but hoist the ailing woman over his shoulder and start off swiftly towards Dharamsala with the distressed boy in his wake.

Upon reaching the village he burst into the crude clinic and found the custodian sleeping in an armchair. "Does everybody sleep all day in this blasted village?" he cried. The old British doctor named Jones woke up with a start and saw Walter with the woman on his shoulder.

He said, "Lay her here" pointing to the unpainted wooden operating table.

Walter placed her frail body where instructed. The doctor put his hand on her wrist to take her pulse. He noticed plastic wedding bangles. He looked up at Walter after thirty seconds or so and said, "She is gone. It must have been either malaria or dengue. The mosquitoes are back and there have been at least three reported deaths in the village already this season."

The boy stood by his mother's bedside. He observed that the two white saabs had backed away. He looked up at them in despair. Dr. Jones, having served in the village for many years and having had to say such words many times before, put his hand on the boy's shoulder and said, "Aaoki ma mar chuki hai (your mother is dead.)"

Walter picked the boy up into his arms. The boy put his arms around Walter's neck and sobbed.

What was he to do now, with a six-year-old boy who didn't speak English, and a flock of sheep that needed to be cared for until marketable? All he knew about the father was that he worked in

Amritsar, but there was no way of contacting him. The town was just too large.

He sat on a chair to consider options. He finally rose, took the weeping boy by the hand and walked towards the temple for a second time in the same day. He went through the same rituals as he entered, and this time when the pandit saw him there were no jokes. It was evident that something was amiss.

He looked at Walter seeking an explanation. Walter said, "His mother died on my shoulder as I was bringing her to the clinic. Dr. Jones says it must have been malaria or dengue fever." He paused and continued, "Now I have this boy on my hands, no way of notifying his father, and a flock of about ten fluffy sheep."

The pandit said, "I know about that poor shepherd woman. In fact, she has been known to be so desperate she steals from residents who come up in the summer. Petty theft, mind you, but still evil. She would then attempt to sell her loot to British soldiers from the cantonment and other white people. That may account for your strange visitor. She just may have had something of value and thought you may be interested in buying it. When these people see white people like you all they think of is 'Money'."

He continued, "But that's neither here nor there; we've got this whimpering boy on our hands. Let's sort out the priorities starting at the lowest...An attempt to find his father in Amritsar would be futile. Even if we found the man, the boy would be left alone all day while his father worked; he would not get an education and most likely mix with street boys and conceivably end his life as a dacoit with a bullet in his chest by age twenty two. The sheep can wait. They can be sold in the market at a fair price any day of the week. That leaves the number one priority, the boy. There are Indian schools in the village and I wish I could say they are good, but I won't. I suggest you take him to the mission school outside the cantonment and talk to Sister Margaret. They take in Hindu and Muslim orphans, lodge them, and educate them to the tenth-standard level at no cost. I don't like the fact that they attempt to convert the boys, but that comes with the package. Christianity isn't a bad religion; our King is a Christian and he is a good man, despite the fact that...Oh forget it. What do you think of my assessment Walter?

"I totally agree. You were rapid with your reply though. I think you must have been faced with similar situations of this nature before."

"Yes I have."

Walter thanked the pandit, walked out of the temple, and headed up towards the mission school.

WALTER AND THE BOY arrived at the mission school in McLeod Ganj after a half hour walk. A middle aged nun greeted him and he said, "Good Day Sister. My name is Walter Elliot."

"My name is Sister Margaret, Good day Mr. Elliot, and who is this boy?"

"I don't know his name Sister. He's a shepherd boy who lives close to my tent on the hillside and his mother has just died of malaria. His father works in Amritsar and is unreachable. I hoped you would take him in, shelter him and give him an education. Based on his height and skills at herding sheep, which I have witnessed, I would judge him to be between six and seven years of age."

Sister Margaret knelt down and exchanged a few words in Hindi with the boy. "His Christian name is Anil, but he knows of no other name. We will call him Anil Norris."

"Do you think that is an appropriate name Sister? After all, 'Anil' is a Hindu name."

She relented, "I suppose it is the correct thing to do Mr Elliot. Anil Kumar it will be. Kumar is a popular name in north India. Please follow me."

After they passed through the gate, Walter saw a few boys playing tug-a-war with a rough rope. Little girls were skipping. All seemed to be happy, laughing in fact, having fun. This pleased him. Then he saw one Indian boy sitting alone looking through a picture book.

Sister Margaret stopped at the Indian boy and said, "This is Amir Khan. He was brought here last week by his father, the village blacksmith. His father wants the boy to be educated rather than grow up to become a blacksmith as well; I commend the father. Too many lower class semi- or skilled-workers don't think a formal education is worthwhile when they can teach their boys all they need to know in adulthood. The boy still only speaks Hindi. He will be a perfect friend for the lad."

"Does the father pay a stipend Sister?"

"He promised to contribute whatever and whenever he can, which was good of him. But most importantly we receive funds from the British cantonment as most of the white students you saw in the playground are soldier's or British civilian worker's children. They return home at the end of each day."

Walter thanked Sister Margaret again and walked away in the direction of the unattended sheep.

## Notes

1. The Honeymoon Bridge collapsed in 1938 to be replaced by the current Rainbow Bridge.
2. Banditry.

# Four

**A WOODEN CART WHEEL** bounced down the swift-running river in front of Walter Elliot as he sat on a downed log admiring the environment. It was a cool October morning, and he had been taking a walk on an old ox-cart track skirting a river not far north of town. There had been an abundant monsoon that year; the current was therefore stronger than usual. It wasn't a deep river, and wasn't very wide; perhaps only reaching a depth of eight feet and fifty feet in width. There were occasional light rapids.

He enjoyed his nature-walks amongst the white oaks, cedars and blue pines of the hills; admiring the freedom of an occasional Himalayan vulture soaring overhead; smiling as the langur monkeys scolded him, an intruder in their territory; watching the squirrels scurry around on tree branches and the ground.

His pleasure was diverted when the large wooden wheel bounced past him, buoyed by the river. He thought that rather strange and rose to investigate. As he followed the river upstream more out-of-place items drifted past; a lathi; some burlap bags of vegetables; rags and a few items of clothing for instance. *'Yes, strange indeed! What was the source of these items?'* he wondered.

As he rounded a bend he saw it. An ox-cart lay half overturned in the centre of the swift running current. A desperate family clung on for their lives. The ox flailed in an attempt to regain control of his burden, or at least to release it. Human cries were emitted, arms were waved. No one heard. No one saw. The only one in that neck of the woods on this particular day was Mr. Walter Elliot, the British recluse who dwelt nearby.

Walter sprung into action. He ran up the bank to a spot adjacent to the scene, and then plunged into the current in order to save lives. Fortunately the cart had been blocked by boulders in mid stream, thus keeping it from being sent bouncing farther downstream. By the time he reached his objective, he was standing shoulder-deep in water. His first thought was of the mother with babe in hands held high. She had managed to keep herself and the child from being swept away by placing one arm between the cart and a rope which was fastened at both ends.

When he reached her he grabbed the neck of her sari and attempted to drag her to safety, but she would not let go of the rope and screamed loudly into his ear. He made attempt after attempt, but she still would *not* let go. After the fifth attempt, and in a state of desperation, he socked her in the side of the head with his hard right fist. That settled her down. He held the babe high in his right hand and dragged the mother towards the muddy shore with his other.

He deposited them both in the mud. The two youngsters – a little girl and a pre-teen boy – were his next priority. He splashed his way towards the two. They were clinging to the same rope the mother had used. After seeing what had happened when their mother resisted, they were cooperative. Again, he dragged both to the shore, this time by their arms.

When he reached the cart the third time he saw the father lying on his back inside the cart with his head above water held up by a large bag of vegetables. His eyes were closed, but he was breathing. This was going to be the greatest challenge of the day. Fortunately, the hinged back of the cart had sprung open and hung flapping in the current. Other bags of vegetables had blocked his body from sliding away into the river. Walter climbed inside. He crawled toward the man and tried to revive him. No result. He then pushed the blocking vegetable bags over the end and dragged the unconscious man over as well. There was nothing he could do, but drag him to shore and see if there was life in his body once he arrived.

Upon reaching shore he pulled the man up onto the grassy bank and laid him on his back; no breath at all. The youngsters helped him roll their father over onto his chest. Walter applied rudimentary artificial respiration he had seen medics conducting during the war. It worked! Bursts of water and slimy black spittle sputtered from the man's distorted mouth. But he was only semi-conscious. The mother and baby sat nearby crying. Just then, the bellow of the ox diverted everyone's attention. They all rose, looked towards the ox and cried out in their local dialect, seemingly meaning "Save our precious ox; he is our livelihood!" Walter understood.

Back into the water he went. Had the ox not been harnessed it would have made its own way to safety. But, of course, it was. Walter knew nothing about harnessing apparatuses of beasts of burden. Then he felt what seemed to be a hand grasp his arm. It was! The young lad had run upstream a hundred feet, jumped into the river, and had drifted down to help. With assistance from the boy and with his own brute strength, the two of them were successful. The ox wallowed to shore, climbed up onto the bank with considerable difficulty and disappeared into the forest.

As soon as Walter and the boy regained solid ground, the boy high-tailed it into the woods in the direction the ox had taken. He returned only five minutes later holding the ox by the nose ring. The mother and girl child ran to the boy, full of joy. The father still lay on the ground; he needed medical attention.

Walter hoisted the family onto the back of the ox in a seating pattern where the woman could keep her husband's head held upright. The woman sat side saddle, so to speak, while the man's legs straddled the beast. The boy holding the baby sat in the rear and the infant between the mother's back and the boy. They marched slowly towards town, with Walter holding a vine he had fastened to the bull's nose ring.

During the half-hour walk, Walter began to feel a release from the guilt he had experienced over the past several years. Tears began to roll down his cheeks.

When they reached Dharamsala, the woman and lad started shouting. They must have been saying, "This man saved our lives," because a crowd gathered behind them, forming a procession as they moved slowly towards the clinic. People ran towards them from all directions. Walter carried the man into the clinic and told the doctor what had happened. When Doctor Jones saw the man he knew immediately what the problem was. He said, "I've seen this man before. He's addicted to opium ... Ever since the Anglo-Afghan Treaty was signed in 1919 ruthless smugglers have been bringing it into British India from Afghanistan by the cart load. There is nothing I can do. The cure is abstinence which, for an opium addicted person, is extremely difficult. He will survive though; he just needs sleep." Walter made his way to the door with the boy holding his hand. The mother sat on a chair with the babe in arms, and the little girl sat on the floor.

When Walter and the boy stepped outside, a virtual throng had gathered. They were cheering. Reverend Whitaker was in the crowd. Walter was overwhelmed, he didn't deserve such respect. When Panditji arrived he patted Walter on the back and said, "Let us escape from this scene. Follow me."

Before they entered the temple, the boy touched Walter's feet and ran off. Inside the temple they sat on the floor. Presently,

Reverend Whitaker appeared at the door and asked if he could join them. "Please do Reverend," said the pandit. Once he was seated they all sat in silence.

After about three minutes Walter asked, "Why are they making such a fuss about the episode? Wouldn't anyone in my position have done the same thing?"

Panditji's reply surprised him when he said, "No Walter they wouldn't risk their lives and hence the livelihoods of their family members to save the lives of people like that. The most daring may have fetched a vine, stood in the water knee deep, and tossed the end of a vine hoping that one or two would catch it and hold on, whereupon he would drag them ashore. None would have done what you did."

He continued, "But leaving that aside, certainly you must feel some of the quilt of past events being released from your soul Walter." Walter gave him a strange look and was told there were no secrets in India, and certainly not in small villages like Dharamsala.

With a frown at Whitaker who simply shrugged his shoulders as if to say, 'I don't know', he said, "Yes Panditji, I began to experience that release you speak of while walking back to town. I had to kill those five Germans. Had I not, they would have killed me and I wouldn't have been here to save the lives of those five people in the stream."

Then Whitaker spoke, "You can return to England now Elliot. You didn't run away from the people of your town. They didn't even know about those tormenting events which occurred in France. The guilt of being amongst them is what drove you to a life of solitude in far off India."

Walter replied, "Reverend Whitaker, I won't say '*for once* I agree with you,' but I will say I do believe you make sense. I adopted India as my permanent home a few years ago, but adoptions can be annulled. Panditji, when I've made final arrangements I'll drop by for my formal goodbye. And after I have, would you please gift my tent to any family of your choice who needs or deserves it?"

"You are most thoughtful Mr. Walter Elliot; certainly I will."

"I will drop by for a final 'good bye' just before leaving town Panditji."

Walter and Whitaker departed. The crowd had dispersed by the time they reached the roadway. They walked away and shook hands at the church. "Take care of yourself Mr. Elliot." Walter made the Indian affirmative gesture and said, "Thank you Pastor. I will."

Walter had some tying of loose ends to attend to before leaving for Britain. First, he walked to the mission school, where Sister Margaret greeted him. "Good morning Sister."

"Good Day Mr. Elliot. How may I help you?"

"Sister, I will be departing for Britain soon and I'd like to come in and observe little Anil before I leave if I may."

"Certainly Mr. Elliot, please follow me."

It was the beginning of the school day and as they walked across the playground towards the wood-sided single classroom he heard the children singing the National Anthem; *'God Save the King'*. It brought back childhood memories.

When they entered the classroom Sister Margaret raised her hand to alert Sister Patricia. She then spoke to the children. "Good morning children."

"Good morning Sister Margaret," they all sang out in unison.

"Children, I would like to introduce Mr. Elliot. He is the gentleman who brought your friend Anil to the mission school."

The children's response rang out again ... "Good morning Mr. Elliot."

Walter said "Good morning children," and offered a deep bow. The children giggled, much to Walter's delight. Anil beamed up at him from the front row. Walter bent down, ruffled his hair and shook his hand.

After they left the classroom Walter said, "Sister, you told me the blacksmith intends to send funds for his boy. I will also send funds for little Anil once I am back in Britain and find employment. Until he is old enough to understand, please read him the letters I send and encourage him to write back when he is able."

"I certainly will Mr. Elliot. You are a very thoughtful man. God be with you."

❄❄❄❄

WALTER ELLIOT STEPPED onto the platform at Delhi Railway Station. The platform was teaming with passengers, porters and street urchins. Women clad in rags with babes in arms begged for alms; dusty rhesus monkeys begged for food titbits; two pariah dogs scrapped below the belly of an irritated horse. Newspaper sellers walked up and down the platform, as did 'chai wallahs' with waxed paper cups of hot tea for sale. Whole families slept at the end of the platform on the hard concrete. Fancily clad women danced in circles around wealthy looking passengers hoping for handouts. And one single woman sat on the concrete with a pan in front of her. Her face was severely scarred with purple blotches all over it.

Walter purchased a newspaper from a vendor. The date was 9th November 1921. Albert Einstein had been awarded the Nobel Prize in Physics for his work with the photoelectric effect. Walter didn't even know what photoelectric effect was. *'Perhaps it has something to do with photography,'* he thought. Whatever it was, it was newsworthy enough for a place on the under-side of the front page.

He noticed a British gentleman dressed in a finely tailored suit and top hat, toting a walking stick. Walter needed to ask directions, but was reluctant due to his Indian apparel. He mustered up the courage and approached the gentleman. He had thought of a good tact; "Excuse me Sir. My name is Walter Elliot. Would you please be so kind as to direct me towards an establishment where I can purchase proper English clothing?"

The gentleman looked him up and down and said, "I should hope so. How on earth did you become Indianised?"

"I've been living in Dharamsala since I returned from France almost three years ago. This clothing is more comfortable and easier to wash."

"I suppose that does make sense Mr. Elliot, but really...My name is Colonel Leonard Raymond by the way. I didn't serve in the recent war, but did my duty on the Transvaal during the late 1890s. I am currently a director in the Secretariat of State for India and am on my way towards Kashmiri Gate on business. Come with me. I'll point you in the direction of the shopping area once we arrive."

While talking as they walked north on Chelmsford Road, Walter asked, "Sir, I'm familiar with the ruckus around Indian railway stations except for two I noticed here in Delhi."

"What were they Mr. Elliot?"

"First there were the fancily dressed women who danced around me after I stepped off the train. They were too well dressed to be regular beggars."

"They are eunuchs, a sad aspect about India. They are former street boys who at around ten years of age were dragged into brothels, castrated, dressed as females, and used by wealthy Indians and I'm ashamed to say even some highly-placed British for perverted fornication. Once they are old enough to realize what has been happening to them and begin to resist, they are thrown back out onto the streets, where they meet other victims and those you saw are what they become...And the other thing that puzzled you?"

Walter asked about the woman with facial scars.

"That is also a sad phenomenon, she is a victim of an acid attack."

"Acid attack? Please explain."

"Acid attacks are usually carried out against women and there are various reasons, but the most common is property disputes. There was a recent article in the *Delhi Times* about that woman written by a British woman who runs an organization that attempts to help them. When that woman's grandfather died, his two sons disputed among themselves as to who should own the house and land it was situated on. One night that woman's uncle sneaked into the house of his brother and sprinkled acid over the faces of his sister-in-law and her two young daughters. The woman you saw was only three years old at the time."

Walter walked in silence mixed with pity for a minute or two and then wanting to change the subject reached into his rucksack and pulled out the platinum locket. He passed it to the Colonel and said, "I found this locket outside my tent one morning. Do you think it's platinum and if so what do you suppose it is worth?"

Raymond rolled his eyes. "You lived in a *tent*?"

"I preferred solitude at that stage of my life, but now I am ready to return to Britain...The locket?"

The colonel inspected the piece. He opened it and saw the gold engraving. He looked at the back and said, "It is surely platinum. And if it weren't for the faint engraving on the back you could get as much as twenty quid. The engraving may devalue it to eighteen." He reinspected the reverse more closely and said, "The initials are much worn, but it seems as though the first one is, or was, a 'W'. You can just make out the beginning of it."

"I have also come to that conclusion."

"If you have enough money to support yourself until you reach Britain you would get a better price for it there. The local money lenders of Delhi are mercenary; they especially attempt to apply their skills on colonizers – people like you and me that is.

"Thank you Colonel...When we met, you said you were off to Kashmiri Gate. What is behind that gate?"

"Oh, Kashmiri Gate was one of the entrances to the walled city of Delhi, founded as Shahjahanabad in 1639 by the Mughal Emperor

Shah Jahan. Back when it was founded, nobles of the Mughal court lived in grand mansions with marble floors and finely tended gardens, and the roadways were lined with beautiful trees. Over the past almost three hundred years however, the mansions are scruffy tenement houses, the gardens no longer exist; commercial establishments stand in their place and the once tree-lined roadways are now lined with street vendors selling everything under the sun. One saving grace is that the glorious Jama Masjid remains. It would be a worthwhile place to visit before you depart Mr. Elliot."..."and while I'm on the subject of Shah Jahan, he also built the Taj Mahal in Agra.

***Jama Masjid***

Once they reached the vicinity of their destination, the Colonel pointed to a line of shops where he would certainly find one or two that sold various types of garments. He advised him to barter for the lowest price, since this is what merchants expected. They always set their starting price high. He then noticed the church.

"Do you see that church across the road?" Walter nodded "That is St. James Church, also known as Skinner's Church. It was commissioned by Colonel James Skinner. He was lying wounded and near death on the battlefield of Uniara in 1800. He prayed to God promising to build a church if he survived. St James, built at his own expense, is evidence that prayer works wonders. The Viceroy attends services there every Sunday. I recommend you take a peek at that as well."

"Thank you for your assistance, valuable descriptions and recommendations Colonel Raymond. I'll be on my way now."

The two shook hands and parted company.

FIVE DAYS after his arrival in Delhi, Walter again stepped off a train, this time in Bombay. He had spent two and a half days sightseeing in Delhi and two and a half on the long railway ride in a third class carriage. The scene on the platform was much the same as that in Delhi. After the racket of rumbling over junctions in the rails and shouting of lower class Indian passengers he was exhausted. He needed sleep.

He was wearing khaki cotton trousers, a white shirt, khadi vest, comfortable British-style shoes, an overcoat and scarf topped off with a fedora hat when he walked out the railway gate at Tilak Nagar.

Bombay with a population of 1.2 million was more than twice that of Delhi at 420,250. He reached into his pocket and transferred his locket to the inside zippered pocket of his overcoat for fear of pickpockets on the crowded streets he saw ahead.

He noticed a corporal of the 'British Indian Army' standing nearby, and walked up to him. "Excuse me Corporal. My name is Captain retired Walter Elliot. Would you please direct me towards a relatively low-cost hotel?"…"and in the morning I'm going to the docks in an attempt to board a ship bound for England, so I seek directions to docklands as well."

"Certainly Captain." The corporal pointed towards the closest road junction and said, "Turn right on that road and you are bound to find several hotels Sir." He then pointed to the west and said, "We are actually on a peninsula. The Arabian Sea is in that direction. The Bombay Docklands are located on the southern shore of the peninsula. I recommend you take a 'tanga', as it would be a very long walk of perhaps three hours."

The corporal continued, "Are you looking for a berth on a passage liner or a cargo ship? Sometimes cargo ships do have space and take on passengers at much more reasonable rates."

"How will I know who to approach for cargo ship passage?"

"Just go to the warehouses. They're all owned by Parsi exporters who pretty well know all the ship captains. One of them will surely introduce you to one."

"What in the devil is a Parsi anyway?"

"I posed precisely the same question to one of my officers when I arrived here and apparently, Parsis are Persians who migrated to South Asia from Persia hundreds of years ago to avoid religious persecution. They are of a separate religion altogether. Most settled in Gujarat a couple of hundred miles north of here, but there are many here in Bombay. They're as sharp as tacks businesswise and very honest."

"Thank you Corporal." Walter walked away towards the indicated hotel street.

THE NEXT MORNING he stepped out of his hotel. It was not the class of hotel a normal Briton resident of India would have chosen, but the only funds he now possessed were from the sale of ten fluffy sheep in the Himalayan foothills. He had a good sleep despite his initial concern about the constant street-racket two stories below his window.

He turned and walked towards the 'tanga' stand close to the gate of the railway station. Sari clad beggar-women with babes in arms begged for alms; cripples sitting on the ground cried out to him; street urchins danced around seemingly teasing him. Walter walked on with an air of indifference.

He approached the 'tanga' at the head of the queue and told him he wanted to go to the docks. The 'tanga wallah' only understood the local language, Marathi. Walter pulled a pencil and piece of paper from his pocket and drew a rough picture of a cargo ship. When he passed it to the 'tanga' driver, the man said, "Achha, Nauka" and motioned for Walter to take a seat. Off they galloped in a two-wheeled cart with the horse's rump swaying back and forth in front of them. Clickidy-click, clickidy-click, clickidy-click...

They arrived right outside the docklands gate. As he walked in, Walter noticed an establishment called 'Ruttonjee Shipping Enterprises', directly across the road. He walked across, entered the establishment and asked to speak to the owner.

Presently a well dressed gentleman walked out of his office and said, "Hello Sir. My name is Alankar Ruttonjee. How may I help you?"

"Good day Mr. Ruttonjee. I'm retired Captain Walter Elliot and I was wondering if you might know of any ships bound for England shortly that could possibly take me on as a passenger."

"You are rather young for a sea captain so I assume you must have served in the Army. Is that a correct assumption?"

"That's correct Sir. I retired after the war in Europe."

"So now you are here in India for some reason which is none of my business; you are short of funds, and that is why you seek passage on a cargo ship rather than an ocean liner."

While smiling Walter replied, "I've been told that Parsis are very good businessmen and thus quick to judge situations. That is also correct."

Mr. Ruttonjee also smiled, "Please take a seat Mr. Elliot. I will soon be walking over to a ship that will be carrying a large load of my goods to Southampton. It is scheduled to depart in two days. I will take you with me and introduce you to Captain Parsons."

After thanking the man Walter sat in a comfortable chair and picked up a copy of the *Times of India*. He was reading a story about the Spanish Communist Party being founded when Mr. Ruttonjee walked out of his office and asked him to come along.

While walking the half mile to SS Royalstar, Mr Ruttonjee asked, "Would you be willing to work as a member of the crew? That way instead of you paying them, they'd pay you."

"That is indeed an interesting option I'd be willing to accept."

"And since you were an army officer, I assume you have a university education. Is that correct?"

Walter smiled and shook his head in the affirmative.

"You just *may* find a position as a junior officer under training. In that case you'd work on shifts at the helm. They would use more experienced helmsmen for entering and leaving harbour, and for navigating the Suez Canal, but it would be safe in open seas. A further benefit would be that you'd be given a cabin above the hull within the superstructure opposed to living amongst forty filthy seamen below decks. All of this of course depends on what Captain Parsons has to say."

"This is her" Walter looked up at the large black hull of the Royalstar and saw the British Red Ensign flying high at the stern. He would be proud sailing under those colours. He and Mr. Ruttonjee walked up the gangway and asked the Negro standing guard duty at the brow if they could speak to the captain.

The man said, "Please watch the gangway Mr. Ruttonjee while I go and fetch him," in a strangely accented voice.

"He knows your name Sir. You must have boarded this ship many times."

"Yes, more than many Mr. Elliot. That man hails from Tanganyika in British East Africa. The Royalstar is crewed mainly by seamen from the colonies, mostly from India and Ceylon, but you'll also see a few from the West Indies and Africa. The cook is from Hong Kong." He paused for thought. "The only white men are seven Brits – the captain, two watch officers, the boatswain, the engineer and two seaman – one is a Newfoundlander the other whites jokingly call 'Goofy Newfie'. He served in the Royal Navy during the war."

Captain Parsons appeared as he walked around the superstructure and made his way aft towards them along the starboard upper deck. Ruttonjee saw him approaching and said, "Follow me Elliot."

They met the captain at the halfway point. Ruttonjee stuck out his hand and said, "Good day Captain Parsons. It certainly is a brisk one."

"Not as brisk as Southampton I suspect Mr. Ruttonjee, and who is this handsome gentleman?"

"Captain Parsons, I'd like to present Captain Walter Elliot. He's a retired army officer who has been living in British India for the past three years. He served in France during the war."

Captain Parsons stuck out his hand while saying, "It's a pleasure to meet you Captain Elliot."

Walter bowed slightly and replied, "My pleasure Captain Parsons," as the two shook hands.

After the niceties the captain turned to Mr. Ruttonjee and said, "That certainly is a huge shipment of khadi. Are you sure you have enough buyers for it all."

"Well Sir, I only have one buyer. That is Ruttonjee Importers in Southampton which I appointed my son Zubin to run. But I don't know how long his customers – the manufacturers of clothing – will stay in business if that movement in Gujarat run by a rabblerouser named Gandhi builds up steam.

"Interesting, please explain what you mean."

"Well, khadi is cotton in rough form which is shipped to Britain, spun and manufactured into clothing, and then shipped back to India and to other countries. It's a profitable business for many including me. This Gandhi fellow's movement is aimed at boycotting foreign goods including cotton and promoting Indian-manufactured goods, thereby creating employment for ordinary Indians. If the movement gains steam, khadi exports will fall by the wayside. The British should keep a close eye on this Gandhi fellow. He's a peaceful-minded chap and it wouldn't surprise me at all if some day he is the figurehead of a non-violent freedom movement."

Captain Parsons was in deep thought…"Actually, although it may hurt both you and me in the long run, Gandhi's movement does make sense. I think I shall inform the owners of the Blue Star Line to brace for the possibility of a forthcoming shock. Their ships carry large quantities of khadi from several South Asian ports."

"You don't have to remind me Sir. I have warehouses in them all."

"Tell me Mr. Ruttonjeee, how did you get the funding to create such an empire in the first place."

"Well Captain Parsons; back in the days when men were made of steel and ships were made of wood, my grandfather owned a shipping company that exported opium to China on company-owned sailing ships. He became a millionaire, as did many of *your* countrymen. My father inherited the business and expanded it. He died relatively young and I inherited a large chunk of my grandfather's fortune… Back to the last topic of discussion, the decline won't happen overnight. If it's successful it may take a few years to gain steam, but you'd be wise to inform your owners just in case"… He paused and said, "Captain Parsons, Captain Elliot is willing to work on board at any position available until the Royalstar reaches Southampton. Do you think you can use him?"

Walter was standing tall with his shoulders back and a smile on his face when Captain Parsons looked him over and said, "Well young man, you look healthy. You were an army officer so you are educated, and since Mr. Ruttonjeee says you are willing to work in any position does that mean you'd even work in the boiler room as a stoker shovelling coal?"

"If need be Captain Parsons."

"Do you realise how hot it is in the boiler room?"

"Well Sir I imagine standing in front of an open hatch chucking shovel-load upon shovel-load of coal into an already raging fires would be an extremely hot place to work. I'd do it though."

"You *are* desperate to get home aren't you, but we have no vacancies in the boiler room; that position is covered."

Walter's shoulders sunk.

"But I could use another helmsman on the bridge. Our two other officers stood watch on watch off all the way from Southampton, but we prefer a one in three rotation. This allows one fellow to take the helm for four hours and sleep for eight before going back on watch for four hours. The system allows eight hours of uninterrupted sleep per day. You would only take the helm on the high seas, mind you. My Chief Bos'n, Mr. Turpin mans the helm while entering and leaving harbour, and while transiting the Suez Canal. How does that sound?"

"You have found the right man Sir."

"Excellent, but remember, there is only one Captain on this ship!" After some chuckling the captain turned to the seaman and said, "Take this gentleman to the wardroom and show him a chair, the bookcase and some old copies of Athenaeum magazine"...He then turned to Walter, "Mr. Elliot please follow this fellow and I'll be with you after talking business with Mr. Ruttonjee."

"Thank you Captain Parsons, and thank *you* Mr. Ruttonjee."

"Think nothing of it. I'd only do it for someone I liked at first sight, and I liked you Mr Elliot. Have a pleasant trip. And say hello to Mama from me!

# Five

**JOSEPH AND MABEL** had found the bungalow recommended by Mr. Richardson to be perfect and had moved in during the first week of November. Joseph was gainfully employed in the shipping and receiving warehouse at the back of the Cassidy's store. Mr. Richardson had driven him to work for the first couple of weeks, but always dropped him off one block away from the store so it wouldn't be perceived as though he was showing favouritism to one of his most junior staff members.

While in the shipping and receiving department however, Joseph discovered that two other fellows lived in Leaside and he decided to tell Mr. Richardson he appreciated his drives to and from work, but would rather make his own way with one of the other fellows he had befriended. His boss patted him on the back.

So Joseph worked his heart out padding and packing precious pieces of china into hardwood boxes and placing them into the backs of delivery trucks, and also receiving and unpacking the same for storage or placement on the shelves of the retail store out front.

Sometimes he whistled while he worked. Further, it was obvious that Mabel was pregnant. The new-born child would arrive in June of 1922 which also brought happiness to his new life in Canada.

❄❄❄❄

IN THE MISSION SCHOOL in Dharamsala young Anil Kumar sat at his desk in a classroom along with about twenty of his new friends. He was dressed in the school uniform. Sister Patricia was giving the English lesson. "Anil, please stand up and say the alphabet."

Anil stood and sang; *"A-B-C-D-E-F-G—H-I-J-K-LMNOP—Q-R-S—T-U-V—W-X—Y & Z. Now I know my ABCs next time won't you sing with me?"*

"Very good Anil … but you don't have to sing the last part. Just stop at Z. Now, what word starts with E?"

"El-ef-fant"

"Excellent! You may sit down now Anil ... Susan please stand."

Susan stood...

After classes Panditji arrived at the mission school gate. He asked the chowkidar to tell Sister Margaret he wished to speak to Anil.

"Ji Panditji" The chowkidar ran off and appeared a few minutes later with Mother Superior.

"Good morning Panditji, little Anil will be with us in a moment or two."

"Good morning Sister Margaret. I have come to tell him I received a letter from Mr. Elliot. He was in Bombay and about to sail to Southampton on a merchant ship. He asked me to tell him he would send him a letter once he gets settled in at home. How has the boy been making out in his lessons in these early stages?"

"I placed him in a class with children about one year younger because he needs to learn the basics before he can advance. He's a fast learner and it won't be very long before he catches up with children of his own age."

"Will you allow me to drop by to pick up Anil and the other Indian boy on Sunday afternoons Sister?"

"Yes, that would be alright Panditji. The other boy's name is Amir ... you could pick them up at twelve noon, but we serve dinner at seven o'clock. So, have them back by six thirty, which will give them time to wash up prior to saying grace."

As the Pandit was thanking Sister Superior, Anil came running towards him with a big smile on his face yelling, '*Panditji ... Panditji.* He threw his arms around the lower part of his body.

Sister Margaret burst out in Hindi, *"Anil, show some respect!"*

"Ji Sister Margaret," Anil stood back a step, bowed his head with his hands in the prayer position and then knelt and touched Panditji's feet."

The sister said "Good boy."

Panditji ruffled the boy's hair and told him about the letter. Anil beamed as he looked up at Sister Margaret who smiled back.

"Sister Margaret has told me I could pick you and Amir up on Sunday afternoons. We could do all kinds of things, walk in the forest, stroll through the village, say hello to Amir's papa, go to the temple, all sorts of things. It will be *your* afternoon."

"Cricket?"

Panditji nodded.

Anil jumped up and down while yelling *"Achhaaah!"*

After that burst of joy Panditji excused himself. "I must be off now. Thank you Sister, and good day to you; I should arrive at the gate at one o'clock on Sunday. Good day Anil."

He slowly walked away, lathi in hand.

SURE ENOUGH ON SUNDAY afternoon Panditji arrived at the mission school gate right on schedule. Anil and Amir were waiting for him dressed in mufti. Amir had a child-size cricket bat propped over his shoulder and Anil was carrying a ball. "It doesn't look as though you want to walk in the forest," said Panditji in the local language, "but we will still have to walk to the village to get to the playing field."

"Ji Panditji," replied one of the boys.

"Would you like to stop and say hello to your papa Amir," asked Panditji, "he may want to join us."

"Tee Kay."

As the three of them walked through the village, everyone they passed paid respects to Panditji. The trio turned down a short lane and encountered Amir's father in front of his blacksmith shop sitting on an overturned wooden box puffing on a hookah. He didn't notice them coming and was startled when Amir ran up and jumped on his back. They both laughed, as did Anil and Panditji.

After the levity had died down Panditji was the first to speak. "We're off to the playground where Anil and Amir can take turns at bowling and batting. Would you care to join us Sri Khan?"

"That would be a wonderful break in my boring life down this dark lane, and besides, my wife is a chatterbox." Again they laughed.

When they reached the small playing field Panditji and Sri Khan sat on a crude park bench in the shade of a pine tree. The boys wasted no time in going onto the field to take turns bowling and batting. As the two men watched, Panditji couldn't help but notice the keenness of Anil's eye-to-hand coordination while batting. He could wallop the ball a fair distance for a seven-year-old. He pondered about cricket leading to a better life for the little boy in the future if his cricket skills turned out to be remarkable. And he knew how he could help him, but he'd have to wait until he reached graduation age from the mission school at the tenth standard level.

As the two boys played Panditji asked, "How is business going Sri Khan?"

"Not so well Panditji," replied Khan. "If given the dimensions, I can make gates, grilles, furniture and railings, and decorative and religious items, but there just aren't many requirements for these up in the hills. At one time my greatest demand was for fixtures, tools, agricultural implements, cooking utensils and weapons such as spearheads. The problem is that I have more axe heads, hoes, hammers, picks and crowbars on hand than this village would require for the next hundred years. Needless to say, business is slow."

"When you say 'furniture' does that mean decorative end pieces for garden or park benches; and with gates and fences I suppose you'd need dimensions?"

"I've constructed the most beautiful decorative benches for the army cantonment up the hill. I produced the end pieces and the carpenter fitted the wooden seats and backs; and yes, I'd need dimensions for gates, railings and fences."

"Please give me a few minutes to think Sri Khan; an idea has just entered my noggin and it may take time for me to assemble it properly" ... ... After three minutes he spoke again, "Everyone in the village would remember that British gentleman who lived in a tent up in the forest." Sri Khan nodded. "Well, he returned to his homeland about a month ago. His father owns a hardware store and he may, just may, be interested in importing items manufactured by you ... he has promised to send me a letter once he gets settled, and when I have his home address I will send him a letter and mention what we just discussed."

"Thank you Panditji. That is most kind of you."

❄❄❄❄

THREE DAYS after Walter Elliot officially became a seaman, the Royalstar was about 500 miles south-east of Bombay on the Arabian Sea. He was at the helm and Chief Bos'n Turpin was standing at his side giving instructions. Turpin turned to the Officer of the Watch (OOW) and said, "Ready Sir."

Mr. Wilkins, the OOW said, "Port twenty."

The helmsman was required to repeat all helm orders while performing them. Walter replied, "Port twenty," and turned to helm twenty degrees to port.

Twenty seconds later Mr. Wilkins ordered, "Midships."

"Midships," Walter replied as he brought the helm back to the centre position.

"Starboard ten."

"Starboard ten."

"Port ten, steer 320."[1]

"Port ten, steer 320," and once he got on course Walter replied, "Steering course 320 Sir."

"Excellent Elliot," said Turpin and then went on to explain, "We are steering into the sea now."

"Into the sea, Mr. Turpin; I thought we were sailing on the sea."

"Alright you smart ass, 'into the sea' means the waves are hitting us straight on...when they are hitting us on the port or starboard bows, or quarters – that's the sides of the after part of the ship – it is harder to stay on course. When we have a stern sea – and please use your noggin to figure that one out – it is extremely hard, especially when it's rough weather because we never know which way the sea will throw us. I'll be back during your morning watch tomorrow." The bos'n walked away and raised the back of his hand in acknowledgment when Walter thanked him.

Walter appreciated the lessons of Mr. Turpin. He had run him through many evolutions over the past couple of days; with lifeboat drill and fire-fighting being the most important.

BANG ... BANG. "You are aiming too far to the right Sir." BANG ... BANG ... BANG. "They're altering away," reported the port lookout, "but it looks as though you hit one."

"Keep a close watch on that boat and for others coming from different directions Lookout, that one could have been a decoy."

"Aye-aye Sir."

It was 30th November 1921. The Royalstar was passing through the narrow strait between Djibouti to the west and Yemen to the east before entering the Red Sea. From high on the bridge, land was visible in both directions, although far away. Walter Elliot was at the helm.

Captain Parsons arrived on the bridge, huffing and puffing. "Those Muhammadin devils again?" he asked.

"Yes," replied the Officer of the Watch ... "there were about four armed men onboard and this time they appeared to be ready to engage." He pointed at the boat off the starboard bow, "It's beyond range of our rifle, and is now running parallel to our course."

"Tell the lookouts to keep a close watch in all directions, as that one may only have been a decoy."

"Already done Sir."

"Good man," replied Captain Parsons, and continued with a chuckle, "You're finally using your head for more than a hat rack." He stepped back and stood near the helm.

Walter was curious; "Would you mind explaining what you meant by 'those Muhammadin devils again Sir? Why do they attack? Were they pirates or something?"

"It goes a long way back in history Elliot....As you would know, the 'Scramble of Africa' by European powers started over a hundred years ago. Just the other day we rounded the 'Horn of Africa,' where British Somaliland and French Somaliland are located. We stopped for coal in Aden a port of Yemen – situated at the heel of the boot-shaped Saudi Peninsula. The British regained control of Yemen just this year; although it may only be temporary. Now, there is a Dervish leader named Husain in British Somaliland who is attempting to persuade colonised territories of the region to join forces and fight for independence of their traditional homelands. Therefore, the coasts of the Red Sea are quite hostile, especially on the African side. With regard to the pirate part of your question, if they gained control of the ship, they would kill all the crew, or at least the white crew members. They'd run the vessel aground and loot all, or most of the cargo. The sides of this ship are too high for that though, so they just shoot at us."

"And what about the Suez Canal Sir?"

"No problems there Elliot, the British have a firm grip."

❄❄❄❄

WILMA AND IRVING HALL were living a happy life in Barnstaple. Wilma had many more friends than she did when she first arrived and Irving had earned several friendships at the Lilico's Pub on the Square in the Town Centre. He and his boss, Stephen Crawford, dropped in at the pub after work a couple of times a week. Irving liked a pint of scrumpy now and then, but was by no means an alcoholic. Wilma did not object.

Little Annie Snelgrove was now attending kindergarten. Jessie walked her to and from school every Monday to Friday. Sometimes

Wilma would accompany them, and she and Jessie would stop at the market on the way back home in the morning. They all enjoyed the Barnstaple Fair each July.

One evening after Annie had been tucked into bed Irving took Wilma into the living room and said, "Dear, Annie has been asking me why her last name is Snelgrove and her mummy and daddy's last name is Hall. She told me children had been asking her and she didn't know the answer." He carried on, "Do you think it would be advisable if we renamed her 'Annie Hall' to simplify matters for the poor child?

Wilma agreed and the paperwork was taken care of within a week.

❄❄❄❄

IN THE LATE AFTERNOON of 19th December, the Royalstar sailed past the Solent, the body of water between the Isle of Wight and Portsmouth, and entered the Southampton East Cowes, the final stretch of water before landing in home port. There had been no further incidents in the Red Sea or Suez Canal. On the western end of the Mediterranean, they had stopped for coal at the Spanish port of Almería located close by the huge iron deposits that British and French mining companies exploited. While moving north in the Atlantic, the temperatures fell quite drastically. Walter Elliot was issued a weather jacket to compensate. He was off duty, but standing on the bridge to watch the approach. Captain Parsons was standing beside him.

"Well Elliot, he said, "we'll be parting ways tomorrow morning. I've written a recommendation letter and will give it to you if you follow me to my cabin after I leave the bridge. That will help you in finding employment, or even to come back to Blue Star Line in the future."

"That's most kind of you Sir. I'd also like to say it's been a pleasure working under your command."

"Don't forget to see Patel the paymaster before you depart. And if you'd like to keep the weather jacket, inform him now and he'll deduct the cost from your remuneration. At 9:30 am on 20th December, Royalstar berthed at Eastern Docks in her home port. Captain Parsons was standing at the gangway when Elliot was about to go ashore. They shook hands, both saying it had been a pleasure knowing each other.

Walter Elliot stepped back into his homeland at 10 o'clock with a pocket full of cash; well, not quite a pocket full, but he thought 30 quid was nothing to sneeze at, especially since it was earned by doing something he enjoyed immensely.

Outside the eastern gate he went to the head of the queue of waiting taxis and told the driver, "The railway station please."

"What will be your final destination Sir?" After being told it was Bedford the driver continued, "That will be the main station, only about 15 minutes from here. You appear to have come off the Royalstar that just pulled in, so I don't imagine you have a ticket yet, and if not, being the week before Christmas you may find it a little hard to get one ... And don't be taken in by unscrupulous counterfeiters as you enter the gates of the station parking area. They'll tell you all trains are fully booked, but they have extra tickets for all destinations."

"Thanks for the warning about counterfeiters, and as regards to availability, the distance is only 95 miles and I'll go third class if need be."

After paying and thanking the driver, Walter picked up his carry bag and walked to the ticket booths outside the station. A couple of seedy looking characters approached saying "All trains are fully booked Sir," but he ignored them and kept walking. The queue at the Bedford booth was ten people long, and seemed to be moving rather well. He was happy he hadn't seen anyone walking away with his head down in a dejected state of mind. When he was third in line a small ruckus broke out.

***"What do you mean no first class tickets,"*** bellowed a gentleman with a fine woollen coat, polished boots and a top hat. ***"Do you expect a self-respecting gentleman like me to travel third class with the likes of him?"*** He pointed at a working class man in the next queue.

The man he pointed at broke the queue, walked the five steps to the so-called gentleman, swung his right hand and knocked the top hat off the ill-mannered offender's head. It landed in a pile of dirty slush on the cobblestone walkway. The hat-swatter stood firm awaiting the consequences, but there were none. All those who witnessed the incident clapped their hands and threw verbal insults at the bad-mouthed gentleman. The champion of the day returned to his place in the queue after receiving multiple pats on the back. The offender grudgingly purchased a third class ticket and walked away.

Walter purchased his ticket and with more than three hours on his hands before departure walked out to the street and approached a café to enjoy an English breakfast, his first in almost three years. As he was about to enter, the person manning the door said, "We're rather busy this morning and all tables are occupied. It should only be five minutes if you don't mind waiting."

"No problem at all," replied Walter. Just then a pretty woman who looked to be a couple of years younger than Walter fell in behind him. And soon a party of four did the same. Walter turned to the group and said, "They're full, but a chap told me it won't be too long a wait."

Two satisfied diners exited and the fellow from inside reappeared a moment later to announce, "I have a table for two available. He looked at Walter and then the woman behind him and said, "We're quite busy this morning for some reason," and then asked, "Would the two of you mind sharing a table?"

Walter was the first to reply, "I have no problem with that," and turned to the woman.

"This man doesn't appear to be a degenerate, so I have no objection, especially since my stomach is begging for replenishment after an overnight train ride from Plymouth."

The man escorted the couple into the rather noisy café to a table beside the window. Walter pulled out the chair with the street view and assisted the woman by pushing it back in as she sat down. He took the room view. Then he wondered if he had made the correct assumption saying, "I assume you *do* prefer a street view rather than watch a bunch of blabber-mouths eating breakfast."

"Yes, thank you Mr…"

"Elliot," he said, "Walter Elliot from Bedford."

My name is Ruby Baker, also from Bedford. I'm waiting for the train to depart as I suppose you are."

"Going home for Christmas?"

"Well, Christmas in nigh, but I'm also going home to stay. Where are you coming from?"

"Considerably farther away than Plymouth; India actually and I'm also going home to stay. I arrived on a cargo ship earlier this morning."

After the waiter arrived and took their orders Ruby said, "So you're a seaman by occupation?"

"No no, far from it. After having lived in India for a couple of years when I returned from the war, I was too short of funds to afford an ocean liner, but found a ship captain willing to take me on as a crew member for the passage."

"What do you plan to do now that you are home?"

"Father owns Bedford Hardware Store on St John's Street. I have big plans for that little store...And you; do you plan to remain in Bedford?"

"Yes, I've been offered a teaching appointment at Bedford School. You'll probably know it's a boy's school dating back to the 1500s. Until they changed the rules last year they only employed male teachers. I'm quite excited about the assignment."

"Yes, it's an excellent school. I studied there until my graduation at age 18, and then carried on to university."

Their breakfasts arrived and they ate with few exchanges of words.

After breakfast Ruby said, "It's been a pleasure making your acquaintance Mr. Elliot, I'm going to go back into the station and read some magazines while I wait for departure."

"The pleasure is mine Miss Baker. I'll stroll around exploring the streets for a while. By the way, there is no Mrs Elliot and if you are also unattached would you consent to me paying you a visit in Bedford from time to time?"

"Certainly Mr. Elliot, I'll be staying with my mother until I find a place of my own and the address is 2 Newnham Road, off the Embankment."

"How convenient, I'll also be staying with my parents until I find a place of my own as well. Their bungalow is situated on Albany road only a ten minute walk from your mother's house."

Outside on the street they shook hands and walked off in opposite directions. Walter in particular was interested in visiting a hardware store in a larger city than Bedford. Within fifteen minutes he walked into one by the name of 'Riggs Hardware'. The elderly owner, Mr. Riggs, greeted him at the door.

"Welcome young man," he said, "is there anything in particular you are looking for?"

"Not really Sir: my father owns a small hardware store in the town of Bedford up north of Southampton. I was fighting in France for four years and have been overseas for a couple of years since then. I've just returned and plan to enlarge the store when I get home. I just wanted to look around and see what type of new products have come out during the time I've been away. Father most likely has no idea."

"I passed through Bedford a few years ago and stopped at a hardware store. I believe it was the only one in town. I met the owner but I forget his name."

"His name is Elliot Sir and I'm his son Walter."

"Yes...Yes. Now I remember. It *was* Elliot," Being a shrewd businessman, Mr. Riggs placed his index finger across his lips and his palm on his chin, looked up at the ceiling and thought, *'since Bedford is located far from here this man's store will not be my competitor so why not show him around'.* "I'd be happy to show you around Mr. Elliot, although not many new items hardware-wise have been introduced in recent years."

So they walked up and down the aisles and every time Walter saw something he knew his father wouldn't have had he took out his pencil and noted it in a little notepad he had acquired in Delhi. He not only noted the item, but the brand name and British manufacturer or that of the place from where it was exported. By the time he thanked Mr. Riggs and departed, his list contained more than twenty-five entries. He was satisfied with his endeavour.

Two hours later he was seated in a crowded third class compartment of the train on his way to Bedford. Babies cried, people verbally abused each other,; violent physical encounters took place... it was very noisy to say the least – in fact, too noisy to even think about reading the newspaper he had picked up before departure. It remained folded on his lap.

Then a squabble broke out between a man and his wife, seemingly about an earlier-made decision on whose parents they'd be spending Christmas with. It got so violent that at one point the man rose, stood in the aisle and removed his belt. As he raised it to beat his wife, Walter jumped out of his seat and arrested the man's arm with his strong fist. The man glared at Walter, but realising he was defeated sat down again.

A gentleman sitting across the aisle said, "Well done young man. You can expect anything from this class of people." Walter realized it was the man who had kicked up a ruckus ahead of him in the queue earlier in the day. He didn't respond to his compliment, but noticing the soiled top hat on his lap did say, "I think your top hat needs cleaning," and walked back to his seat.

The transit took longer than expected, as people in large numbers boarded and climbed on board the carriages. It was 11:30 pm when the train finally arrived in Bedford. Not wanting to disturb his sister's sleep at that hour he walked across the road and entered the 'Beds for Bedford Hotel'. He didn't have to wake up a sleepy clerk because he was standing at the reception desk waiting for guests that arrived every night on the late train from Southampton.

"You need a room for the night I presume Sir."

"Yes please," replied Walter, "just for one night."

"That's the requirement of most of our late train clientele," he said, "that'll be fifty pence for the room and if you choose to have breakfast in our dining room that is not included. Here's the key for room number 10 on the ground floor. It's down the corridor in that direction." He pointed to the left.

Walter reached into his pocket, fished out fifty pence and passed them to the clerk, saying "Thank you." He was somewhat surprised that he was not required to sign a register. As he walked away he noticed the same gentleman from the train standing in a queue at the registration counter.

The room was well-appointed, with a single bed, arm chair and an attached bathroom. He undressed and lay down beneath the sheets and woollen blanket. He slept well that night, rising at seven-thirty in the morning. After a bath he dressed, picked up his belongings and left the room.

As he walked through the lobby on his way to the small dining room, that same rude gentleman was standing at the registration desk shouting at the top of his lungs to the daytime receptionist, ***"What do you mean no receipt? I'm on a business trip and must account for my expenses. I wasn't even required to sign your register last night when I checked in. This hotel is avoiding taxes!"***

Walter didn't pause to see the outcome of the confrontation; he simply walked past and into the dining room for breakfast. After a spread of scrambled eggs, bacon and fried sliced tomatoes, complemented with two slices of buttered brown toast, he paid his bill and left the hotel.

He stood on the sidewalk while establishing his bearings. He then turned east and walked about five hundred yards to Midland Road where he turned left onto River St., then up past the Stage Coach Depot and eventually to the next right and stopped at 10 Bruce Street. He walked up the pathway, raised the brass knocker and rapped three times on the door. A little boy who appeared to be about seven years of age opened the door.

"Are you Master Charles?" Walter asked.

"Yes Sir."

"May I please talk to your Auntie? Just say Mr. Walter is at the door."

The boy looked up at the man while studying his face with a sense of recognition in his eyes, then said, "One moment please Mister Walter." He disappeared into the interior of the house in a flash.

Moments later Joan appeared at the run, Charles at her heels. When she reached the door she threw her arms around her older brother and cried, "Walter ... Walter, I'm so glad you're finally home." Her eyes welled up. Then she turned to young Charles and said, "Charles, this is your Papa. He's been away for a long time. You were only four years old when he left and you just turned seven last month.

Charles extended his hand and said, "Hello Papa, pleased to meet you," not fully understanding what this meant.

Joan said, "We shall walk up to see Mother and Father after lunch, but please let us just sit down for the morning while you tell us the adventures of your times in India."

"Before we start, I'd like to tell you while waiting for the train in Southampton, I had breakfast with a woman from Bedford named Ruby Baker. Her family lives up on Newnham Road. When I asked if she minded, she said I could visit her from time to time. She's a pretty woman, very pleasant and unattached."

"I'm not friends of the Baker family, but I do know them by sight because they attend our church. I think they'd be wonderful in-laws if romance is your intention.

"Let's wait and see," said Walter.

"Now, tell us about India."

"Can we wait until we're with Mother and Father this afternoon, or I'll have to go through the whole story twice?" asked Walter adding, "not that it's a bad story. It's quite pleasant actually. Do you have one of those new-fangled telephones yet?"

"Yes, it's in the dining room."

"... and what about Ma and Pa?"

"The same with them, why?"

"Well, I haven't had a roast beef meal since I left for India. You most likely know that Indians don't eat beef. So we can walk down to the market where I'll purchase a large roast of beef and we can invite Ma and Pa over for dinner this evening after Donald gets home. When you call, just say you have a surprise for them. Then I'll tell my story to the whole family. How's that?"

"Excellent idea Brother. You and Charles can start getting to know each other in the meantime while I start to prepare an early lunch. Or perhaps you'd prefer to catch a few winks before lunch."

"I think an early snooze may be the best thing or I'm liable to fall asleep during dinner. Where is Donald by the way?"

"Oh, He's down at the playing field having his early morning round of cricket with friends. He'll be home in time to wash up and dress for church. Would you like to join us at church this morning?"

"No; Ma and Pa will be there and that would spoil our surprise for this evening. I'll just go up for my snooze now instead."

"You know your way. The guest room is always set up."

MR. AND MRS. ELLIOT arrived at the house at 6 pm that evening and were overjoyed to see Walter. During the three-course meal he told them all about his life in India: the village of Dharamsala; sights of the Himalayas; his tent in the small field beside the forest and stream; the locket; the shepherd boy; 'St. John's Church in the Wilderness' and the parson; his friendship and conversations with the village pandit; the sad story of the shepherd boy's mother; the stream emergency; the mission school; his journey back to Bombay; the Parsi shipping agent; the sea voyage; everything, including why he went there in the first place. Afterwards he answered questions for a full hour. One question was, "What do you intend to do with the locket?"

He pulled it out of his pocket passed it around and said, "I have plans for this treasure which I don't want to reveal until the time comes." Everyone accepted his explanation.

Afterwards he turned to his father and said, "Pa, I assume your hardware store is still the only one in town. Is that correct?"

"Yes Walter. That is correct; why?"

"I'd like to join hands with you and expand the business. Is that plot next door where the dry goods store burnt to the ground still standing empty and if so is it still for sale?

"The answers to your double question are, yes it is and yes it is." After laughter subsided, Mr. Elliot continued, "If purchasing it is part of your plan it may be rather difficult with only the store as collateral."

That's where Donald joined the conversation, "Why don't the three of us retire to the drawing room after dessert and tea. Then you Walter can describe your plan and I'll tell you a way you may be able to solve the money aspect. As you know Walter I work for a bank. I'm now the loans manager."

"Congratulations Donald," said Walter, "you've advanced up the seniority ladder considerably since I left home. When you returned from the war and got the job I think you were a clerk under training."

"Thank you and yes I was."

After dinner the three men entered the drawing room. Mr. Elliot the elder lit his pipe and Walter explained his plan.

Two months later 'Elliot & Elliot Hardware and Garden Centre' had been incorporated. They had acquired the necessary start-up funds from a wealthy investor under agreeable terms with the assistance of Donald. The lot had been paved with cement and a wooden shingled roof supported by thick square concrete posts stood over it. A thick wire fence was affixed to the posts.

Walter hadn't sent a letter to Panditji in Dharamsala since the short one he wrote while still in India. So, one evening he sat down and wrote a letter to him which described a plan that had come to mind throughout the renovation process of the new establishment. He also enclosed a letter of encouragement to Anil Kumar, the shepherd boy, in the same envelope.

❄❄❄❄

THREE MONTHS AFTER his conversation with Mr. Khan, the village blacksmith, Panditji received a letter from Walter Elliot. As he read it, it became obvious that Elliot hadn't received the letter that Panditji had also sent, but its content surprised him. Elliot had thought of the same idea that had been discussed with Mr. Khan. He even sent an order for a number of axes, picks, crowbars (hooked and straight), garden gates and fence sections with dimensions, railings for outdoor steps, steel-based garden tables with diameters for wooden tops, and decorative park benches. There was even an order for dozens of flower pots of various dimensions for the village potters.

He also gave the name of a shipping agent, 'Ruttonjee Shipping Enterprises', in Bombay and told Panditji he'd send a letter to Mr. Ruttonjee telling him he'd pay for shipment once the order had been delivered to Bedford by the importers warehouse in Southampton. Knowing that his request wouldn't be denied Walter had even enclosed twenty pounds to cover the cost of raw material and shipment to Bombay. Everything had been thought of in detail.

Panditji would translate the order into Hindi and give it to Mr. Khan in the morning, but first he'd take the letter addressed to Anil Kumar up to the mission school and read it to the boy.

❄❄❄❄

SMACK; SMACK; another baby cried in Toronto. Mabel Benning lay in a sense of relief after delivery of a baby. The doctor held the child up and said, "It's a girl Mrs Benning."

"May I hold her doctor?"

"Yes, of course. She seems to be perfectly healthy." He passed the slimy body to Mabel.

"Welcome, Bettina Joan Benning. Thank God you have come safe and sound." She then kissed the child's forehead and passed her to the doctor's waiting hands.

"I assume Mr. Benning is in the waiting room?"

"Yes he is Doctor."

The doctor passed the baby to the nurse standing by, and departed in the direction of the waiting room. Once there he saw a single man sitting on a chair with his eyes closed and head turned towards the ceiling. He seemed to be whispering. Assuming he was praying he gently placed his hand on the man's shoulder. When Joseph's eyes opened the doctor said, "Congratulations Mr. Benning. It's a healthy girl; no complications whatsoever."

With eyes turned skyward Joseph said, "Thank you Lord," then turned to the doctor and said, "Thank you doctor. May I go to Mabel's bedside?"

"You can see her Sir, but only through a window in the hallway. And you can see Mrs. Benning and the baby together if you come back tomorrow at 10 am, your wife will be nursing the babe at that time...Come."

The two gentlemen walked through the door and down the hallway. The doctor entered the delivery room and opened the curtained window. Mabel turned her head to the right and saw Joseph with an earlobe-to-earlobe smile on his face. Joseph pointed at his chest, put his hands together and looked skyward, to tell her he'd been praying for her. She smiled.

After four minutes of blowing kisses back and forth Joseph indicated in pantomime that he'd depart now, but would be back at ten o'clock the next morning; he pointed at himself, flickered his fingers to indicate walking, pointed back to the spot he was standing, put ten fingers up, pointed at his watch, and slowly mouthed the word *to-mor-row*. They both smiled again and he waved while turning to walk away.

While walking past the waiting room Joseph heard the words, '*stillborn*' and '*boy*'; and a man burst into tears. He looked to the left and saw a doctor standing in front of a man who had his elbows on his knees and palms over his face; he was weeping. Joseph hesitated. *I* can't just stand here. Should I keep walking? Should I ...?

He walked over to the man, sat down beside him and put his arm around a shaking shoulder and drew him close. The man put his head on Joseph's shoulder and bawled out loud while wiping his eyes and blowing his nose into a handkerchief. Joseph looked to his right and saw a group of five spectators standing in the passageway to the lobby watching. He waved them to go disperse, but nobody heeded. But when the man finally raised his head from Joseph's shoulder they all hustled away.

The man said, "Thank you Mister ...?"

"Benning" Joseph replied, "Joseph Benning, and *your* name Sir?"

"George Jackson, Mr. Benning ... and thank you again. I'll be alright now."

As Joseph was walking down the hallway a nurse took his arm. He stopped and looked down at her. "You're a good man Sir."

He simply replied, "Half an hour ago it could have been me," and walked out of the door to the sidewalk.

## Notes

1. 320 degrees on gyro compass (invented in 1908).

# Six

**AAAAAH; SWOOSH; CRACK; SLICE!** Although bamboo lathis are heavy and hard when dry they were no match for the weapons the six dacoits employed when they attacked Ahmed Shah's ox cart and sliced the head off his driver.

The night before, as he bowed towards Mecca for Isha'a, after the fundamental words of praise he thanked Allah for his new-found prosperity and for that of other villagers who were benefitting from the manufacture of goods for the British market. Mr. Elliot had sent a letter which told him to keep sending shipments coming as frequently as he could without sacrificing quality. With that, he had hired a helper and engaged the services of a blacksmith, carpenter and potters from a neighbouring village.

Since Amritsar was the closest city where trains with box cars stopped, goods needed to be transported from the foothills by ox-cart. Mr Ruttonjee, the shipper from Bombay, had informed him that it would be more economical if shipments were delivered by rail to his warehouses in the seaport of Karachi. Ships bound for Southampton usually departed from Karachi on a bi-weekly basis.

On a Monday morning in the summer of July 1925 he set out for Amritsar. The foothills portion of the narrow dirt road down to the plains had grass between the tracks. Trees overhung the road. If two ox carts met head on it was extremely difficult to pass each other; the drivers of each had to cooperate by disembarking from their seats and guiding their ox so that only one set of back-front wheels remained on the track. All ox cart drivers were skilled at the evolution. Mr. Shah always sat beside the driver, rather than have him make the journey alone.

Then one day as they twisted and turned down the road, a group of six dacoits sprang from the forest all armed with deadly fifteen inch long kukris even though they were not Gurkhas.

***Kukri – traditional Gurkha knife.***

They came from both sides of the track, jumped on board, and started slashing. One swift blow on the back of the neck of Sunil the driver left his head dangling by a narrow strand of flesh at the front. Mr. Shah suffered a flesh wound on the back of the upper portion of his right leg as he managed to jump to the ground and start running back up the roadway. Assuming they'd be in Amritsar and finished dealing with their corrupt buyer before he even reached his town, only a half-hearted attempt was made to catch him; the sole pursuer stopped and returned to his cohorts after only thirty seconds of chase. Then they started their own passage down towards the city.

Mr. Shah however, looked over this shoulder and noticed he was no longer being pursued, so as soon as he rounded the first bend he stopped. He removed his loosely bound turban and wrapped it around this wounded leg. His kurta was white, which would contrast with the darkness of the forested surroundings, so he had to engage great stealth as he turned and followed the cart. He'd wait until they rounded bends before advancing to the next waiting point.

Eventually he heard another cart advancing from behind. He hailed them down. They recognized him and stopped. Ahmed told them what had happened, then he looked into the back of their cart. It was empty with the exception of a couple of rugged rucksacks. He was told they were on their way to Amritsar to purchase fresh fruit and vegetables for the village. He asked if he could join them.

Once on board he told them what had happened and laid out his plan to recover his precious goods and cart. "We won't be able the pass that cart. The roadway is just too narrow, so stay behind by at least a quarter of a mile. The dacoits will eventually see us and most likely send one of their own back to investigate. He'll look into the back of your cart and noticing it's empty and thus worthless, he may ask if you saw a man walking back towards Dharamsala. He won't recognise me, as the incident only lasted about fifteen seconds and all bearded Muslims look the same to them. Just say, 'A man emerged from the forest behind you after you had passed.

He must have been off the track to defecate, but he did go upward toward the village when he emerged'." The four men in the cart all agreed to comply. "I'll explain how you can help me once we get to Amritsar along the way.

"Ji Sri Shah."

THE OX CART that had picked up Ahmed Shah entered the outskirts of Amritsar approximately four hundred yards behind the culprits. They followed them until they turned down a lane to the warehouse of the crooked dealer with whom they dealt. Then, according to plan Ahmed and two of the men jumped off, and the cart carried on to its original destination.

Ahmed concealed himself in the shadows across the roadway, and the cart men ran off in different directions. He kept his eyes peeled in three directions, the dealer's establishment and the directions the others had taken. Then he saw one of them approaching. He was being followed by the shipping agent who normally sent his goods to Karachi. He walked towards them and indicated that they should stand back about a hundred yards until the other fellow arrived.

Ten minutes later Ahmed saw the other cart man running ahead of two mounted British officers of the Imperial Police; they were armed with repeating handguns. Ahmed walked towards them before they could be seen by the dacoits and asked them to stop. He described what had happened and reached up under his kurta to retrieve money and the invoice for his goods that he had strapped with a cloth to his upper leg close to his groin. He then pointed to the man who he normally dealt with and the man verified that it was true. Then he told them where the culprits were unloading the crates containing his belongings.

The senior officer told the cart men they could carry on and Ahmed and his shipper to remain where they were. The cart men remained to watch the spectacle of an arrest and possibly a violent one. The Imperial policemen remained mounted and trotted down the short lane towards the dacoit's delivery point. A lookout saw them coming and ran inside to alert his companions.

When the policemen witnessed this they drew their weapons and waited. Within seconds the five dacoits ran out of the door and attacked the lawmen. But the bullet is mightier than the kukri; when the smoke cleared three dacoits lay dead on the ground. Two were seriously wounded and also on the ground writhing in pain.

The sound of shooting had attracted the attention of at least fifty townsfolk. Once the action was over they all ran towards the downed dacoits. The police realized they didn't have a hope in hell of saving the pain stricken dacoits and bringing them to justice; the mob would obstruct them. So they simply entered the warehouse and arrested the dealer. When the mob had walked away the policemen emerged to find the two bandits clubbed to death, as they had expected. They told Ahmed he could enter and retrieve his goods and took the dealer to the local lock-up.

Ahmed and his shipping agent entered the warehouse and found that the goods were still crated, but one was on the floor. It was still blocked and tackled so they simply hoisted it back onto the cart and departed.

Once his goods were safely in the warehouse of his shipper Ahmed drove his ox cart out of the town centre and along part of the Grand Trunk Road towards Khalsa College in order to visit his son Amir who was studying Business Administration. Ahmed had earned enough to pay the tuition for his son to enter this prestigious university that was administered by Sikhs. The students were therefore mainly Sikh, but those belonging to other religions were not disallowed from applying.

Amir's Hindu friend Anil was also studying Business Administration at Khalsa. Walter Elliot had paid for Amir's two years of grammar school and the lad had earned a scholarship due to his high grades and his natural ability to wallop centuries in cricket matches.

❄❄❄❄

BY 1930 WALTER ELLIOT was aged thirty-six. He and Ruby Baker started dating shortly after Walter returned to Bedford from India in 1922. They had quickly fallen in love and were married on Saturday, 17th May 1923 at St Paul's Church on St Paul's Square in the town centre of the market. Charles was now seventeen and wore glasses. He had a nine-year-old stepsister named Enid. Both Ruby and Walter loved the children equally. Charles would graduate from Bedford Grammar School in June the following year and wanted to further his education at the Leicester University where he planned to study civil engineering.

Elliot & Elliot Hardware and Garden Centre was doing better than had been anticipated, much to the credit of Walter – a younger, fresh co-owner with a dream, leadership skills and a determination to succeed. The business was receiving an average of ten shipments of garden furniture and pottery from Dharamsala per year. Even after shipping charges the prices were significantly lower than British-made products of the same style and quality. Customers especially liked the quality of the decorative gates, garden benches and the beauty of the clay pottery of all sizes; some large enough to root a small cedar tree.

Two retailers from other towns, noticing the popularity of these products, approached Walter during the course of a six month period to enquire if he'd consider placing orders for their establishments. Walter complied, thus making Elliot & Elliot not only a retailer, but also an import agent.

ONE DAY WALTER received a letter from an old childhood friend named Francis Marlatte. Walter and Francis had served together in the same regiment during the war. They had communicated frequently throughout the years. Francis had emigrated from England to Canada after the war and now lived in Moose Jaw, a town located in the province of Saskatchewan about 40 miles west of Regina the capital.

In the letter, after a short paragraph about family affairs, Francis encouraged Walter to sell Elliot & Elliot and come to Moose Jaw to live. He said that Moose Jaw was in dire need of another hardware store and a man with Walter's experience in retailing of hardware products could be very successful if he established one.

Walter wrote back telling Francis he'd give it serious thought. And he did give it *very* serious thought over the following month.

A month after receipt of the letter he led Ruby by the hand to the drawing room. She noticed the serious look on his face.

"This looks serious Dear; what is it?" she asked.

"Ruby I believe I've told you I have an old friend named Francis Marlatte who lives in Moose Jaw, Saskatchewan – a province of Canada."

"Yes you have," she said "and I believe you exchange letters now and then."

"My, memory seems to be slipping...but yes we do exchange letters and I received one from him last month urging us to pack up and move there. He said Moose Jaw is a wonderful place and in dire need of another hardware store, and we could earn a prosperous living if we were to set one up."

"What are your feelings on the prospect Dear?" he asked.

"Well," she said, "first there's Charles's desire to study civil engineering. I wonder if there's a university close to this Moose Jaw place you speak of that teaches it ... And then there is *your* baby – the business. What would you do with that?"

"Knowing of Charles's ambition, Frank told me the University of Saskatoon – 125 miles north of Moose Jaw teaches civil engineering. Saskatoon is even closer than Liecester." He paused for a moment and added. "And a couple of weeks ago you told me my sister Joan said that Donald is no longer happy in his banking job."

"That's correct Dear. When you arrived home he was the loans manager. However, it seems he has reached the pinnacle of his aspirations. Other more junior men have been bypassing him, for instance just last week his own assistant was promoted to assistant bank manager. Donald was so depressed he couldn't even eat his dinner when he got home that night. Joan said he was close to tears when he told her."

"Do you think he'd be interested in owning a fifty-one percent share in the company? He could hire an experienced manager and we'd earn dividends while living abroad."

"Fifty-one percent would deprive you of making key decisions. Why not the other way around with you owning fifty-one percent and him forty-nine?"

"Well," said Walter, "I've thought of that, but we'd be located a quarter of the way across the globe and some decisions in business need quick answers or solutions. The way I suggested would give him that power."

"Yes, that makes sense, so today is Saturday. Let's invite them over for dinner tomorrow evening. We could put the prospect to both of them after we finish eating."

"Good idea," said Walter.

AFTER A FINE ROAST ham dinner on Sunday evening both families retired to the drawing room for tea.

Once everyone was seated, Donald was the first to speak. "Walter, Ruby told Joan you have an interesting proposition to put to me, but wouldn't tell her what it is."

"I like a man who doesn't believe in small talk Donald," said Walter, "and that is, in fact, true. I do have a proposition. First, one simple 'Yes or No' question ... Are you still happy with your banking job?"

*"No!"*

Walter then went on to explain what Ruby and he had previously discussed. When he finished he said, "another 'Yes or No' question; but this time if the answer is 'Yes', please tell us why...The question is: Does this proposal interest you?"

Donald quickly glanced at the smiling Joan before turning his focus back to Walter, "Yes this does interest me. I have a very competent friend named Robert Harrison who would jump at the prospect to be my assistant in an endeavour like you have established. His father is the pastor of the local Baptist church and has taught Robert all the principles of being a decent clean-living individual. He is also hard working and was blessed with a business-oriented mind. Until recently he was a manager at the Raymond Tractors plant that closed down. He is now unemployed. The two of us could work together and expand the business as is also your objective Walter."

This is where Charles joined the conversation, "What about my plans to become a civil engineer? And then there are all my friends. What about these two things?"

"Mr. Marlatte knew about your ambition and assured me the University of Saskatoon not far from Moose Jaw teaches civil engineering. He also has a son your age named George and he'd become your first friend, and introduce you to others. Your charming personality would enable you to make a lot more friends on your own."

Charles didn't respond, but seemed to be satisfied.

"Ruby and I are both onboard for this proposal so another question: How much notice do you have to give to the bank Donald?

"Only one month."

"Good. Submit your notice on Monday and report to Elliot & Elliot next month to commence your orientation. Bring your friend Robert along with you. The orientation should take us a minimum of three months and once I'm satisfied we'll hire an attorney to handle the paperwork."

Walter then turned to Ruby. "When I'm satisfied Dear," he said, "If you don't mind, I'll move on ahead of you and the kids. I'll find a suitable house, purchase it and start setting up shop. This should take around six months. When I'm ready, I'll send you a telegram and tell you that you can pack up and join me."

"No, I don't mind Dear. In fact, if *you* hadn't suggested it, *I* would have.

ONCE SATISFIED, WALTER boarded an airplane in London airport bound for Toronto. In Toronto he took another flight to Regina, Saskatchewan. Then there was a westward bound railway ride of about two hours to Moose Jaw. He had placed a phone call to his friend Francis who was waiting for him at the station in the centre of the town. They embraced when they met each other after so many years apart.

Frank took Walter home, introduced him to his wife Sylvia and showed him to the spare bedroom where he was told he could stay as long as he wanted. After dropping his bags in the room Walter went down to catch up on recent events in their lives. As could be expected, Walter's Dharamsala experiences dominated most of the conversation.

Walter didn't waste any time. The next morning when Francis came down for breakfast he found his friend sitting in the living room scouring the real estate ads in the 'Regina Leader-Post' for a suitable-sounding residence and a retail establishment in Moose Jaw where he could set up shop. Francis told him he'd introduce him to the agent who had helped him and Sylvia find their present abode.

A month and a half after his arrival in Moose Jaw, Walter had purchased a two story, four bedroom house located on Fairford Street near the corner of Athabasca Street East. Once the house was furnished he sent for his wife Ruby and the two youngsters.

The real estate agent showed him a rundown auto repair shop on Main St. West that was for sale. It had ample paved parking space in front and a paved portion of the property in the rear, which was connected to a rutted gravel delivery lane. He made an offer and was just awaiting acceptance. Much to his surprise the offer was accepted by the elderly owner with no back and forth bargaining a week after being presented.

Walter then hired a working crew and got to work in restoring the place into a decent looking establishment. Two months later what would soon become 'Elliot Hardware and Garden Supplies' had hardwood floors and shelves. He had set up the garden supplies space in much the same style as his enterprise back home in Bedford. He left half the paved front vacant for parking.

Elliot Hardware and Garden Supplies' was fully stocked and running by October 1932. Charles would enter Saskatoon University in September of 1933 and his new friend George would also enter the same university to study Business Administration.

# Seven

**BY 1933 JOSEPH BENNING** was 43 years old. He and Mabel were living a happy life. Their first-born child, Betty was eleven and Molly a second daughter was nine years old. Joseph had advanced up the totem pole at work and was now the senior salesman of the floor of the Cassidy's retail store. A few years earlier the family had also purchased a larger two story house located at 37 Macnaughton Road in Leaside.

The family lived close enough to Bethel Baptist Church to walk there every Sunday morning for services. Joseph had followed through on the seed planted in his head back before he left Barnstable; he was now the mentor of the local Baptist Boys Brigade.

On Sunday afternoon of 16th July Joseph was walking from his home towards his church. He and the family had attended the morning service and after lunch Joseph was on his way back for the afternoon mentoring session of the Baptist Boys Brigade.

As he passed a small park he saw a young fellow sitting by himself on a park bench. He was gazing at the sky as an airplane was on the glide path to land at Malton Airport. A group of about seven other boys were playing street hockey on the roadway half a block away. Joseph walked over and sat beside the boy.

He said, "Hello young man, my name is Mr. Benning. What's your name?

"Billy Cunningham Sir."

"I saw you looking at that airplane a moment ago. Do you like airplanes?"

"Yes Sir. I will fly airplanes some day."

"Hold on to that belief Billy and someday you will. Oh, I see you even have a book about flying in your lap. But wouldn't you rather be playing street hockey with those boys up the road on a Sunday afternoon rather than reading?"

"I would but the other boys' mothers won't let them play with me. They say I'm a 'bastard'. I asked my mother about my father and she told me I don't have one, but I am twelve years old and have learned enough to realize that that is impossible. I told her this but she won't change her story."

"So you have no friends?"

"No friends Sir."

"I am on my way to a place where you'll meet a lot of new friends. This is a group of boys about twelve years old who I speak with every Sunday afternoon. We discuss many things about growing up and so on. They call me Uncle Joseph."

"Will they treat me the same way as those boys up the street?"

"Not at all Billy; I've taught them to respect all worthy people, and believe me, you *are* worthy of respect."

JOSEPH AND BILLY CUNNINGHAM entered Bethel Baptist Church, and once in the vestibule they climbed down the stairs to a basement conference room. Joseph's boys were all there and standing around chatting. When they noticed Joseph and the new boy enter they rang out with "Good afternoon Uncle Joseph."

"Good afternoon fellows," he turned to Billy, "I'd like you to meet my new friend Billy Cunningham. He lives in Leaside not far from my house. He wants to be an airplane pilot when he grows up."

When the introductions were completed Joseph said, "Ok boys; you can take your seats now." They all sat down on chairs arranged in a semicircle and Joseph took his seat in the centre, facing the boys.

"This week boys, we're going to talk about *self belief*; this is not belief in God Almighty, but belief in your own dreams and believing that you can make them come true by doing whatever is required. Do you all understand what I'm talking about?"

There were only a few weak nods. "Ok, this afternoon while on my way here I came across Billy looking at an airplane overhead. I went over and spoke to him and he said he wanted to be an airplane pilot when he grew up. I asked him if he'd like to join us and here he is."

"Billy, do you believe you can become an airplane pilot someday?"

"Yes Sir."

"Do you know what you'll have to do to become an airplane pilot?"

Billy smiled and said, "I'll have to learn how to fly one."

There were a few snickers from the group which pleased Billy.

"That's true Billy but you smiled when you said it which must mean you realize there's more to it." Joseph looked at the other boys and asked, "Can anyone tell us what Billy will have to do to learn how to fly an airplane?" Three boys raised their hands. Joseph chose Ronnie the oldest.

"Since we're supposed to be talking about believing in dreams today Sir, first he must have a strong belief that he *will* become a pilot someday; and then ...

EVENTUALLY BILLY was introduced to Joseph's daughter Betty. The first meeting was in October after a church service. They discovered that they were in the same Grade but in different schools. They interacted at Sunday school picnics and other church events. Sometimes they clandestinely met on Saturdays and went to a matinee at the movie house on Bayview Avenue.

As the years went by and they had reached the age of nineteen they had become sweethearts. Betty kept this to herself, knowing full well her mother Mabel wouldn't have been delighted – in fact, she'd be angry at the prospect although Betty didn't know the reason for her dislike of William.

❄❄❄❄

IN 1933 A GERMAN by the name of Adolph Hitler was causing the British and many European countries concern.

Hitler was born in Austria on 20 April 1889 and raised near Linz. He moved to Germany in 1913.. He joined the German Workers' Party, the precursor of the NSDAP in 1919 and became leader in 1921. In 1923, he attempted a coup to seize power in Munich. The failed coup resulted in his imprisonment, during which time he dictated the first volume of his autobiography and political manifesto *Mein Kampf*. After his release in 1924, Hitler gained popular support by attacking the Treaty of Versailles and promoting Pan-Germanism, antisemitism, and anti-communism with charismatic oratory and Nazi propaganda. Hitler frequently denounced international capitalism and communism as being part of a Jewish conspiracy.

The Nazi Party was the largest elected party in the German Reichstag, which led to Hitler's appointment as Chancellor on 30 January 1933. Following fresh elections won by his coalition, the Reichstag passed the Enabling Act, which began the process of transforming the Weimar Republic into Nazi Germany, a one-party dictatorship based on the totalitarian and autocratic ideology of National Socialism.

Hitler aimed to eliminate Jews from Germany and establish a New Order to counter what he saw as the injustice of the post-World War I international order dominated by Britain and France. His first six years in power resulted in rapid economic recovery from the Great Depression, the effective abandonment of restrictions imposed on Germany after World War I, and the annexation of territories that were home to millions of ethnic Germans – actions which gave him significant popular support.

❄❄❄❄

ON 26TH SEPTEMBER 1936 Allan Snelgrove knocked on the door of 157 Rumsey Road in Leaside. This was the address on the last letter from Joseph Benning to his friend Mrs. Wilma Hall; the house where Joseph supposedly lived. An elderly gentleman answered the door.

"Is this the residence of Mr. Joseph Benning?" asked Allan.

"No Sir." replied the man, "We purchased this house from the Bennings about five years ago and they left no forwarding address."

"Thank you Sir."

Allan walked back to the sidewalk where his wife Norma, son Donald and niece Annie were standing. He informed them of what the man had told him.

ANNIE HALL HAD TURNED twenty back in Barnstaple on 24th July 1936. She was a qualified elementary school teacher having graduated in June 1935 from St Mary's Girl's Teachers College near her home town. Her mother Wilma Hall had passed away from breast cancer in June 1934 at the age of fifty-four.

After Wilma's passing Irving Hall had fallen into a state of deep depression. Irving's employer Stephen Crawford noticed a dip in Irving's performance and knew the reason. He tried to no avail to help him put the death of his dear wife behind him and get on with his life. But Irving just wandered about aimlessly at work and at home, due to his loss.

One evening Annie answered the door and welcomed Norma and Allan into the house. After small-talk, Allan was the first to speak about the reason for the visit.

"Annie, Irving, we plan to immigrate to Canada. Do you happen to know the address of that nice gentleman Joseph Benning who left Barnstaple several years ago? Wilma had been his friend and had introduced him to his now wife Mable. I believe Mr. Benning and his wife settled in Toronto."

Annie replied, "There are a few old letters from Mr. Benning in the possessions of Mother. Perhaps I can find one, and surely there will be one with his home address on the envelope." She excused herself and ran up the stairs.

While she was out of ear-shot Irving spoke. "Would it be too much of a burden to take Annie along with you Allan and Norma?"

"But what about you Irving, don't you need someone with you at this point of your life?"

"I'll be out of this depression soon folks. Annie and I went to the movie house last weekend and watched Charlie Caplin in his film *Modern Times*. It was the first time I had laughed out loud in two years. So as I said earlier, would you consider taking Annie along with you?"

"Did I just hear mention of my name?" asked Annie when she arrived back holding an envelope."

Norma and Allan looked at each other and both smiled. "Annie, your father has just suggested, or I should say 'requested' that we take you along with us. What do you think of the idea? Surely there will be opportunities available for qualified teachers like you in Toronto."

Anne was wide-eyed and speechless for a moment. Finally she turned to Irving and said, "I'd love to...but what about you Father?"

"I'll be just fine Annie. Jessie is still here cooking and doing the housework, and I just told Norma and Allan about laughing out loud when we went to the movies last weekend. When I pass on the attorney Mr. Starling will ensure that my Will is handled properly. You'll inherit the house."

"I'm not worried about your Will Dad; it's you I worry about!"

"As I said Annie, go ahead, widen your world; explore beyond the horizon; accept new challenges around every corner; enjoy life while you're still young."

"You didn't say all of those things Dad, but thanks for your encouraging words and approval...Aunt Norma, Uncle Allan, I accept your offer."

SO THERE THEY STOOD in front of the wrong house. "Now what?" asked Norma.

"Well," said Allan, "I suggest we go back to the hotel, read the newspaper and try to find an employment agency. Perhaps they will know of an establishment in need of a good pharmacist."

"That makes sense," said Norma.

When they walked back into their hotel they asked the receptionist if he knew the whereabouts of a good employment agency.

"What is your profession?"

"Pharmacist," said Allan.

"No need for an employment agency," replied the receptionist, "my brother-in-law owns a drug store in Port Credit – a town to the west of Toronto. He is in desperate need of one.

"Drug store?" asked Allan.

"I believe in Great Britain you refer to them as 'phar-macies'."

"Thank you. Yes we do...I was about to say we don't do business with 'drug dealers'."

The man smiled and said, "I'll just give him a ring and you can speak to him." After making contact and telling his brother-in-law the purpose of the call he passed the phone to Allan.

The two spoke for about five minutes and when Allan put down the receiver he said, "He wants to meet me at his shop this afternoon at four o'clock. You folks can wait here and explore and I'll take the bus out to Port Credit. He told me his establishment, 'Lakeshore Drug Store', is located ten stores to the east of the bus stop at 1245 Lakeshore Road. The owner's name is Mr. Watson"

"That sounds good to me Allan, what about you kids?"

"Sounds good," they both replied.

ALLAN WALKED into Lakeshore Drug Store clad in his Sunday best at ten minutes to four and was greeted by an elderly gentleman. "Are you Mr. Watson?" asked Allan.

"Yes I am and I assume from your British accent you must be Mr. Allan Snelgrove. My friends simply call me 'Soapy' after Watson's

Soap. If I accept your application I may give you that privilege after some time. May I please see your credentials?"

Allan passed the gentleman his Army retirement certificate, his resumé and a farewell letter from his last employer which ended with the words, '... and I wish you and Norma good fortune in Canada'. After being impressed with what he read, and a few more rudimentary questions Mr. Watson asked, "When can you start?"

"My wife, two youngsters and I are currently staying in a hotel in Toronto…I'd like to purchase a house and move in before I commence. Do you know of any three bedroom houses for sale, or the address of a real estate agent?"

"There's a nice bungalow at the corner of Ruby Street North and High Street West that I pass on the way to and from work every day. A 'For Sale by Owner' sign went up last week. There is no phone number so I suppose that means a person should simply knock on the door. It's in a good location and won't be on the market for long. I'll draw you a map and you can walk up now if you wish."

"Thank you Mr. Watson. I'll do that."

"Here's my business card," said Watson, "give me a call tomorrow and let me know what you think."

WHEN ALLAN WALKED into the hotel room he found Norma, Annie and Donald reading magazines. He said, "I'm hired and not only that, I've found the ideal three bedroom house to live in."

"Wonderful," replied Norma, "can we go out and see the house tomorrow morning?"

"I asked the owner Mr. Potter exactly the same question and he said his door was always open to friendly people, and especially to prospective buyers."

"How much does he want for it?"

"He's asking fifteen thousand dollars, so I stopped by the drug store on the way back to the bus stop and asked my new employer, Mr. Watson, if that was a reasonable price. He said it was, but advised me to offer twelve and settle somewhere in between."

The following morning Mr. Potter welcomed them to his house. He escorted them around, explaining a few intricacies and showed them the large back yard. There was a driveway that ended at a garage just past the rear of the house. The master bedroom had an attached bathroom; the two young folks would have to share the other one. The kitchen was well-appointed and there was a large dining and living room.

After a tour of the house Allan said, "Mr. Potter, do you mind if we have some privacy for a couple of minutes to discuss what we think?

"No problem whatsoever Mr. Snelgrove," said the gentleman as he walked into the kitchen.

After Mr. Potter had disappeared, Norma was the first to speak. "Excellent Allan; I really think it'll be a perfect house for all of us," She turned to the young folk, "What do you folks think?"

"I agree," said Annie, "as long and I can have the bedroom that looks out onto the backyard."

Donald said, "That's alright with me. I also like the house."

"I'll go into the kitchen and conduct some bargaining with Mr. Potter. You folks wait here. It shouldn't take long."

He walked into the kitchen to find Mr. Potter drying the freshly-washed dishes. "May we sit at the table and talk for a minute Sir?" asked Allan.

Once seated, Mr. Potter asked, "So what does your family think?"

"Well Sir, being located on an intersection they were a little concerned about traffic noise at night, but besides that they are pleased."

"There is very little traffic during the day, and after ten o'clock there is virtually none, so traffic is nothing to worry about."

"Alright then," said Allan, "You are asking fifteen thousand for the house. I offer you twelve thousand." He reached in his pocket, pulled out one thousand dollars in cash and placed it on the table saying, "And here's a deposit."

Mr. Potter said, "Make it thirteen-five and we have a deal."

Allan had already drawn up a bill of sale in layman's language with only the price, amount of deposit and signature lines left blank. Potter watched as Allan filled in the blanks, signed it and passed it to him for his signature, after which they shook hands.

Within a month, the Snelgroves and Annie Hall had moved into their new residence in Port Credit. Norma was a stay-at-home housewife and Allan was working happily at Lakeshore Drug Store.

Annie in the meantime had acquired a Grade three teaching position at Clarkson Public School about four miles farther west of Port Credit on Lakeshore Road. She knew there were separate schools in Ontario; the separate schools being for Roman Catholics and public schools for Protestants, but since they didn't ask during the interview she didn't voluntarily tell them she was Catholic. Had they, she would have been truthful.

# Eight

# World War II

**CHARLES ELLIOT AND GEORGE MARLATTE** stood in the middle of the potential officer's line outside the Canadian Army Recruitment Centre in downtown Toronto. There were approximately twenty-five men ahead of them and the same number behind. The line for 'other ranks' stretched around the corner of the intersection to the rear. The date was Tuesday, 12th September 1939; two days after King George VI had accepted the Canadian declaration to participate in the war with Germany. Their plan was to join the Canadian Army and fight in Europe. Charles was, by then, married to Marnie, a pretty young woman he had met while in university. George was married to a woman named Dorothy.

Their wait was only half an hour before they stood in front one of two desks, with an Army Captain and a Corporal assistant seated on the opposite side of each. They were told to take seats in front of the desk. Charles had carried out some research and knew what papers to bring along, so he was holding his graduation diplomas, and birth and marriage certificates plus a few other documents. Charles was a qualified civil engineer.

"So you want to join the Army Mr. Elliot, is that correct?" asked the recruiting officer.

Charles noticed that the officer also wore spectacles and said, "That is why I am here Sir."

"May I see your latest eye test records?"

Charles shuffled through his papers and passed them over.

After a quick look, the officer said, "Your eyesight is even lower than mine. I wasn't permitted to fight in Europe and that's why

I'm sitting here at this desk...May I see your graduation certificate please?"

Charles placed it on the desk and waited.

"Aha, you're an engineer. That means you can still join and stay on this side of the Atlantic and teach others to carry out engineering tasks of combat. What do you think of that prospect?"

"Well, I'd rather be serving in Europe, but if I can't then I'd be happy to serve the war effort by training others."

"Good. Please go to the second door down the hall – the one marked 'Engineering' and speak to the officer inside. He'll explain the roles of engineers in combat."

Charles walked down the hall as instructed and knocked on the door. A private soldier answered and said, "Please come in Sir. Captain Armstrong will call for you once he's finished talking to another potential officer. In the meantime you can read what is expected of an Army Engineers here." He handed a sheet of paper to Charles. It read:

> *The mission of the Army Engineers is to contribute to the survival, mobility, and combat effectiveness of the army. Their responsibilities encompass the use of demolitions and land mines, the design, construction and maintenance of defensive works and fortifications, urban operations (hostile room entry), breaching obstacles, establishing and maintaining lines of communication, and bridging. They also provide water, power and other utilities, provide fire, aircraft crash and rescue services, hazardous material operations, and develop maps and other engineering intelligence. In addition, Army engineers are experts in deception and concealment, as well as in the design and development of equipment necessary to carry out these operations. The official role of the combat engineer is to allow friendly troops to live, move and fight on the battlefield and deny that to the enemy.*

Five minutes after reading the document the private came back and told him Captain Armstrong was ready to interview. After entering and introductions the captain told Charles to take a seat. He looked over Charles's documents and spoke.

"I see that you have already been rejected for combat duties in Europe. Would you still be willing to stay on the home front and instruct other young engineers?"

"It wasn't my intention when I walked in the main door half an hour ago, but the answer to your question is 'yes', but after reading some of the requirements I would need some training myself."

"Did you work at all after graduation?"

"Yes, I was employed by Cousins Construction for about a year. But they mainly conduct marine construction; the building of dock facilities, and dredging of harbours or channels mostly."

"Yes, you will need some training related to the occupation and also on how to deliver instructions. That is carried out in New Market, Ontario and that is also where you will instruct those going to the other side. We have a competent engineer who served in the Great War who has volunteered to lend his assistance when required. Are you happy with what's been said so far Mr. Elliot?"

"Yes I am Sir."

"Then please report back at ten o'clock next Monday morning for your medical. If you prove to be fit, then the signing process will take place immediately after. Your basic training will commence on," he reached for his calendar, "Monday 2nd October. Any questions?"

"Yes Sir, you said 'basic training'. Is that training on becoming an engineering instructor? Or does it imply something else."

"Basic training is where we train you to be a soldier. It'll only last six weeks. You will commence your engineering instruction immediately afterward and that's carried out at the same base. Just report back here at 8 am on 2nd October for transport to New Market, Ontario."

"Thank you Sir," said Charles as they shook hands.

"I wish you well Mr. Elliot. The private soldier outside the door will escort you to the medical examination room."

George was waiting for Charles on the sidewalk when he emerged. He said, "I've been accepted for combat duties and will commence my basic training in New Market on 2nd October."

Charles replied, "I was rejected for combat but will remain on this side and instruct engineering to others who will be going to Europe. I will also commence my basic training on the same date as you. We'll most likely be in the same class.

❄❄❄❄

"MOM, DAD I'm going to sign up."

"Sign up for what Donald?" asked his father Allan.

"The Army Dad," said Donald, "what else did you expect on this particular date? Didn't you hear, Canada declared war on Germany three days ago."

"Donald, Donald! I lost my only brother Andrew in the last war. I don't want to lose my only son in another."

"It's my duty Dad. It's the duty of all able bodied men to do the same, and I was hoping you would congratulate me, but I am old enough to make my own decisions and will do it with or without your blessing."

Allan walked away and entered the kitchen in order to inform Norma. He heard the front door close behind him.

Two hours later Donald Snelgrove stood in the same line as Charles Elliot had stood two days earlier. He arrived back home six hours later and when he encountered his father said, "You are looking at an officer in the Canadian Army. I report for training on Monday 2nd October."

Not a word was spoken at the dinner table that evening, but during the few days remaining before Donald's departure Allan warmed up. The duo sat together on garden chairs out front for three hours on Sunday afternoon just talking about whatever came to their minds. On Monday morning Allan and Norma escorted Donald to the recruitment centre where he boarded a bus to New Market, as did the parents of many other would-be warriors. Tears rolled down Allan's cheeks while he waved as the bus pulled away.

❄❄❄❄

*"HOWEVER MATTERS MAY BE IN FRANCE or with the French Government or with another French Government, we in this island and in the British Empire will never lose our sense of comradeship with the French people. If we are now called upon to endure what they have suffered we shall emulate their courage, and if final victory rewards our toils they shall share the gains, aye. And freedom shall be restored to all. We abate nothing of our just demands – Czechs, Poles, Norwegians, Dutch, Belgians, all who have joined their causes to our own shall be restored.*

*What General Weygand has called the Battle of France is over... the Battle of Britain is about to begin. Upon this battle depends the survival of Christian civilisation. Upon it depends our own British life, and the long continuity of our institutions and our Empire. The whole fury and might of the enemy must very soon be turned on us. Hitler knows that he will have to break us in this island or lose the war. If we can stand up to him, all Europe may be freed and the life of the world may move forward into broad, sunlit uplands.*

*But if we fail, then the whole world, including the United States, including all that we have known and cared for, will sink into the abyss of a new dark age made more sinister, and perhaps more protracted, by the lights of perverted science. Let us therefore brace ourselves to our duties, and so bear ourselves, that if the British Empire and its Commonwealth last for a thousand years, men will still say, This was their finest hour."*

The orator was Sir Winston Churchill, Prime Minister of the United Kingdom. The venue was the British House of Commons. The date was 18th June 1940.

WHEN WILLIAM CUNNINGHAM had read the speech of Churchill in the *Globe* the next day he had just finished his third year at university. Mr. Benning had told him in order to become a pilot he must be a graduate. He had one year to go before graduation, but with a burning desire to go to Britain and get into the fight he decided to go to the Royal Canadian Air Force recruiting office in downtown Toronto and see if they'd accept him as an officer anyway.

"Do you wish to become a non-commissioned airman, commonly known as ground crew, or an officer?" asked the recruiting officer?

"An officer," replied Bill, "I want to become a pilot."

"What is your education?"

"Three years of university Sir," said, Bill proudly.

"All officers must be university graduates. This war is expected to last for a few more years yet. I advise you to complete your final year and then come back at this time next year."..."What type of officer do you wish to become if accepted?"

"Pilot Sir," said Bill.

"I'm afraid that would be impractical Mr. Cunningham. Training of pilots takes a long time. All crew members of bombers and fighters are officers however. Of course there's the pilot; then the navigator; forward gunner who is also the bomb aimer; middle gunner on some aircraft; the flight engineer; wireless operator; and the tail gunner. But if you remain in the RCAF when the war ends, there will be nothing holding you back from eventually becoming a pilot if that is your desire...So, do you wish to wait and come back next year?"

"Thank you for the briefing Sir; I *will* come back next year because since I was a boy I have always dreamed of becoming an airplane pilot. This will be part of the process."

They shook hands and Bill walked out of the office.

IT WAS LATE afternoon on the same day he had talked to the recruiting officer as William sat in a street car making its slow transit up Bayview Avenue. He disembarked at Millwood Road and walked the two blocks down to Macnaughton where he turned left. When he reached house number thirty-seven he stood on the sidewalk outside in hopes that Betty, his girlfriend, would see him and come out. Since Betty and Bill had become sweethearts, every Saturday night during their dating years Mrs Benning sat in the living room until the couple came home, had kissed on the doorstep and Betty had entered the house.

Bill faced the house and soon saw the curtains move slightly; he speculated *'that must have been Mrs Benning,'* while knowing perfectly well why she dreaded the thought that her daughter may end up wanting to marry him some day; it was because there was never mention of his father and Bill had no explanation to provide.

Presently he felt a hand on his shoulder. He turned to face the friendly smile as Joseph Benning said, "What are you doing standing out here in the heat young man?"

"I'm waiting for Betty to see me and come out Sir. I have something important to tell her. If she's not at home I'll wait here."

"Is there anything about your important message you can share with me Bill?"

"Yes Sir, but I'd rather tell you outside. I don't want Mrs Benning to hear it without Betty present."

"Come," said Joseph, "let's sit on the garden chairs."

Once seated Bill said, "Sir I intend to join the Royal Canadian Air Force."

"Wouldn't it be advisable to finish your university education before you do Bill? Officers require a university education, and certainly pilots do."

"That's exactly what the recruiting officer told me. He advised me to finish my schooling and come back next year." Bill explained other aspects about what he'd been told then added, "So that's what I've decided to do...but Sir that's not the end of it." He paused for a long spell.

"Go ahead Bill; spit it out, you know you are like a son to me."

After he mustered the courage he said, "I'd like to marry Betty before joining and going to Britain."

Joseph was in thought ..."I'm sure you realize there is always a chance in war that when a man leaves he may not come back. That's the sadness of war, and I saw so much if it during the last one in France...Being a war widow is sad enough, but being a war widow with a child is even worse."

"I've been thinking of that ever since I left the recruiting office a couple of hours ago Mr. Benning. But Betty is a God fearing, kind and compassionate woman, and she's also beautiful. I'm sure a good man would find her; they would fall in love and eventually marry... and this time even with Mrs Benning's blessing." Bill smiled as he said it, as did Joseph. "Regarding the war widow with a child aspect, we'd take the necessary precautions until I leave Sir."

"You have my approval Bill. You wait here if you don't mind."

"In fact, I'd prefer to Sir. If Betty is at home, please send her out."

Betty didn't appear immediately, but fifteen minutes later he saw her walking 'Perky', her two-year-old male Pekinese dog, across the park and towards the house. She didn't even notice Bill sitting on the lawn chair until she was halfway up the driveway. When she did she exclaimed, "Bill, what are you doing here on a Wednesday? We usually don't see each other until Saturday evenings."

"Come and sit down for a few moments Betty; I have something to tell you."

Betty sat beside Bill and took his hand. Perky stationed himself between the two lovers. Then, much to both of their surprises Perky lifted a back leg and urinated on Bill's pant leg.

*"Perky; how could you be so rude to Bill. He loves you too!"* yelled Betty.

"Don't scold him Betty. Congratulate him on his response to the training your mother has given him."

"*Bill,"* cried Betty as she burst out laughing.

After she had recovered she asked, "So what do you have to tell me Billy Boy?"

Bill got right to the point, "I'm going to join the RCAF as soon as I graduate. Officers require a university education, so it won't happen for another year.

"I read in the *Globe* this morning that Sir Winston Churchill's 'finest hour' speech yesterday may inspire many young Canadian men to join the Army, Navy or Air Force. Congratulations Bill I believe you are doing the right thing, although I hate the thought of losing you."

"Thank you Dear, but that's not the end of what I want to say."

"Carry on then. Please tell."

Bill rose from the garden chair, placed one knee on the ground and extended the other while keeping his foot on the grass. He took one of her hands looked her in the eyes and said "Bettina Joan Benning, will you be my lawful wedded wife?"

"Let's stand up for my reply Bill." They rose, faced each other, held hands and again looked each other directly in the eyes. "Yes William Cunningham, I accept. I will be your loving and faithful wife, and we'll marry before you go away."

They threw their arms around each other and for the first time Betty wasn't afraid that her mother was most likely watching. Once they released each other they walked hand in hand up the remainder of the driveway and into the house.

ONCE INSIDE MABEL CAME storming towards them from the living room. "Betty, your father told me about Bill's plan to join the RCAF and fight in the war and I welcomed the prospect".

"Because I may not return," interjected Bill.

Mabel ignored him and continued; "But what was that disgraceful act of passion afterwards, and that in front of all the neighbours? Surely joining the Air Force wouldn't merit such a display when there'd be a chance of you losing your boyfriend. Don't tell me you..."

"Yes Mom, we plan to marry before he leaves around this time next year."

"Oh good grief," cried Mabel as she walked slowly back into the living room with spectacles in one hand and the other holding a handkerchief over her eyes.

Joseph and Betty's younger sister Molly had been standing in silence observing the confrontation.

Bill said, "It's time for me to leave now Betty." He kissed her on the cheek, shook Joseph's hand and left.

Once the family had joined Mabel in the living room she cried, "Betty how could you do this? Joseph, how could you give your approval to this? Haven't you heard the expression, *like father; like son?* For all we know, his father may have deserted his wife and son; for all we know he may be serving life in prison for murder; for all we know his mother may have been a shameless street-walker and that's why she doesn't even know who his father is. But whoever he was, he was a bad man who didn't care about the consequences of his actions...Mark my words Betty; he'll *break your heart* some day."

❄❄❄❄

HA HA HA HA! In the evening of Friday 12th January 1941 laughter broke out from a table occupied by three Royal Canadian Navy officers at the joint Army, Navy, Air Force Mess at Gander air station in the Dominion of Newfoundland and Labrador. They were permanently stationed at the RCN radio monitoring station on the base. A laughing officer was pointing at one of the three Air Force officers at another table.

The Air Force officers had set out from Trenton, Ontario earlier in the day and would be flying on to Britain in the morning.

"What are they laughing about?...Why are they laughing Art?" yelled Flying Officer Bill Cunningham.

Art Westlake, who had been trying to appear to be uninterested finally gave in and replied. "I was in the washroom a minute ago and one of those sailors boys walked in. When I finished I washed my hands, but when he finished he didn't. As he walked out I said, 'In the Air Force we wash our hands after we urinate', and he replied, 'In the Navy we don't piss all over our hands when we drop a leak'." That caused loud laughter from poor Art's companions. Officers from other tables came over and asked what was going on. Art was the laughing stock of the whole mess.

When the reverie had died down a navy officer stepped up on to the two-foot high stage and, cried out, "D'ya hear there;[1] May I have your attention please." Everyone hushed and turned to hear what he had to say. He then started his story.

"A ground-pounder (soldier) goes to the toilet to pee." Then to everybody's delight he marched up to an imaginary toilet and in pantomime came to a halt, conducted a right turn, and stood at ease. He then he pretended to undo his zipper, pull out his penis and pee. Once finished, he zipped up, came to attention, conducted a left turn and marched off. Once the light laughter had subsided he said, "A matelow (sailor) goes to the toilet to drop a leak." Again in pantomime he staggered up to an imaginary toilet, almost falling over before getting there. He pretended to unzip and pull out his penis – still struggling to stay standing. Once he started to urinate, he staggered everywhere; at one point facing the audience and yelling '*Watch out*!' He then pretended to zip up, and while staggering away managed to avoid slipping and falling on his own urine. This time the whole room laughed much harder. Finally the navy officer raised his hand; everybody waited for act three. Then he said, "An Air *Farce* guy goes to the toilet to *urinate.*" Giggling erupted. He then pretended to walk up to a toilet; he looked both ways to ensure privacy, turned around backwards and sat down to ease his bladder. This time there was pandemonium as laughter erupted from tables of everyone present; even from that of Bill and his companions.

WILLIAM CUNNINGHAM had graduated from the University of Toronto in June 1941. A month later he and Bettina Benning were married at Bethel Baptist Church. The following day the newlyweds took a train to Niagara Falls for a short four-day honeymoon. Once completed the couple returned to Toronto, and the following day, Bill reported for duty. Betty accompanied him to the departure point and after they embraced and kissed she passed him a straw-stuffed horse, small enough to carry in his uniform pocket. She told him it was for luck. She wept as they waved and blew kisses at each other when the bus drove away, knowing there was a possibility they'd never see each other again.

The rudimentary military training, carried out at Trenton Air Force base, was only two weeks long and mostly consisted on how to march, salute and apply survival tactics if airplanes were shot down, but crew members managed to parachute into enemy occupied territory. When that phase had been completed crew members were trained in the necessary skills at specific positions in bombers. Bill was trained to be a forward gunner cum bomb aimer. The forward gunner sat in a transparent half bubble-like turret perched in front of the fuselage from where he would fire a machine gun at enemy aircraft. Once closing in on the target area he would be told over the intenal voice system to drop to the viewing bubble below his turret where he would lie on his stomach and peer through a rectangular hole, and once the target was in sight, release the bomb load. When that task was completed he'd announce 'Bombs away' and go back up top and resume his position as a forward gunner for the trip to home base. Much of the training was carried out in simulators.

AFTER THE SHORT BREAK in Gander, Bill Cunningham and other officers he had trained with at Trenton boarded Hudson bombers and were transported to various airfields in County Yorkshire in north eastern England. He had trained with fellow Canadians and a few Australians and New Zealanders, but when he arrived at the airfield near Leads he was surprised to see men from so many other parts of the world – both officers and ground crew men, some not even out of their teens. There were airmen from several British colonies and some from occupied France, Poland and Czechoslovakia.

All Air Forces of the Dominions – Canada, Australia and New Zealand – were merged into the Royal Air Force bomber command to simplify matters. The Canadian Army, however, remained a separate entity.

The new arrivals were given the day following their arrival off, but were in their bombers ready to go in the early afternoon of 22nd August 1941. At this point of the war, raids had been mostly carried out in daylight and were on naval ports and military bases. Unlike Hitler and his Blitz, the British were still reluctant to attack densely populated industrial cities which would inflict massive civilian casualties.

BILL SAT in the forward gun turret of a Lancaster bomber waiting for the pilot to be given the signal to take off. Soon he was sky-high looking down on the British Channel. Their destination was the sea port of Kiel just south of Denmark on the narrow entrance to the Baltic Sea.

***Lancaster Bomber in flight***

It wasn't long before Luftwaffe Messerschmitt fighters were upon the fifty-five RAF bombers that had taken off on this mission. Bill fired his machine gun in anger for the first time. He fired at one that seemed to be targeting another bomber to his right because it flew above his own aircraft. He heard a large explosion behind his head and quickly looked back to see if it came from the Messerschmitt or the bomber it was targeting. Had it been from the friendly bomber, the fighter would have swung back and attempted to take his aircraft out as well. He was pleased to see the friendly bomber next door. He had successfully taken out his first enemy fighter.

Just then he was told it was time to drop into the fuselage and take his position as the bomb aimer. He lay peering through the rectangular whole until he heard the navigator's words, "Drop when ready aimer."

When Bill clearly saw the target area below, he pulled a lever and released the bomb load. He announced *"Bombs Away!"* and rapidly returned to his forward gun turret.

❄❄❄❄

*"THE NAZIS ENTERED THIS WAR under the rather childish delusion that they were going to bomb everyone else, and nobody was going to bomb them. At Rotterdam, London, Warsaw and half a hundred other places, they put their rather naive theory into operation. They sowed the wind, and now they are going to reap the whirlwind."*

These were the words of Air Marshal Arthur Harris – later referred to as 'Bomber Harris'– after he had been placed in charge of RAF Bomber Command in February 1942.

***Air Marshal Arthur (Bomber) Harris***

During the same month, Prime Minister Winston Churchill's friend Professor Frederick Lindemann, the British government's leading scientific adviser with a seat in the Cabinet, had presented a seminal paper to Cabinet advocating the area bombing of German cities in a strategic bombing campaign. It was accepted by Cabinet and Air Marshal Harris was directed to carry out the area bombing directive. It was hoped it would become an important part of the total war waged against Germany.

AS THE SUN WAS SETTING on the night of 30/31 May 1942 Bill Cunningham's Group 5's first mission under the newly conceived plan, was the 1000 bomber raid on Cologne, approximately 40 miles inside the German border with the Netherlands. Attacking bombers would include: Wellingtons; Stirlings; Halifaxes; Whitleys; Lancasters; Manchesters; and Hampdens from several airfields located across Yorkshire.

Once Bill and other crew members were inside their Lancaster they were told the destination city. No one besides the navigator and the pilot knew the destination prior to entering the fuselage. Nobody else needed to know. German spies and double agents were everywhere. At 8 pm they were running down the runway.

The attacking bombers approached Cologne in waves; 1000 bombers all at once would cause too much confusion, and possible mid-air collisions. By the time they were over the Netherlands, radar stations detected them and the Luftwaffe Messerschmitts were upon them shortly afterward. An air battle ensued, with German fighters attacking British bombers and escorting Spitfires attacking German fighters. Fighters from both sides, and bombers went down in flames.

Bill's Lancaster was in the fourth wave of approximately 100 bombers of various types to close in on Cologne. The sky above was dark, but ahead all Bill could see was orange from the flames of burning buildings and factories below. While in his turret he saw flashes of bright orange all around him due to mid-air collisions and explosions of bombers and fighters hit by flak. It took astonishing courage to endure the conditions while flying at night over occupied Europe, running the gauntlet of German night fighters, anti-aircraft fire and mid-air collisions. The nerves of these young men were stretched to breaking point, but Bill's Lancaster pushed on.

Finally, much to Bill's relief, he was told to ready himself to drop the load. He was in position and ready to drop within seconds. It seemed to be an eternity before he heard the command, 'Drop when ready Aimer'. Bill adjusted his focus, pulled the lever and exclaimed, *"Bombs Away!"*

With that, the pilot conducted a sharp turn to starboard and circled southward. He steadied up at a heading of due south for ten minutes before altering to starboard again and setting a course of 315° on the compass. Northwest would take them and the other returning bombers with them back to England.

"Crossing over Belgian border," announced Art Westlake, the navigator. '*Not that it makes much difference*', thought Bill, '*Belgium's still occupied*'. So he kept a close lookout for incomings as he sat in his turret. He was remembering the words in the pre-flight briefing–*The Luftwaffe normally concentrate on east-bound bombers because they are heading towards targets, but don't hesitate to engage returning aircraft, under the logical theory of one less aircraft to return on another night.*

When one was upon them, it came in upwards under the port wing. The breakers cut in to prevent the middle gunner from shooting off the wing of his own aircraft. Bullets ripped through the cockpit, surely killing the pilot and possibly the navigator.

❄❄❄❄

KA-BOOM A LANCASTER exploded as it hit the ground nose-first. Two airmen in parachutes witnessed the horror as they floated to the ground while imagining the anguish of their companions left inside the aircraft when they realized they were going to perish within seconds.

After each had landed and ditched his parachute the two airmen ran toward each other not knowing which of their friends they were going to encounter. When they came face-to-face the forward gunner and the navigator cried out each other's name; "Bill!" ... "Art! I thought you'd be a goner Art," Bill cried, "He came in under the port wing and the safeties cut in preventing mid-gun Harry from engaging."

Art said, "One round whizzed past my forehead so close I swear I felt the wind in its wake, but it blew poor Jeff's brains out. Shall we go to the crash site to see if there are survivors?" He asked.

"No sense in that Art. Certainly the Germans will be here shortly to see if anyone parachuted to safety. In the slim chance that there are survivors, they'll certainly be severely injured or burned half to death. They'll be taken as prisoners and patched up. So, let's get outta here before the Krauts are upon us."

Bill took a magnetic compass and a little flashlight with a red lens and checked for the westerly direction. As he did so he said, "I prayed I'd never have to use this thing, but perhaps I didn't pray hard enough."

Art replied, "As Shakespeare wrote in Hamlet, Bill, *'Words without thought to Heaven do not go'.*"

"We don't need your Shakespeare now buddy. Something is rotten in the state we're in and we need to get the fuck outta here," said Bill.

After gaining their bearings, they started running across open fields. After forty-five minutes of jogging they stopped for a breather. Bill knew Art well. He knew him to be an expert navigator, but not a leader. He said, "Art, I'll take charge of getting us repatriated if you have no objections."

"Please do Bill."

"Okay, we'll travel by night and lay low during the daylight hours; perhaps under the shade of a tree or something else like an abandoned farm wagon."

"Good idea Boss."

By travelling at night they could take advantage of roadways. Several times they heard oncoming German vehicles with headlights partially blacked out except for a narrow strip in the centre. When this occurred, the two airmen were able to dive into a ditch, thus allowing the vehicles to pass without seeing them. They'd allow them to open to about half a mile before coming back up to the roadway to proceed. Other times they heard eastbound bombers making their way to other doomed target cities.

❄❄❄❄

ON SATURDAY MORNING 6th June 1942, Betty Cunningham was sitting on the garden chair on the front lawn of 37 Macnaughton stroking her little dog Perky after their morning walk. Earlier in the week she had read of the 1000 bomber raid on Cologne, Germany. According to the *Globe* story, the city was virtually flattened with the exception of the Cathedral. She wondered if Bill's squadron was part of it.

While she was sitting there a blue car with an RCAF crest on the front door pulled up and parked in front of the house. An old corporal emerged and walked up the driveway. He was holding an envelope in his hand. He saw Betty sitting there and asked, "Are you Mrs. Bettina Cunningham?"

"Yes I am," replied Betty with a horrified look on her face.

Knowing what she was dreading he said, "Yes it's true Mrs. Cunningham. Your husband William's Lancaster failed to return from the raid on Cologne a few nights ago."

Betty wailed, "No, No. Oh Lord tell me it's not so," but she knew it was. She buried her face in her hands and wept, while the corporal stood beside her. After a few minutes she recovered enough to ask, "Is there any hope at all that he survived?"

"All I can say Madam is that all crew members wear parachutes, so yes there is hope, albeit slim."...After a short pause he said, "I must leave now Mrs. Cunningham. There are several other wives and mothers in Toronto I must inform." He walked back to the car, and drove away. Betty buried her face in her hands again.

As she turned her eyes skyward to pray Joseph Benning walked up from behind. He allowed her to finish praying before placing his hand on her shoulder. Betty rose, threw her arms around her father and wept on his shoulder.

Mabel Benning stood at the window watching, but emotionless.

## Notes

1. Standard opening to any announcement to the crew over the ship's main broadcast.

# Nine

**ON THE FOURTH NIGHT** of Bill and Art's journey homeward they saw the lights of what appeared to be a village. Being famished and thirsty Bill decided to approach and see if they could obtain proper food and drink. Until then, they had been eating grass and roots, and drinking stale water from ponds.

As they approached the village they made their way to a dwelling on the peripheral which appeared to be a farm house. Bill reached deep into the pocket of his trousers and laid his hands on the little stray-fill horse Betty had given him for good luck. Being in occupied Belgium he assumed the residents would be friendly, but prior to advancing to the back door they saw a water pump. They started cranking the handle and fresh ground water spurted out. They scooped water in their hands and drank. The squeaking of the handle alerted the resident and the back door opened. A silhouette of what appeared to be a middle aged woman appeared on the back porch.

Bill approached her with his hands in the air to indicate he wasn't armed. From the dull light of the kitchen behind her she noticed his RAF uniform and in English said, "Come inside quickly; both of you!"

Once inside, the woman said, "Please sit" ... She pointed to two wooden kitchen chairs at a table. She sat on the third. "I see you are Royal Air Force officers. Was your aircraft lost?"

"Yes it was Mrs ..."

"Knaaper," she replied.

Bill continued, "Thank you Madam Knaaper. My name is Flying Officer William Cunningham and this is Flying Officer Arthur Westlake, but you can call us Bill and Art…Our aircraft was shot down while returning from Cologne a few nights ago. We were fortunate enough to parachute to safety."

"It must have been a harrowing experience."

"Yes it was Madam."...Not wanting to linger on the subject he asked, "What town is this and where is it located?"

"This is Genk, a coal mining town in eastern Belgium. You British calculate your distances in miles, so give me a minute" She paused for ten seconds and added, "The German border is roughly 15 miles due east and Amsterdam is 50 miles to the northwest of here."..."Now, you must be famished. We used to raise pigs, and other families raised cattle or sheep, but the enemy confiscated all of the livestock to feed their own...All I can offer you are some of last year's potatoes and carrots we grew in the small garden out back."

She continued, "Being a coal mining town, there are many German soldiers about; including the Gestapo. They use the coal for the furnaces in their industrial cities. They rarely leave the town centre so we can offer you refuge in our attic until you are ready to carry on with your journey. All I need is your acceptance; nothing else. After all, you are our friends and your troops will eventually liberate us."

"Do you have a family, Madam Knaaper?" asked Bill.

"Yes, my husband Jeroen. He works 12 hours a day in one of the collieries. He'll be home shortly."

"Will he approve of us staying for a few nights?"

"I rule the roost in this family. He'll approve or I'll bonk him on the head with my rolling pin," replied Mrs. Knaaper.

"Mrs. Knaaper, we will accept your generous offer for a few nights, but will then carry on with our westward trek. We want to get closer to the coast and wait until the inevitable invasion takes place, be repatriated and go back across the Channel to rejoin our squadron, and then continue the fight."

"I admire you both for that Flying Officer Cunningham; very dedicated to the cause indeed."

"Soooo! Entertaining two young men while I'm at work, is it Elisabeth? ... Oh! I see they're two British airmen no less," said Mr. Knaaper with a chuckle as he entered the kitchen.

"These two gentlemen from the Royal Air Force have just gone through a harrowing experience Jeroen," replied Elisabeth, and went on to tell their story plus the fact they they'd be hosting them for a few days.

"You have my consent...as if you need it," said Jeroen.

Elisabeth then said, "You are both roughly the same size as Jeroen. Would you like some civilian clothing to wear on your journey?"

"Thank you Mrs. Knaaper, but we've been advised it wouldn't be wise to wear civilian clothes. If ever we were stopped and asked questions we wouldn't know the language, and in that case may be mistaken for spies and shot."

"Yes, that makes sense."

After the two airmen had gobbled down their potatoes and carrots, they enjoyed a cup of tea while Mr. Knaaper entered the bedroom. He picked up a step ladder and placed it under the trap door to the attic. He then called out, "Would one of you young men please help me by passing up the quilt and blanket?" Bill did the needful after Mrs. Knaaper passed them to him.

Before he dozed off Bill said, "No hogging the blanket Art!" Art didn't hear. He was already snoring.

❄❄❄❄

BOOM; BOOM, RATA TAT TAT; landing craft exploded before reaching shore; ships were sunk; aircraft zoomed across the chaos below firing their machine guns; some were shot down. This was at about 05:30 am on 19th August 1942, the day Canadian soldiers first set foot on the European mainland as combatants. They were part of a raid on the French port of Dieppe.

Second Lieutenant Donald Snelgrove egged on those of the troops in his platoon who made it to the beach alive. However, they got pinned down behind a wall on the inland side of the beach by machine gun fire from German bunkers high on the cliffs surrounding the port. They could not advance.

At 10:30 am when Allied Commanders ordered a retreat Snelgrove cried "*Retreat*! Able bodied men assist the walking wounded." He latched one arm around a soldier with blood stained combat pants and assisted him halfway across the beach before they were both mowed down by machine gun fire. They were both dead before they hit the sand.

NORMA AND ALLAN SNELGROVE read about the Dieppe Raid in the evening edition of the *Toronto Star*. The report said:

> *Although valuable lessons were learned from the Raid on Dieppe, a steep price was paid. Of the 4,963 Canadians who embarked on the operation, only 2,210 returned to England, and many of these were wounded. There were 3,367 casualties, including 1,946 prisoners of war taken; 916 Canadian soldiers lost their lives.*

Norma and Allan prayed that their son was not part of the raid. Their greatest fears came true when a telegram arrived two days later saying that their son Donald had fallen at Dieppe. Norma, Allan and their niece Annie were grief stricken.

Since so many Canadian lives had been claimed, foreign correspondents of the *Globe and Mail,* and the *Toronto Star* stationed in England delved deeper into the disaster. Some reports filed described the raid as an *'experimental operation to test the German defenses'.* Others described the fallen soldiers as *'sacrificial lambs'*, and went on to describe the raid as a *'fiasco'.*

Norma and Allan were furious from these reports and blamed one man – Sir Winston Churchill – for authorizing the raid in the first place.

❄❄❄❄

BETTY CUNNINGHAM READ the *Toronto Star* every evening and learned of the sacrifices of Canadian servicemen fighting in the war. Reports had earlier said the *Star's* opposition and criticism of the Nazi regime during the 1930s saw the daily become one of the first North American newspapers to be banned in Germany.

While reading she noticed stories of downed airmen who had survived and made their way to neutral Spain, where they were picked up and repatriated to Britain. Other times she saw names of downed airmen who had survived, but had been captured by the Germans. She hoped Bill's name would appear in one of those stories some day. She was heartened to learn that the Geneva Convention stated in times of war opposing forces would report names of captured combatants to each other and detainees must be incarcerated in humane conditions.

Betty also wanted to supplement the family income by paying her mother and father for putting her up while Bill was away. Although they insisted it wasn't necessary she was determined, and besides that she was quite bored. She was a trained secretary, but then one day while reading the want ads she came across something that seemed to be exciting. It was an opening for waitresses in the dining rooms of pleasure cruisers that sailed on the Great Lakes from Toronto to Sault Ste Marie, Ontario, with a side excursion into Georgian Bay. She jumped at the opportunity whole-heartedly. Therefore, at 8:30 am on Friday 3rd July 1942, she stood at the head of the line at a door on the second floor of a downtown office building which was the cruise company's recruiting centre.

At nine o'clock a middle-aged gentleman wearing a double-breasted suit arrived at the door and said, he'd be ready as soon as his secretary arrived. Five minutes later a woman who appeared to be in her early thirties arrived and entered. Not long after Betty was called into the office.

Introductions followed then the gentleman, Mr. Johnston, asked, "Will your husband approve of you being away from home for two weeks at a time Mrs. Cunningham?"

"My husband William is, and I hope not *was,* an airman whose aircraft was shot down during the Cologne raid a couple of months ago. I've been told not to give up hope, as all crew members are fitted with parachutes," replied Betty.

"Do you have children?"

"No Sir, I don't."

"And why do you think you are suitable for this job; what excites you about it if anything?"

"Well Sir, I am courteous; I know my manners; I show respect for all mankind regardless of race, creed or colour; I've been told I have a great sense of humour; and, I stand up for myself when challenged or verbally assaulted – all attributes I think are necessary for such a career choice. With regard to the excitement portion of your question, I've never travelled far from Toronto and I'm excited about the prospect of making new friends among the other waitresses and about seeing new places." She added with a smile, "It shouldn't be too hard to teach me the art of being a waitress; after all, I serve my mother and father supper every evening with no complaints and believe me, my mother is the world's greatest complainer."

"Ok Mrs. Cunningham, that is enough, but there is something I want to stress should you be hired."... After a short pause to see if he had her full attention he continued, "Under no circumstances are crew members – male or female – permitted to fraternize with paying passengers, whether on board or ashore. Do you understand?"

"Yes Sir, I'm a married woman so there is no chance of that happening.

"Thank you Mrs Cunningham. We have others to interview. You will be hearing from me one way or the other in a couple of days."

"Thank you Sir." Betty walked out of the office feeling confident. When she arrived home she told her mother and father what she had done. They both congratulated her on her initiative.

On Tuesday morning at ten o'clock, the pedestal-type telephone rang at 37 Macnaughton Road. Mabel unhitched the receiver and placed it against her left ear, while she lifted the speaker up to her mouth, "Hello," she said.

"Hello," said the voice on the other end of the line, "May I please speak to Mrs. Cunningham?"

"May I tell her whose calling?"

"Yes, my name is Samuel Johnston from the Lake Star Steam Cruiser Line."

"One minute please Mr. Johnston."... Mabel cried out, *"Betty; you have an important phone call."* Betty came running, wondering if it was about William.

"Mr. Johnston," whispered Mabel.

"Hello Mr. Johnston; its Bettina Cunningham speak-ing."

"Good day Mrs Cunningham. Are you still excited about the prospect of becoming a Great Lakes sailor?"

"I sure am Sir."

"Excellent. Please report to SS Maple Leaf tomorrow morning at 10 o'clock. She is berthed at Pier One at the foot of Bay Street just west of the island ferry terminal. A Mr. Angus Young will be standing at the head of the gangway to greet you and the other waitress who was hired. Mr. Young is the food and beverage manager of the Maple Leaf. He'll show you both around the ship, answer any questions you may have and explain tasks you'll be expected to perform... Do you have any questions I can answer now Mrs. Cunningham?"

"No Sir; you have made yourself quite clear. I will be at the Maple Leaf tomorrow morning at 10 o'clock."

"Good Mrs. Cunningham. I wish you well in your new position. Good day."

"Good day to you Sir. And thank you for calling."

Mable had been standing by listening. When Betty replaced the receiver she said, "Congratulations Dear." Then she laughed as Betty conducted a mock jitterbug dance beside the dining room table. It was good to see happiness reappear into her daughter's life.

❄❄❄❄

AT NEWMARKET, ONTARIO, about 30 miles north of Toronto, Captain Charles Elliot stood in front of a class of Canadian Army engineers who would be bound for Britain after training.

"The next phase of your training," said Charles, "will be on Bailey bridges."

"A Bailey bridge is a type of portable, pre-fabricated, truss bridge. It was recently developed by the British for use in this war. After the invasion of Europe by British, Canadian and American armies, the Germans will destroy their bridges behind them as they retreat, so the Bailey bridge is expected to see extensive use."

He continued, "A Bailey bridge has the advantages of requiring no special tools or heavy equipment to assemble. The wood and steel bridge elements are small and light enough to be carried in trucks and be lifted into place by hand, without requiring the use of a crane. They are strong enough to withstand the weight of tanks. But they must be assembled under the direction of men taught the methods. That is where you fellows will play a big part."

Charles continued, "Now if you look out into the centre of the field you will see a 200 yard long culvert, which was especially dug for your Bailey bridge training. You'll also see a flat-bed truck with the parts on the back."

"Today, I will take charge of directing you fellows on how to erect one. Tomorrow one of you will take charge under my direction."... "After the invasion when you are pursuing the Germans to Berlin you will use non-commissioned infantrymen to do the bull-work while you direct them. Some may have taken part in the evolution numerous times and may even be able to take charge themselves, but we must assume that none have experience."

"Are there any questions before we start?" No hands went up. "Good. Let's get at it. Follow me."

❄❄❄❄

ON THE SATURDAY after he and his wife had sheltered Flying Officers William Cunningham and Arthur Westlake in their attic, Jeroen Knaaper sat at a table with three close friends in the café near his house. The men met regularly on Saturday evenings.

Most of the talk was about the ongoing war. They speculated on where and when the invasion would take place, and about the number of RAF bombers that had been shot down over their homeland. At one point the man sitting next to Jeroen whispered, "An RAF airman who had parachuted to safety knocked on our back door last month. We invited him in and served him dinner."

"That's nothing," blurted out Jeroen. "Elisabeth and I have two RAF airmen hidden out in our attic."

A friend said, "Watch your tongue Jeroen. You never know who may be listening."

A man named Bernard Overall, sat nearby. Jeroen was facing the man when he made the announcement of the RAF airmen in his attic. Overall held an open book in his hands and his head faced downward. His eyes, however, were focused on the quartet of men sitting at the nearby table. He was eavesdropping and heard what Jeroen Knaaper had proudly proclaimed. Mr. Overall winked towards Knaaper and smiled, he then turned his eyes back to his book.

The next evening after dark Overall walked 100 metres ahead of a Gestapo officer and three enlisted men. When he was close enough to the Knaaper residence he hid himself behind the trunk of a large tree and waited for the Germans to reach him. Once they were close enough he pointed to the Knaaper's house and waited to watch.

The foursome walked up to the door and went into the house through the unlocked front door. Jeroen and Elisabeth, who were eating dinner sprang up and backed toward the rear wall. A soldier blocked the back door so they couldn't run off. They had developed a strategy. The officer nodded to one of his soldiers who spoke French, indicating it was time to address the couple.

"You have two British airmen sheltered in your attic. Where is the attic? Tell us quickly or you will both die here and now!" the soldier yelled.

Knowing they meant business, and would find it with or without his aid, Jeroen led them to the bedroom and pointed at the ceiling hatch. He also pointed to a step ladder propped against the wall.

The officer, who spoke English, climbed the ladder, with torch in one hand and pistol in the other. He poked his head and arms through the hatch and before long spotted William and Art lying flat on their stomachs. He raised his Luger P08 and shot a hole in the roof for emphasis. He then shouted, "Come down, you have been found."

Both William and Art obeyed.

When they passed their hosts Bill passed Mrs. Knaaper the stray-stuffed horse Betty had given him for luck. The officer allowed him to say a few words, "I'm alive, so this lucky horse my wife gave me for good luck has served me well to date. Now I pass on its magic to you Mrs Knaaper."

"Thank you William," she said with tears in her eyes.

As the two airmen were being escorted out of the front door, the French-speaking soldier turned to the Knaapers and said, "You may want to patch the hole in your roof before the rains come.

The couple stood on the threshold watching as the two airmen were marched away handcuffed to each other. All that was visible were their silhouettes, but they saw a man walk out from behind the tree to join them.

Mr. Knaaper smirked and nodded when one of the soldiers passed him what he presumed were food vouchers, and walked away in a different direction with a recognisable limp. Jeroen said, "I know that limp Elizabeth. He *will* pay for his traitorous deeds."

Elizabeth, however, thought it strange that she and her husband had not been shot, because many others had been shot for sheltering RAF officers. The smirk on her husband's face was also puzzling; and the fact that the door was simply unlocked when it was normally bolted seemed strange to her.

WILLIAM AND ARTHUR were taken to a temporary lock-up to await the next train bound for Germany with Jews from Amsterdam, and possibly with other captured airmen. Their temporary home was more comfortable than their hideout in the Knaaper's attic. It consisted of six huts to accommodate up to twenty or so individuals and an outdoor closely-knit barbed wire fenced in a 200 square metre area with no vegetation. There was a fenced in 8 metre wide, 200 metre long corridor leading to a railway platform. All sides of the compound were guarded by soldiers bearing machine guns.

Bill and Art heard voices in two of the buildings and speculated they were of Jews dragged from their homes in the town and surrounding landscape. The Jews weren't allowed to walk around outside and breathe fresh air while waiting for the train to arrive. Only captured combatants were allowed this – what their captors called – *'luxus'* (luxury).

Two days after being incarcerated Art said, "Do you hear it Bill?"

"Hear what?"

"It sounds as though a train is coming."

Bill perked up his ear. "Yes Art," said Bill, "I believe you're right."

Five minutes later a freight train stopped at a platform at the end of the compound corridor. The doors to the huts in the compound were opened one by one and the captive Jews were ushered into boxcars.

"What are those yellow symbols on the arms of some of them Bill?" asked Art.

"They are the 'Star of David', Art."…"Ever since 1939 all Jews in Germany, and now its occupied countries, have been required to wear one on their arm as a prelude to deporting them to ghettos in occupied Europe."

"Will they be gassed?"

"I don't think so Art. Hitler is evil; but I can't even perceive the fact that he could be *that* evil."

The two airmen watched in a state of sympathy as at least 500 Jews walked past them. Once at the train they were jammed elbow to elbow into the boxcars already teaming with those from Amsterdam and other towns along the way. The two airmen were put in another car, one directly behind the engine. They were the only occupants so they speculated it must have been reserved for other airmen. Once their door had been secured the steam engine began puffing and the train commenced moving eastward again.

FIVE HOURS AFTER BOARDING the train; on a transit that otherwise would have taken two, the train stopped again. The doors to the boxcar behind the engine rolled open. There were some loud orders in German. Bill and Art didn't have to be told what the words meant. They rose from the sitting positions and climbed down to the platform. They were immediately ushered to a small truck built to transport prisoners; not only Prisoners of War, but also domestic prisoners to or from jail or court. It wasn't long before the vehicle stopped at Stalag VI G[1], the closest POW camp to the Netherlands border. It was run by the Gestapo.

The Gestapo commandant, who Bill speculated held the rank of Major, emerged from his office when they arrived. He wasted no time. He looked Bill in the eyes and in English said, "Name?"

"William Cunningham."

He turned to Art, "Name?"

"Arthur Westlake."

Bill asked, "Will our commanders be informed that we have been captured?"

"No!"

Bill began to protest, "But the Geneva Convention ..."

"We *shit* on the Geneva Convention; we take our orders from *Der Führe*," the major interjected.

He then reached up under the collars of each and ripped their lightly chained dog tags free. He inspected them for confirmation, pocketed them, and issued an order to four soldiers. And by the looks of the rectangular concrete building standing in front of them, Bill knew the order wasn't *'Take them to their luxurious accommodation'.*

## Notes

1. The 'G' represented Gestapo. Stalags with an 'A' were run by the German Army.

# Ten

**WAITRESSES, COOKS, MUSICIANS, PASSENGERS** and dishwashers in the dining room or kitchen of SS Maple Leaf stood around a five-foot tall oak arched-top radio listening to the CBC news on the evening of 6th June 1944. This was the day of the massive Allied invasion on the beaches of Normandy; a day termed as D-Day.

The listeners didn't know whether to rejoice or pray, or simply cry. On the one hand, they knew many combatants of land, air and sea would die, and on the other, they knew the war would soon be won and their sons, husbands or brothers would hopefully return unscathed. The CBC announcer said there would be more news in the morning.

The orchestra went back to their instruments and played hymns. Betty Cunningham walked up to the conductor and made a request. She took the microphone and after the opening chords she sang ...

*O Lord my God, When I in awesome wonder*
*Consider all the worlds Thy Hands have made;*
*I see the stars, I hear the rolling thunder*
*Thy power throughout the universe displayed*

*Then sings my soul, My Saviour God, to Thee*
*How great Thou art, How great Thou art*
*Then sings my soul, My Saviour God, to Thee*
*How great Thou art, How great Thou art!*

*When through the woods, and forest glades I wander*
*And hear the birds sing sweetly in the trees*
*When I look down, from lofty mountain grandeur*
*And see the brook, and feel the gentle breeze*

*Then sings my soul, My Saviour God, to Thee*
*How great Thou art, How great Thou art*
*Then sings my soul, My Saviour God, to Thee*
*How great Thou art, How great Thou art!*

*And when I think, that God, His Son not sparing;*
*Sent Him to die, I scarce can take it in;*
*That on the Cross, my burden gladly bearing*
*He bled and died to take away my sin*[1]

Given the reverence of the hymn and the occasion, nobody clapped, nor should they have, but everybody smiled and nodded their heads as she walked away. Others, both passengers and crew members sang their favourite hymns. Everyone on the ship, regardless of station in life, was united that evening.

In the morning a different announcer told listening Canadians more than 156,000 soldiers, six infantry divisions, plus armoured units, had landed on five beaches along a 100 km sweep of coastline in Normandy and also behind enemy lines. The Americans were assigned to the beaches code-named Utah and Omaha, the British to Gold and Sword, and the Canadians to Juno. A battalion of Canadian paratroopers landed behind German lines, as did three divisions of British and US paratroopers on the flanks of the main invasion force. The announcer said it was the largest seaborne invasion ever attempted.

Those listening to CBC that morning were told that by the end the day total Allied casualties, both dead and wounded, reached more than 10,000, including 359 Canadians killed in action. Hundreds of Germans were also killed and captured. French civilians died due to bullets and bombs raining around their seaside villages. Although none of the Allied forces succeeded in reaching their inland D-Day objectives, the Normandy beachhead itself was secured, which would allow successive waves of troops, tanks, artillery and other supplies to come ashore. On Gold Beach the British engineers began constructing floating "Mulberry" harbours made out of massive barge pieces towed across the Channel.

❄❄❄❄

"BILL CUNNINGHAM WHAT brings you home so early!?" exclaimed Mable after answering the door of 37 Macnaughton Road. "We were told you had survived, but we thought you'd remain to continue the fight."

Bill simply replied, "I wanted to stay until it ended, but they sent me home early… Is Betty around?"

"She's on a Great Lakes pleasure cruise with Chris Stensson," she said and grinned.

Bill took a small note pad and a pen out of his uniform pocket, scratched down some digits and passed them to his mother-in-law.

"Here is the phone number of where I'll be staying. Please give it to Betty when she returns." He walked away with a devastated look on his face.

While Betty and Bill were dating she had introduced him to Chris Stensson, her first cousin. Afterwards, she had told him that when Chris was a ten-year-old he had asked her father if he could marry her when they grew up and that her father had said, 'Chrisie, you don't breed cattle that way'; thinking it may have sounded a little crass to Bill she reminded him that her father's family had been cattle breeders in North Devon.

AT AROUND NOON two days later, the phone rang at the home of Rebecca Cunningham. Bill picked it up, "William Cunningham speaking," he said.

*"Bill … Bill!"* exclaimed Betty, "Thank God my prayers have been answered. I was informed you'd been repatriated, but didn't expect you home until the war was won."

*'Obviously,'* Bill thought but instead said, "I'm home now and on standby to go to Burma to fight the Japs."

"Dad will be so happy to see you. You must come to supper tonight, and bring your mother along with you … we eat at 6 o'clock as usual," said Betty.

"By the way Bet, how was your recent trip? Is there anything I ought to know about it?"

"It was pleasant enough. There's nothing you ought to know except that it was the last of the season due to an early icing up of the Welland Canal…So, will you both come for supper tonight?"

"I can't speak for Mother because she's out shopping, but set the table as if she'll attend and if she doesn't simply remove her setting."

"Can't wait to see you Bill. Love you, bye bye."

"Love you too, bye for now Bet."

When she replaced the receiver Betty walked into the kitchen to inform her mother. Before she could say anything Mabel said, *"I heard,"* in a very distasteful manner.

Betty retaliated, "And for the sake of God, Bill, Dad and me, don't snub your nose at them. Bill must have gone through hell over there. I expect it will take some time for him to recover from it. He doesn't need to be treated like scum. He's a war hero in my eyes, and in the eyes of our country and King."

Betty then picked up the phone and called her father at work. When Joseph took the receiver she said, "Dad, we'll be having a special guest for supper tonight. Please arrange to be home early this evening."

"Who is it pray tell?"

"It's a surprise Dad, but you'll be delighted to see the person."

"Is 5 o'clock alright?"

"Perfect Dad."

"Ok. I'll be there at five."

After hanging up Betty turned to her mother and said, "And don't you spoil the surprise when he gets home by telling him who's coming Mom!"

Mabel had never received a direct order from her daughter before and knew she meant business. "I won't Dear."

Betty was sitting on the living room winged armchair at 5 pm. It was dark and she took note of every set of car headlights coming along Macnaughton Rd. or Cameron Crescent where the two streets joined at the tip of the triangular park across the street. At 5:15 Joseph's '38 Dodge pulled into the driveway. She ran to the door as he entered and said, "Hi Dad. I trust you had a good day," and quickly returned to the armchair before Joseph even had a chance to answer face to face.

He called after her, "Yes I did Dear."

Due to her interest in the window he had a pretty good idea of who the surprise guest was going to be and smiled. Mabel was standing by watching. He smiled at her and said, "I can't wait to see him." Mabel returned the smile.

At 5:30 pm Betty jumped up from the armchair and darted to the front door which opened onto the driveway. She didn't even stop to close the door behind her. She ran down the driveway, met her husband at the halfway point and threw her arms around him. Tears rolled down her cheeks as the cried, 'Bill; Bill; Thank *God* you are home. I missed you so much. Not a night went by that I didn't pray for your safe return. My prayers have been answered."

"I did a lot of praying along the same lines too Bet," he said as they walked hand in hand up the driveway.

When they opened the door that her mother had closed after her departure, Joseph and Mabel were standing in the vestibule. Joseph embraced him and said, "Welcome home Son."

Bill and Mabel simply shook hands. Mabel said, "Your mother is not with you so I assume you are alone. Is that a correct assumption?"

"Yes Mrs. Benning, she chose not to attend."

"Shall we go to the living room to chat?" asked Joseph.

"You folks go. I'll return to the kitchen and finish cooking the meal," said Mabel.

Once seated in the living room Joseph asked, "So, what can you tell us about your experience Bill?"

"All I'm up to saying at this moment is that my bomber was shot down over Belgium on return from the '42 raid on Cologne. The navigator and I managed to parachute to the ground and the remainder of the crew perished." His eyes welled up and Betty, who was sitting beside him on the chesterfield, stroked his hand while waiting for him to recover.

Eventually he carried on. "A friendly Belgian couple hid us in their attic and a collaborator turned us in...We were taken to a Gestapo Stalag and incarcerated. When I arrived I asked the English speaking major in command if our headquarters would be informed and he said, 'No'. I reminded him of the Geneva Convention articles and he said, and these were his words not mine, 'We *shit* on the Geneva Convention. We take our orders from *Der Führer'*."..."A couple of months after D-Day we were being transferred further inland and my friend Art Westlake, and I and a few others managed to jump from a moving cattle car. Art and I made our way to Amsterdam where the Germans had capitulated[1] to Canadian troops on 8th May and we were eventually sent back across the Channel."

He paused, pulled out a pipe and asked, "Do either of you mind if I smoke?"

"Please go ahead Bill," replied Joseph.

Bill thanked his father-in-law and carried on where he left off. "Upon return I expected to be sent back to my squadron and carry on with the fight to the finish, but they disallowed it."

“Why was that Bill?” asked Betty.

“Because after the so called ‘Great Escape’ earlier this year, Hitler declared that any recaptured POWs would be shot.”...“I pleaded with my Wing Commander. I said, ‘Give me the dog tags of your corporal administrator. There are no ranks on dog tags,’ but he just said, ‘Unlike Hitler, we play by the rules,’ and sent me home instead. I’m now supposedly on standby to go to Burma to fight the Japs, but I think I was just told a fable. It won’t happen... After the war in Europe is won I expect Canadian involvement will end.”

They all sat in silence for about ten minutes, while Betty stroked Bill’s hand.

Soon, Mabel entered and announced, “Dinner time.”

The three others walked in silence and took their places at the table.

There wasn’t much talk at the table that night, but at one point Joseph asked, “Do you plan to remain in the Air Force when it ends Bill?”

“Yes Dad, when we first met back while I was still a young lad I told you I would fly airplanes some day. That is still my main goal in life and remaining in active service is the best chance to realize that dream without paying for it...Sadly, there will be a shortage of pilots when the war ends because they are situated in a position inside the fuselage the farthest from the escape hatch when the aircraft has been doomed to an explosive crash when it hits the ground. We lost so...so many good pilots...I mean good *men*. The death toll won’t be tabulated until it’s over, but I expect it to be over 10 thousand Canadians.”

“Where do you expect you’ll be stationed when it’s over?” asked Mabel.

“My hope is RCAF Clinton. It’s situated near the town of Goderich, Ontario on the coast of Lake Huron. I spent some time there during initial training. It’s a nice little town with a cart wheel shaped roundabout in the centre. RCAF Clinton is also where they conduct pilot training.”

Betty caught Mabel’s eyes and gave her a look that said, ‘Don’t you object Mother’, and once that was established said, “Bill, we have a double bed in one of the bedrooms upstairs. Why don’t you stay the night, and tomorrow being Christmas Eve we’ll set out early and go down to Niagara to re-live our honeymoon?”

Joseph said, “Wonderful idea Bet! You can borrow the Dodge to get you there and explore the Niagara Peninsula. What do you think Bill?”

“Well…Mother will be spending Christmas with Aunt Dorothy and Uncle Herb, so I guess it will be alright. Yes, let’s do it.

## Notes

1. Thrown in the towel without firing a shot

# Eleven

**'VICTORY IN EUROPE TODAY'**, were the big bold evening headlines of the *'Toronto Star'* on 8th May 1945. As he sat in the living room armchair of their Goderich house William Cunningham read the story that followed with mixed emotions. He was glad it was over of course, but bitter because he wasn't allowed to fight to the finish.

Betty, who was in her fifth month of pregnancy, walked into the living room and said, "Why have you got such a glum look on your mug on a day like today Bill?"

"Because I've been sitting on my ass at a desk pushing paper for the last five months while my friends were there to finish them off you idiot! I had good reason to want to bomb the *shit* out of them…'On standby to fight in Burma' *bull shit*! That was just a way they thought could appease me. There were never any intentions to send me to Burma. They simply lied! If it didn't mean losing the opportunity to become a pilot at government expense I'd resign my commission tomorrow. No more questions!"

"I was going to suggest we go to the mess tonight and celebrate the victory with your friends, but can now see that's out of the question."

*"Totally!"* replied Bill. "I won't be having supper tonight Betty. I'm just going up to read for a while and then turn in, and hopefully fall asleep early."

That evening Betty just stood and watched as the man she loved climbed slowly up the stairs.

When he reached the bedroom Bill sat in a chair near the window to take advantage of the setting sun. He picked up his copy of '*Grapes of Wrath*' by John Steinbeck. It was about an Oklahoma family who had lost their farm in the Great Depression and were suffering their way across the dusty plains to California in hopes of finding employment. It was a Pulitzer Prize winning novel, but on this particular evening Bill found it a wee bit depressing given his present mood. After reading about five pages he set it aside and climbed under the covers on his side of the double bed. By the time he was snoring, haunting memories of his confinement in Stalag VIG entered his mind in the form of nightmares, as did thoughts of his wife having an affair with her first cousin, Chris Stensson. When Betty slid under the sheets two hours later he didn't even stir.

WHEN BETTY CLIMBED out of bed at 6 o'clock the next morning she was alone. She put on her dressing gown and went downstairs. Bill was nowhere in sight. She was bewildered until ten minutes later when he entered the front door and said, "Good morning Dear. I went to bed so early I woke up at five and have just enjoyed a nice walk down to the town circle and back. This is such a nice town." He added, "And I'm so sorry for calling you an idiot last evening. I'm the idiot for saying such a terrible thing."

"That's alright Bill. I can only imagine the torment you must have suffered in that lockup that made you so desperately want to go back and fight to the end."

"I'll tell you some day Bet, but I'm just not up to it yet. In fact, when I was to brief my senior officers back in Britain after my return, at one point I broke down and wept openly."

"I understand. I can wait until you're ready Bill."

They engaged in light conversation over breakfast and when finished Bill went upstairs to wash, shave and dress for work. He came down forty five minutes later, kissed Betty and was off for the day.

TEN DAYS LATER BILL was informed that officers and ground crew members had started arriving at RCAF Station Trenton; the station from which they had departed Canadian soil five or more years earlier. Bill knew they'd all be given one month of earned leave and when it expired they'd be transported to various Air Force stations across the dominion. Bill had also been given the same amount of leave when he arrived home.

When officers and non-commissioned members who were posted to Clinton arrived a month later Bill started going to the mess after work to meet and engage in conversation with those who would become his new friends. On the first night this happened he arrived home at 8 pm instead of his normal six.

Upon arrival Betty said, "Bill, you could have at least given me a phone call and told me you'd be late. Supper has been ready since 6 o'clock." Betty was a little annoyed.

"Sorry Dear, said Bill. "Let's just assume it will happen every night for a while and reschedule supper for 8 o'clock until I've heard all the stories I want, or perhaps I should say, *'don't want'* to hear."

"Yes alright Dear."

BILL CONTINUED to go to the mess after work and share conversation with fellow air force officers. When he asked other repatriated POWs about the living conditions of camps run by soldiers of the German army, he was appalled when one fellow told him that the one in which he had been interned allowed prisoners to walk or march around freely in the daytime, and play volleyball on a court that had been installed for entertainment. Further, their captors were in the process of building a swimming pool, but stopped construction when Allied forces had gained a beachhead on the coast of Normandy.

When asked about his own experiences Bill spoke of the sadness of seeing the crew members of his bomber perish when it hit the ground and explode while he and his buddy parachuted to the ground. He told about being hidden in the attic of a friendly Belgian family before being betrayed by a collaborator. He mentioned seeing the Jews being stuffed into overcrowded boxcars. He said he didn't even learn about the holocaust until he was told after his repatriation.

When asked about his internship in a Gestapo stalag all he could say was "solitary confinement for almost two years." When asked for details he simply shook his head. He would not – *could not* – add more without the embarrassment of breaking down.

The more he listened to stories of others the more bitter a young man he became. '*Those bastards wouldn't allow me to go back and take out my revenge*' he thought each night as he sat on a chair on the back porch simply staring into space, despite the mosquitoes buzzing around his head.

When he reverted back to his regular schedule of arriving home at 6 pm, Betty would often say, "Let's walk down to the lakefront park, sit on a bench and watch the sun set over the lake," but Bill would refuse.

❄❄❄❄

ON THE MORNING OF 7th December 1941 the Japanese had entered the war when they conducted a sneak-attack on the U.S. Naval Feet in Pearl Harbour. By mid-1942 they had overrun the

Malay Peninsula and were about to occupy Burma, with an overall objective of occupying all of South Asia.

Both Anil Kumar and Amir Shah volunteered for the war effort and joined the British Indian Army when the Japanese entered Burma, and the Indian National Army (INA), formed by Subash Chandra Bose, was assisting them by leading them along the Grand Trunk Road with a motive to eject the British from India. Although both Amir and Anil had a university education there was only a smattering of Indian officers, so they became private soldiers. Due to their fluency in English, and thus their ability to translate orders from their British commanders, it didn't take long before they were both promoted to the rank of corporal. They had been assigned to different regiments. Before departure both had sent letters home informing their next of kin what they had done; Amir's letter was sent to his father who then lived in Amritsar and Anil's was sent to Panditji in Dharamsala.

The Americans dropped atomic bombs on the cities of Hiroshima and Nagasaki on August 6 and 9 (1945), respectively. The Japanese surrendered to Allied Forces on 15th August (1945) approximately a week later. Upon his release from the Army, Amir made his way directly to the home of his parents in Amritsar. Anil, however, was never seen or heard from again. Panditji received a letter saying Anil Kumar had been killed in action.

Panditji informed Walter Elliot by letter.

❄❄❄❄

DURING WHAT WAS ESTIMATED would be her last two weeks of pregnancy Betty took an air force bus down to Toronto. Upon arrival at the drop off point she then took a taxi to her mother and father's house. Both Betty and Bill thought she'd get more professional treatment in a large Toronto hospital rather than one in the small town of Goderich. Bill would travel down the day after the child was born. Bill hoped for a boy; Betty didn't care as long as the child had two legs, two arms, and a strong beating heart.

Two days later the roster for the first class of pilots was posted on the bulletin board outside the regulating office. When he was informed, Bill ran half a mile from his office building to check the list. When he arrived there was a cluster of officers standing in front of it. A few cheered while more walked away with a dejected look on their faces. When Bill got close enough to read it, his name was at the top. "Yaaa hooo," he exclaimed and ran to the nearest telephone and called Betty.

She was delighted for him. "Congratulations Bill, when Dad gets home I'll tell him your dreams and prayers have been answered. "When does the first class start?" she asked.

"Monday 15th October. You and the babe should be home by then ... but I have one request...Please allow me the pleasure of informing Dad when I get there. He was the first one to hear my dream when I was just a boy. I hadn't even told my mother. So, goodbye Dear and I'll be there once the baby is born."

"Goodbye Bill and I won't let 'the cat out of the bag' with regard to Dad. Once again congratulations."

At 10 pm on 27th September Betty went into labour. She called her dad who was just getting ready to turn in for the night. Joseph helped her down the stairway and out the door to the Dodge. Mabel rang the hospital and told the receptionist to expect them. She then hustled out to the car and climbed into the back seat with her daughter. She silently prayed, '*Oh Lord, please don't make me become a midwife along the way*'.

When they arrived two male nurses were standing with a four-wheeled stretcher at the top of a ramp leading to the front door. They rolled the stretcher to the car and eased Betty out of the back seat and onto it, and then rolled her up and through the front doors and to the maternity ward. They handed her over to the female nurses and walked away. When they encountered Mabel and Joseph following they escorted them to the waiting room.

Two hours later at about 01:30 am the doctor walked into the waiting room. There were only two people present– one with her head turned skyward and one bent over with clasped fists. They were both in silent prayer.

"Excuse me folks," Mabel looked up and Joseph sprang to his feet. "It's a perfectly healthy eight and a half pound boy."

"Praise the Lord," exclaimed Joseph, while Mabel wiped tears from her eyes.

JOSEPH PHONED BILL the first thing the next morning and congratulated him.

Bill said, "I'll be on the bus this morning." The bus, however, was late getting away and he arrived at the hospital after visiting hours. He left but was there the next morning when visiting hours commenced. He reported to reception and was escorted down the corridor to a point where he could stand in front of a curtained window. A nurse inside opened those curtains, and when she did

Betty was nursing the babe. He had a clear view of his son's face and took out an HB pencil and a small note pad, and wrote 'What a handsome child Betty', in big block letters. When he showed them to her she smiled and nodded.

When Betty and the baby were discharged she and Bill took a taxi directly to the home of Rebecca Cunningham and asked the driver to leave the metre running and wait. Mrs. Cunningham held the babe in her arms for about fifteen minutes and asked what his name would be.

"Herbert, after Uncle Herb, but we'll simply call him Herbie until he grows up" replied Bill.

"Good choice."..."I assume you're bound for the Benning's house now, and if so, please carry on."

Bill had to return to Goderich shortly after Betty and the babe's release. Betty remained with her mom and dad for a week before boarding another Clinton-bound bus with the babe in her arms.

❄❄❄❄

WHEN V-E DAY was announced, Charles Elliot decided not to remain in the army but began to seek an engineering position in Toronto, rather than return to his hometown of Moose Jaw. He and his wife Marnie now had two children; David born in 1940, and Margaret born in 1943. They gave their daughter the affectionate nickname of 'Maggie'.

The family purchased and moved into a house in Oakville, a town located on the shore of Lake Ontario about mid-way between Toronto and Hamilton.

Charles sent resumés to several Toronto-based engineering companies seeking employment. He waited five weeks before he was contacted by McNamara Construction, which was mainly engaged in dredging of harbours and construction of docking facilities throughout southern Ontario.

When he arrived at the Toronto office of the company, he was escorted to the office of Paul McNamara, the president, who told him to take a seat. Although it was all on his resumé he questioned Charles about his job during the war; his education and other pertinent information. Once satisfied McNamara escorted Charles to his new department, introduced him to the chief engineer, Mr. Louis Dawson, and departed.

Dawson said, "Welcome to McNamara Charles...how would you like to be addressed: Charles, Charlie or Chuck?"

"I've been called all of them Mr. Dawson, so whatever you'd like."

"Ok, Chuck; you can simply call me Lou. I'm sure you were told by Mr. McNamara that you are on a six-month probation period. That means if we're not satisfied with your performance after six months you'll be let go."

"No he didn't. I suppose he was leaving it to you to tell me. But I'm confident I can live up to your expectations."

"I hope so Chuck, because you seem to be a good man and you are a veteran to boot." Mr. Dawson escorted Charles to a desk and said, "This will be your desk. Please sit and wait. I'll be back in a couple of minutes." He left the office.

He reappeared five minutes later holding a folder full of papers and diagrams. "These are government specifications for a job the company just completed at Kingston, Ontario. Before one month has expired I want you to tell me how you would tackle the job if you were in charge. Look the specifications over and write down a plan. If you have questions about the company equipment inventory my extension number is thirty-three."

Three weeks had expired before Charles presented his plan. During the process he had called Mr. Dawson to ask pertinent questions such as: what type of pile-drivers and dump scows does the company have; and what about tug boats to tow the scows out to the lake for dumping?

When he handed the report to Mr. Dawson, his boss took it to Mr. McNamara. After the two had studied it, they both walked to Charles's desk. The company president was the first to speak. He said, "I only wish you were with us a year and a half ago. Had we used your plan we would have saved more than a hundred thousand dollars. Well done Charles. Your six month probation period has now expired."

Charles was delighted. He said, "Thank you Sir," and clasped McNamara's outstretched hand.

CHARLES WAS ALSO HAPPY his father and mother, Walter and Ruby, had fit in well with the Moose Jaw community. Walter had made several friends, including William Hawke, owner of Moose Jaw Heating and Plumbing. Their individual businesses complemented each other in several ways. Mr. Hawke was about ten years older than Walter and he had set up shop in 1909.

Ruby too had several friends; most of whom she met at the church. She taught Sunday school on Sunday mornings and had set up a day care centre for the children of war widows who were forced to work rather than be stay-at-home housewives, which would have been the case had their husbands survived. Elizabeth and Walter were leading happy lives.

That happiness increased when they received a letter from Charles describing his first month at McNamara Construction.

❄❄❄❄

THE STARBOARD ENGINE FAILED on a Vickers Wellington bomber as it flew westward past the coastline of Lake Huron. The aircraft took a sharp turn to starboard. The pilot worked frantically to bring the aircraft back on course as it drifted slowly downwards. The co-pilot said, “Give the port engine more juice Bill.”

Bill Cunningham gave the engine more fuel and worked the controls. Within a minute of the engine failure the aircraft was on an even plain. The co-pilot, who was actually the instructor, then switched on the power to the starboard engine, which he had purposely shut off. He then said, “We can return to base now.”

The wannabe pilot looked down through the mist as the aircraft flew over the town of Goderich on the shore of the lake. He could make out the roundabout in the town centre, but not the house where his wife would probably be feeding his 11-month old son Herbie at that time of day.

As the aircraft was on the glide path into RCAF Clinton the control tower operator constantly guided Bill by saying: “On glide path...below glide path...left of glide path...above glide path.” Bill worked the controls until the aircraft made a perfect landing.

Bill had four months to go if all went well until he would earn his wings and be promoted to Flight Lieutenant.

A month later, at the normal time, Bill walked into the house after work. He stood in front of Betty and said, “Do you notice anything different?”

Betty had eyes of a hawk and it didn’t take long before they homed in on the wings on the left breast of his uniform. “Congratulations Billy Boy. Your boyhood goals have been achieved.” She then picked up the phone and asked the long distance operator to dial the number of her mother and father in Leaside. Mabel answered. “Hi Mom,” Betty said, “Is Dad home yet?”

"He's just walking up the driveway. Just wait a moment… or is there anything I can do for you?"

"No Mom, I must speak to Dad."

Bill was standing by. He tapped Betty on the shoulder and when she turned around he pointed to his own mouth, while flapping his fingers against his thumb. Betty passed him the mouth piece and receiver.

Joseph took the phone and said, "Hello Dear, I trust everything is alright?"

"Hi Dad; it's me Bill."

"Oh, hello Bill. It's good to hear your voice."

"Dad, I have something to tell you…Today I received my wings at a small ceremony on the base. I am now a qualified airplane pilot."

Oh Bill, I'm so proud of you. Well done…I could tell you were sadly depressed when you returned from Britain and even considered surrendering your commission once you got your wings. Is that still your intention, or do you plan to remain in the air force?"

"I'll stay Dad and I now believe I'll command a squadron or at least a contingent before retirement."

"Hold onto that belief Bill, because as Napoleon Hill wrote in his bestselling book, *'What the mind can conceive and believe, the mind can achieve'*…Now, may I please speak with Bet? And once again, congratulations."

"Thanks Sir. Goodbye." Bill passed the phone to Betty.

Most of their talk was about little Herbie before she hung up the phone. Bill went upstairs to change into 'civvies'.

During supper Bill said, "All trainees of the first group also received their wings today. Tomorrow evening there's going to be a celebration dinner at the mess and then most likely a little gaiety afterwards, so I'll be home late."

"How late Bill?" asked Betty.

"I should be home by 10 or 11 o'clock."

"OK, but please don't drink too much."

"Who, me?" replied Bill with a mock innocent smile on his face.

BILL, HOWEVER, did drink too much at the celebration party and arrived home at 2 am as drunk as a sailor after drinking eight to ten tots of rum.

Betty had given him until midnight to arrive before she gave up and went up to bed. She left the bedside lamp on Bill's side of the bed lit. When he entered the bedroom she woke, but remained motionless. Her head was facing the alarm clock and she saw the time in the dim light. Bill fell onto the bed after undressing. He was snoring within ten minutes. The lamp remained switched on.

During breakfast Betty asked, "At what time did you arrive home last night Bill? I waited up reading, but gave up at midnight and went to bed."

"You just missed me Bet. I arrived home a little bit after twelve."

"Yes," she replied, "I suppose two hours is a little bit when compared to the number of hours in a day."

Bill raised his voice while saying, "If you already knew, then why did you ask?"

"Simple question," she said, "I just wanted to hear your answer!"

Bill slammed both fists on the table hard enough to cause the cups and saucers of their half finished tea to rattle. He left the table, put on his wedgie and walked out the front door.

"Little Herbie, who was sitting at that table in a highchair started to cry. Betty consoled him while thinking, '*Bill is certainly not the same man I married,*' but not taking into account what he must have gone through during his confinement in a Gestapo stalag.

She could tell he had recovered when he arrived home that evening so she told him some news that she thought would cheer him up even more.

"I had a visitor this afternoon Bill," she said.

"Who was it?

"Chris Stensson. His lake boat is on an overnight visit to Goderich and he..."

Bill interrupted, "Did he serenade you on his fiddle beforehand?"

"No, he arrived unannounced, but are you insinuating....?"

Bill sat in silence, so Betty continued.

"I remained faithful to you for over three years while you were away. Why on earth would I start being unfaithful after you arrived home?"

Bill would not – *could* not – say '*your mother*' for fear of causing a rift between his mother-in-law and Joseph, his father figure. Instead, he just bowed his head.

Again, they ate supper with the exchange of few unnecessary words.

Herbie, who could now say the words 'Mama' and 'Papa', and wave bye bye, sensed that all was not well between his mother and father. That evening he refused to open his mouth when Betty tried to feed him.

Bill noticed it and picked his son up and took him to an armchair in the living room.

While on his knee he held his son close and stroked his head lovingly. Once he thought it was time, he took Herbie back to his highchair and the youngster cooperated with his mother. He ate.

Betty said, 'Thank you Bill. He needed that. He's your son and he loves you, and I'm your *faithful* wife and I also love you."

"I love both of you too Bet."

# Twelve

**BRITAIN GRANTS INDIA INDEPENDENCE,** or something similar, was the headline of newspapers around the world on 15th August 1947. Most papers attributed India's march to independence to Mahatma Gandhi and his philosophy of non-violent protest called '*satyagraha*', but that didn't tell the full story.

'*The Toronto Star*' was one of the few English language newspapers that got it right. Their editor did give the Mahatma due credit, but he went on to write:

> *"India got its freedom as a result of Britain's exhaustion after the two world wars and its replacement as a global power by the new superpowers, USA and Russia. There is no way that Britain could have held on to its Indian empire much longer. The British Indian armies had played a significant role in the allied victories in the two world wars. Post-1947, had the British delayed the granting of independence, the battle-tested troops of the Indian Army – the Army that had underpinned Britain's world dominions for well over a century – would have soon rebelled, forcing an ignominious retreat on the British. There had already been a rebellion in the Indian Navy and the trial of returned INA (Indian National Army) prisoners of Subhash Chandra Bose had rekindled the spirit of fervent nationalism. The tinder being dry; the call for an armed insurrection by a national leader would have led to a number of mutinies across the length and breadth of India. Had law and order broken down it would have engulfed the British. The two-century edifice of the British Raj would have crumbled overnight. It would have led to large-scale massacre of the British."*[1]

PRIOR TO DEPARTURE British officials sat in heated discussions with Hindu and Muslim leaders to discuss the independence of India and the creation of Pakistan to the northwest and East Pakistan to the central northeast. The Radcliffe Line, thus split the province of Punjab by majority of religion; one side would become part of Pakistan while the other would remain as India. Another Radcliffe Line broke up the province of Bengal; the eastern part would become East Pakistan and the western portion West Bengal, India.

As the British returned to their beloved homeland in a blaze of glory, wide scale violence erupted as Muslims and Hindus came face to face along the lines, with as many as five hundred thousand deaths.

***Mahatma Gandhi by Sagarpuro***

Gandhi died not long after from an assassin's bullet at a prayer meeting, hardly more than a mile from where Nehru, the anointed Prime Minister ruled the new nation. Had Gandhi not been killed by Nathu Ram Godse's bullet, he would have died of a broken heart, unable to bear one of the worst slaughters in Indian history, possibly the largest non-war slaughter in world history.[2]

❄❄❄❄

AMED SHAH HAD been living in Amritsar for the better part of the last war. When violence started erupting after word leaked out about the partition of India, he and his wife decided to go up to Dharamsala, where they thought they would be safer. Ahmed's first stop was the temple where he found Panditji in his normal position on the floor. When Panditji saw him, he rose and welcomed Ahmed home.

"How have you been doing in keeping the peace Panditji?" asked Ahmed.

"There were a few minor scuffles at first but when I showed my face they stopped, shook hands and walked away. Then I had an idea. I met with the Imam at the Masjid and suggested we hold a town meeting in neutral territory. We chose the mission school and just about all of the adult townsfolk attended, as did Mr. Whitaker, pastor of 'St. John's in the Wilderness Church', and Sister Joan, the new Mother Superior of the mission school."

"I was the first to speak. First I introduced Mr. Whitaker who said he was born in India and it is his homeland. He would remain in town and the church would remain open. Sister Joan said that the mission school would remain open but with the departure of British soldiers of the cantonment there would be a lack of pupils. She would still get financial assistance from the church authorities in Delhi and Rome, and pupils from all religions would be welcome, upon payment of a small stipend."

"The Imam, a rather reclusive fellow, chose not to speak. I asked him if he intended to remain in town and he nodded. So it was my turn to address the crowd. In short I told them we had been living together as brothers and sisters for generations and why should ignoramus decisions made in far away Britain by our former colonizers change that? I predicted that wide scale violence would erupt shortly as Hindus from newly established Pakistan and Muslims from India met face to face at that invisible line. I begged any Muslims in this town who would rather go to Pakistan to wait a year until things settled down."

"I think that was enough Mr. Shah. Do you have any opinions?

"Excellent Panditji; you are still in control in this town. You are the only one that people, regardless of religion, listen to."

"Now, what about your business arrangement with Mr. Elliot since the war ended?"

"Well Panditji, since Mr. Elliot's brother-in-law took over operations in Britain after Walter Sir emigrated to Canada, shipments have dried up, but I received a letter from my son Amir urging my wife and me to shift to Delhi. He owns a house in Nizamuddin located on the outskirts of the capital and has a well paying job at a company called the Bajaj Group. He told me that Nizamuddin was where the Mughals had first settled after defeating Lodhi Dynasty. There are several tombs of great Mughal emperors such as Aurangzeb and Safdarjung in the vicinity.

I sent him a letter saying we accepted his proposal and will make our way down when the violence ends."

❄❄❄❄

TURMOIL HAD ALSO erupted in the lives of Betty, Bill and Herbie Cunningham in Goderich, Ontario by mid-August 1947. Betty and Bill were at each other's throats almost nightly as they both accused each other of being unfaithful.

Betty's claims were valid. Bill's were not. Regardless of the truth, little Herbie cried his heart out during each eruption. He wanted – in fact *needed* – harmony, not conflict.

Betty finally told Bill their son had to get away from the turmoil and that she was taking him down to Toronto for a week or so.

"Go ahead," said Bill blandly.

She and Herbie took a bus to Toronto and Joseph picked them up at the terminal in his old Dodge.

During the drive to the house Joseph asked, "Now that Bill has earned his wings has he cheered up at all?"

"Yes Dad," said Betty, "but now there is something else bothering him."

"What is it?"

"He thinks I am having an affair with Chris Stensson of all people, and has taken to having his own affairs."

"Chris Stensson! Where on Earth did he get that notion?"

"I asked him precisely the same question Dad, but he refused to answer."

As they were pulling into the driveway Joseph said, "As you may guess, I'm extremely disappointed in Bill. We will keep this conversation between ourselves though. I don't want to hear your mother say, 'I told you so...*like father; like son*'."

"I certainly agree with that Dad."

Betty and Herbie stayed in Leaside for two weeks. Before Herbie's bedtime Joseph would take him to the living room, perch him on his knee and tell him nursery stories. One evening Joseph was telling the story of 'Little Red Riding Hood and the Big Bad Wolf'. When he got to the part about when the girl arrives at her grandmother's house, she noticed that she looked very strange. Little Red then said, "What a deep voice you have!"..."The better to greet you with", responded the wolf..."Goodness, what big eyes you have Granma!"..."The better to see you with", responded the wolf..."And what big hands you have!"..."The better to hug you with", responded the wolf...and lastly, "What a big mouth you have"..."The better to *eat* you with," responded the wolf!" Herbie understood, he giggled at the first three answers and said, "Oh no!" at the last, and buried his head in his granddad's shoulder. Joseph laughed and Herbie eventually did the same.

Betty and Herbie returned to Goderich two weeks after their arrival in Leaside. When they arrived at the house at approximately 8 pm there were no lights lit. Betty entered, took the suitcase up to the bedroom and then came down to cook supper for the two of them. Herbie asked, "Where Papa, Momma?"

"I don't know Dear. We'll just eat alone tonight. He'll be home after we go to bed."

"During breakfast, Betty knew better than to ask where he had been the night before, so she answered questions Bill asked about Joseph and other things. She told him that she, Joseph and Herbie had gone to the Canadian National Exhibition one afternoon and how their son had laughed while on the 'merry-go-round', and that he had won the 'Child Personality Contest'. She reached into her handbag and showed Bill the little silver-coloured trophy with a black plastic base.

BY NEW YEARS DAY 1948, the time between intimate bedroom sessions between the couple had increased to at least a month and a half. Then in late January they were invited to a birthday party of one of Bill's friends which was held at the officer's mess on the base. They had come home a little tipsy that night and had made love for the first time since the night before Remembrance Day in November.

At breakfast the morning after a *'Yeller and Screamer'* erupted over the aroma of the perfume worn by a woman who was constantly smiling at Bill during the party. Betty was convinced she had smelled it on his uniform several times.

Eventually, Bill slammed his fists on the table. He stood up, but this time didn't depart as usual. He looked Betty straight in the eyes and calmly said, "Betty, I'm outta here. I love you dearly, but I won't be back until you're ready to own up, and when that happens I'll do the same and stop."

"But I have nothing to own up about," replied Betty.

"Then take Herbie down to Leaside. Your wretched mother and your wonderful father will certainly put you up until the divorce papers are signed and sealed, and you find someone else to love."

He kissed her on the cheek and then kissed Herbie with a tear in his eye.

He walked slowly out of the house.

BETTY AND HERBY LEFT Goderich the next day with the help of a highly-respected man of the town named Bob Flynn. He owned a pickup truck. He helped Betty move all of her belongings and those of Herbie into the open back of the truck and prepared to drive them down to Leaside. Mr. Flynn knew both Betty and Bill, and before leaving his own house to go to that of the Cunningham's he had phoned the base and told Bill what he had been asked to do. Bill said, "Yes Bob, I know all about it. She's leaving." Betty didn't notice Bill standing in the freezing cold at the intersection where the pickup truck turned right onto the southbound road towards Toronto. He had tears rolling down his cheeks.

Herbie sat on his mother's knee most of the way and gazed out of the window. He saw aluminium water tanks and windmills in farmers' fields. While passing through villages he pointed at snowmen. As Mr. Flynn shifted gears Herbie's eyes changed direction to see what he was doing. It was a Saturday morning and Betty had phoned her father early that morning and told him they were coming. He was waiting in the driveway when they arrived. Betty threw her arms around her father and sobbed on his shoulder. Joseph stroked her back.

After the four adults had carried all of Betty and Herbie's clothing and other possessions upstairs to their bedrooms, Flynn would accept no payment, but Joseph insisted and paid him twenty dollars – a good daily wage.

Herbie, being only two and a half years old, did not understand what had just taken place, but he immediately noticed the tranquillity in his new home; there was peace and love, not constant spiteful confrontations between his Mama and Papa. He didn't know he may never see his father again.

But he did; on at least two occasions before he turned three years old, there was a knock on the door. Herbie ran to answer it alongside his Nanny. On those occasions his father stood on the driveway between the two houses and his Nanny would allow them ten minutes to interact. Herbie would play peak-a-boo with his father from behind the open door. He didn't understand why his Nanny wouldn't allow his father to enter the house, or why she wouldn't let him climb down the few steps to the driveway so his father could pick him up and hold him.

Betty wasn't home during these peak-a-boo sessions. She had secured a secretarial job at McNamara Construction; she could type faster than a lightning bolt and take dictation in shorthand from the fastest of speakers. After a few quick training sessions she had mastered the art of filing the McNamara way.

WHEN SPRING OF 1948 came Herbie's granddad would take him for walks and point out the robin red-breasts digging for worms, and listen to their *cheerful carol* songs. And then there were the blue jays with their *rusty pump* voices picking up last year's acorns on the ground under oak trees. His granddad would also point to the evergreens and tell his grandson how to identify each by the shape of their foliage and length of their needles. And then there were the hardwoods – maple, elm, and oak. He'd tell Herbie how to identify them by the shapes of their leaves.

On one of these occasions Herbie said, "Granddad look," as he pointed at a birch tree; "why that tree white?"

"It's a birch tree and Mother Nature made it that way Herbie."

"Mama Nature, who dat Granddad?"

"Mother Nature made the trees, the clouds, the birds; everything."

A bond of deep love for his granddad was developing in Herbie's heart and mind.

One Saturday while his granddad was in the living room he called Herbie to his side. Herbie ran to his granddad and jumped onto his lap. Joseph said, "Adam and Eve and Pinchme went down to the river to bathe. Adam and Eve got drowned; who do you think was saved?"

Herbie replied, "Pinch-me," so his granddad did. Both of them laughed each time over the course of six-months they played that game. The pinches didn't hurt.

When Herbie was much older he wrote to his mother saying, *'I have no conscious memories of my early life in Goderich. The first childhood memory I can put a date to is 22nd September 1948 when Nanny, Granddad and I went to the hospital to view you and Lawrence. He was born on 20th of September 1948; eight days before my third birthday. The outside walls of the hospital were beige and there was a cobblestone driveway that arched up from the street to the hospital front doorway'.*

When he told his mother this she was amazed at how far his memory stretched back, but was also relieved that it didn't stretch as far back as Goderich.

There were other memories, however, that may have predated the first one Herbie could put a date to. For instance; the peek-a-boo sessions with his father; wearing a sun suit one hot summer day and sitting in a galvanised wash tub full of cold water. And then there was the time his granddad ran to the front window to wave at some expected guests, and Herbie running to the window as well but accidently knocking over one of two matching clay vases and breaking it. His granddad smacked him on his bum and

Herbie ran to his mother crying, not because it hurt, but because he thought the one man he loved so much had turned mean on him.

The vase had two hunters carrying muskets, and trees of a forest embossed on the sides. The pair was manufactured in the late 19th century, and Joseph and Mabel had brought it with them to Canada. Later Joseph painstakingly glued the parts together and Herbie inherited it along with its double many years later.

AFTER LAWRENCE WAS BORN Betty phoned her ex-husband, Bill Cunningham and said, "Congratulations Bill; you have another son. I called him Lawrence."

Bill's replied, "Tell Chris Stensson. Certainly, being a member of the Stensson dynasty he can afford the support payments," and hung up the phone.

The newborn baby introduced new emotions to Herbie's innocent heart; jealousy and hurtfulness. Up until his new brother came into this world Herbie had always been the centre of everyone's attention. Afterwards, when people entered the house few would even stop to ruffle his curly hair; they simply made their way to the crib to see the new baby.

Betty's younger sister Molly married William London. His uncle Bill had not served during the war and thus had two sons; Robert and Bruce, older than him, and a daughter named Joan who was born about a year after Herbie. While on the street one day Herbie said to Bruce, "If we hada knowed everyone woulda liked Lawrence more than me we wunta bot him"

Bruce laughed and laughed, and told all the other kids what he'd been told. They also laughed.

Another new emotion followed. In the late 1940s it was safe for children as young as three and a half to play on the park at the junction of Macnaughton Road and Cameron Crescent. Herbie played with Billy Baxter and Ronnie Butcher; both his age, and a boy named Dennis a year older. One evening Herbie was riding his little tricycle around the house and when he entered the narrow portion of the hallway between the stairway and kitchen he was frustrated because he couldn't conduct a U turn. At one point he exclaimed, "*Fuck*!"

Mabel, his nanny, ran out and said, "That was a bad word Herbie. Who did you hear it from?"

She coaxed him by showing him the wooden spoon. Herbie had felt the sting of the wooden spoon on his bare bum before so he lowered his head in shame and whispered, "Dennis," while fully understanding he was betraying a friend.

"You tittle-tattled on me," said Dennis the following morning.

His Nanny must have gone up and scolded Dennis's mother after the 'fuck' exclamation the night before.

When Dennis saw Herbie bow his head and was about to cry he said, "But that's OK." So this was another new emotional experience for Herbie; that of guilt.

WHEN HERBIE'S little brother became a toddler he began harassing Perky, the doggie that had urinated on Bill's pant leg on the day he was about to propose to Betty. Perky was getting old at this point and started snapping at Lawrence. The adults decided it was time to put Perky down. Afterwards, when Herbie cried his nanny said, "Big boys don't cry Herbie." And every time he cried, regardless of the reason for the tears she said those five words and they affected him in a negative manner well into adulthood. The next evening Joseph came home and gave Herbie a straw stuffed golden teddy bear to make up for the loss of Perky. It worked. He loved teddy and took him to bed every night. He also brought home a black and white China Scotty dog with a chipped ear which couldn't be sold. He had painted the chipped spot black and told Herbie, "This will belong to you some day."

One morning Herbie walked into his mother's bedroom while she was dressing. When he saw a furry thing between her legs he exclaimed, "Hey, what's that," and after she had quickly covered it up he said, "Lemme see it again!"

Betty said, "No!"..."and don't come into my bedroom again when the door is closed without knocking."

"IS THAT A MANSION Mom," asked Herbie when he first encountered the home of his grand aunt Annie out in Sheridan. His aunt Annie – Joseph's sister – was the matriarch of the Stensson family who owned Sheridan Nurseries.

"Yes Herbie," replied Betty, "I suppose you could call it a mansion." The massive house stood on top of a hill and had a rock garden out front with a sun dial in the centre. To the east of the sundial near the edge of the garden was a wooden honey bee hive, with drawers that could be pulled out to collect the fresh honey. At the foot of the downward sloping rock garden, there was a bare patch and then rows of shrubs stretching almost to Lakeshore Road about half a mile away.

His aunt Annie had four sons – Bill, Fred, Chris and Howard, and a daughter Betty. Herbie addressed the sons as 'Uncle' and Betty as 'Auntie'; but in fact they were all second cousins.

Herbie played with Karen around his age and Laurie a few years older; both were daughters of one the five siblings that had come from Annie's womb. The Leaside clan visited Sheridan on at least three occasions while Betty, Lawrence and Herbie lived with his nanny and granddad.

"HERE THEY COME HERBIE" cried Herbie's nanny in October 1951 when Herbie was five years old. All the children in his school and others in the vicinity were given the morning off to witness history in the making. He was in Grade one.

Hundreds of people waving Union Jacks lined the sidewalks of Bayview Avenue as a cavalcade of black limousines escorted Princess Elizabeth and Prince Philip, the Duke of Edinburgh northward in the direction of Sunnybrook Hospital. They stood in the back of a convertible limousine waving to the crowd. Once at the hospital they would interact with wounded World War II veterans who were still undergoing treatment.

Four months later, on 6th February 1952, Herbie was the first in the family to hear the CBC radio announcement that reported the death of King George VI. He was in the dining room eating his porridge for breakfast. His nanny had just walked through the dining room and had entered the kitchen while singing the hymn *'I Come to the Garden Alone'*. Herb jumped from the chair, ran to the kitchen and told her the sad news. She cried, but Herbie didn't because of course, *'Big boys don't cry'*.

At the beginning of classes that day, without the teacher even prompting them, Herbie and his Grade one classmates all sang 'God Save the Queen'; one of the two national anthems sung in Canadian schools at the beginning of the day, according to the teacher's choice. The other was *'The Maple Leaf Forever'*.[3]

"I FIRED SOMEONE today," said Joseph one evening at the dining room table as the family was about to eat supper.

Herbie was horrified by his granddad's words. He associated *'Fire'* with the phrase *'Ready aim Fire!'* he often heard while watching his favourite cowboy show 'Hop Along Cassidy' on the new black and white television set in the basement of the Gibbons; their next door neighbours. He couldn't imagine a man as good as his grandfather actually shooting someone.

Betty asked, "Why did you fire the person Dad?"

"He had been taking too many coffee breaks on company time, and when I told him so he said some bad words to me, which I'd rather not repeat."

Herbie thought this was a rather harsh punishment, but forgave his Granddad just the same.

"YOU CAN'T BREATHE under water Dear. You must bring your head up and take a breath of air"...On weekends of the summer of 1952, Betty would take Herbie to the local public swimming pool and began teaching him how to swim. She started with the 'dead man's float' and once he had mastered that; the 'dog paddle' was next. By the end of the summer he was able to do the 'forward crawl'. She told her mother and father, "Herbie was born a natural swimmer."

In December 1952 Betty took Herbie and Lawrence aside and said, "Boys; you'll soon have a new father, brother and sister."

Lawrence was too young to really understand the significance of the statement, but Herbie wasn't. He asked, "Does that mean we'll have to leave this house and live somewhere else?"

"Yes Herbie it does. Your new daddy will be Mr. Elliot. His wife died a couple of years ago, and he has a son named David and a daughter named Maggie; that's short for Margaret."..."Anyway, I am going to marry Mr. Elliot. The Elliot's live in the town of Oakville, not far from here and we can visit Nanny and Granddad from time to time."

After the conversation Herbie just gazed into space. Up to that point his granddad had been the only father-figure he had a vivid memory of in his life. He just didn't know what to say.

CHARLES ELLIOT HAD WORKED his way up to Chief Engineer at McNamara Construction since he joined the company shortly after the war ended. Paul McNamara, the company president had also promoted Betty to the position of his private secretary. More senior secretaries attributed Betty's promotion to an ego flaw of McNamara saying she got the promotion due to her beauty. They may have been correct. Some even suggested she and her boss were having an affair, not realizing that would have been unthinkable for Betty.

The attraction between Betty Cunningham and Charles Elliot began one day when they sat together at the same table in the lunch room for their mid-day meal. As they spoke, they discovered they had a great deal in common; the most significant in Betty's mind was that they were both religious and both single parents. After that first lunch together they sat with each other every day. Sometimes he would wait for her to enter and vice versa.

Afterward, if time permitted and they didn't have something important on their desks needing immediate attention, they'd take a half hour walk on University Avenue where the office was located.

It wasn't long before they fell in love and Charles proposed to her. Theirs wasn't a deep love, but they both realized that would come later. The fact that they both needed a good second parent for their children played a big part, and Betty accepted his proposal.

Betty and Charles married on 14th February 1953 and went on a short honeymoon to the Caribbean island of Haiti. Upon their return, Betty and the boys were moved out to Oakville. Herbie was in Grade 2 and moved into a new school that he didn't like. He didn't like his new brother David either. The feelings were mutual. All of a sudden David had to share his private domain – his bedroom – with a new brother just short of five years younger than himself.

It was winter and thus cold. On the first night Herbie asked, "Can we please close the window David?"

David gave him a sharp reply, "NO!" Herbie shivered all night and asked his mom for another blanket in the morning.

Two months after moving to Oakville, the family packed up and moved again, this time to the small village of Hudson, Quebec located on 'The Lake of Two Mountains', a wider portion of the Ottawa River near Montreal. His new father had been recruited by another construction company in Montreal. Herbie therefore entered his third Grade 2 class of the 1952/53 school year.

HUDSON IS LOCATED on the south shore of the Ottawa River about 60 km west of Montreal. What is now Hudson was once part of the Seigneurie de Vaudreuil, which was granted to the Marquis Philippe de Rigaud de Vaudreuil in 1702. Early colonists included a number of voyageurs. The fur trade was Hudson's earliest industry. In the early 19th century, the French-speaking population was augmented by Scottish employees of the Hudson Bay Company and by farmers emigrating from Cumberland, England. Since then the town had attracted both English- and French-speaking residents. The majority of the residents were English-speaking. Descendants of many of those pioneer families, both English and French, still lived in the town. A remote village in the days of travel by horse and canoe, Hudson was drawn into the orbit of Montreal and the wider world with the inauguration of travel by steamboat and especially (in 1890) by the arrival of the Vaudreuil-Prescott Railway Company (later CPR). Improved transportation made the village accessible to cottagers and to permanent residents willing to commute to their jobs in Montreal. But the town still maintained its rural character [Source: Hudson Historical Society].

## Notes

1. From an article titled 'Looking Back: Gandhi Legacy Factor As A Backdrop To India's Global Aspirations' by Vinod Saighal, and published in Delhi-based Diplomatist Magazine April 2017 edition (www.diplo-matist.com).
2. Same source as above.
3. O CANADA didn't become the National Anthem until an act of Parliament made it so in 1980.

# Part - II

# THIRTEEN

**'YER GONNA DROWN KID** *if you don't think fast'*, thought Herbie. He was in a perpendicular position with this legs straight up and his head under water. The front of his bathing trunks had hooked on the knob at the bow of John Wright's row boat in the middle of Pine Lake.

The boys were playing a game in which one boy commanded the boat and four or five others would try to get in and throw him out and become the current commander. Herbie had just made an attempt to get in over the bow, but the commander had seen him, swung him around and had given him a push. That was when his bathing trunks hooked to the bow-knob.

He could arch his back so his head was above water and yell 'Help', but nobody heard his cry; there was already too much yelling on all sides of the boat. So he would take a breath of fresh air and let his head submerge again to release the strain. But he knew he couldn't do this forever; it took great effort. He put his arms behind him and made one fruitless attempt to arch his back far enough for his hands to reach the gunwales but to no avail. Then an easier tactic about saving his life came to his mind. So, after taking another deep breath he bent forward, grabbed the corded belt of the bathing trunks, undid the tied bow and slithered out naked. He then popped up to the surface, put his bathing suit back on and made another attempt at getting into the boat, but this time over the port side.

IT WAS THE SUMMER of 1954 and Herbie would turn nine in late September. Two weeks after the boat crisis incident Herbie walked into the kitchen from the backyard and whined, *"Mom, there's nothing to do."*

His mom gave him her normal brush off answer, "Oh go jump in the lake."

Twenty minutes later he walked back into the kitchen soaking wringing wet from sneakers to ball cap and said, "Hi Mom."

She turned around and exclaimed, "What happened to you!"

"You told me to go jump in the lake so I did."

Once the word got around, the whole neighbourhood got a laugh out of that one.

Herbie's new family was still in the merging phase. Herbie and his little brother Lawrence had begun calling their new father 'Dad' right from the start, but both David and Maggie called their new mother 'Betty'.

Herbie asked his mom, "How come they call *our* mother Betty, and Lawrence and I call *their* father Dad,"

Betty replied, "Give them time Herbie, their real mother died not long before Dad and I were married. They'll call me 'Mom' soon enough."

Then one day Herbie and Maggie walked in the kitchen door from outside and Maggie said, "Hi Betty; what's for dessert tonight."

Betty said, "Lemon meringue pie"

Maggie replied, "Oh boy; my favourite. From now on I'm going to call you 'Mom'.

This pleased Herbie immensely.

By Christmas Day of 1955 David was also calling Betty 'Mom'.

Their new house in Hudson was located at 94 Ridge Road, at the corner of Melrose. From the front door one could look down over the roof of the house across the road and see Pine Lake.

Only a few years before the Elliots moved to Hudson, Pine Lake didn't exist; it was a creek with a large swamp on the Cameron Road side. The men of the families living on the lakefront and those living close by got together and cleared all the dead trees from the swamp and built a dam at the edge of Cameron Road. Soon Pine Lake was established. The families then founded the Pine Lake Club and the Elliots were invited to become members. This meant they would be allowed to swim at the beach at end of Cedar Avenue. Most of Herbie's close friends were members of the Pine Lake Club. These included Peter Dudgeon, Donald Kempt, John Wright, Ian Wyllie, and Russell Kirby. Other close friends included Walter Perkins, Peter Habib, Norman Canyon, and Kathy Stewart but they lived too far away to be members.

Charles Elliot was by no means a rich man, but he did have a high-paying job in Montreal. That meant the family could afford memberships to the Whitlock Golf Club, the Hudson Curling Club and the Hudson Yacht Club (HYC). Charles Elliot owned a speed boat that he moored within the HYC-owned enclave. He also bought David a motorboat with a Johnson 10 HP outboard motor. David would sometimes take his two new brothers fishing in the middle of the lake; once Herbie caught a medium-sized speckled trout, which his mother cooked for supper.

"LET'S GO TO SIMON'S FARM," said Peter Dudgeon one day.

All four of the boys he was playing with that day said, "OK, Let's go."

So they walked up Cameron Road past the Roman Catholic cemetery to where the gravel road became even more rural-looking due to grass growing between the two tire tracks (sometimes they'd walk up Cameron with the sole purpose of picking brown-eyed Susans or black berries for their mothers). Once they reached the forest they jumped over the ditch and started their trek through the undergrowth of the forest. They passed an abandoned maple sugar shack along the way and it wasn't long before Herbie cried out, "*A skunk*!"

They all raced through the prickly scratchy underbrush while the pungent fumes seemed to chase them to the far corner of the farm near the creek that filled Pine Lake. When the smell had subsided, they walked across the pasture towards the barn.

Simon's was a dairy farm and the boys passed the herd of cows grazing in the field. Mr. Stirling Simon was a kindly gentleman farmer who allowed the boys to enter the barn to see the bull in his stall and to watch the pasteurising of milk through a glass window inside the stable. They always wondered though as to why the old bull wasn't allowed to go to the field like the cows.

"Look, here she comes," cried Peter as nineteen year old Rhoda, Mr. Simon's daughter, walked across the drive-way carrying a large bucket of water with great difficulty. They all considered Rhoda to be the prettiest girl in town.

Herbie ran towards her. "May I help you Rhoda?" he asked.

"Why Herbie; how kind of you. A bucket of water is very heavy, but I can handle it alone thank you."

Herbie walked along beside her as she made her way to the bull pen. "He needs his water," she said as she emptied the bucket into the water trough.

Then Peter piped up, "Rhoda, why is he locked up all day? Why can't he go out into the fields like the cows?"

"The cows are in the fields to graze – that's to eat grass – not to play. If we let him go to the fields with the cows he'd be chasing them around all day and they wouldn't get enough to eat. After we lock the barn door at night we let him out and he plays another type of game with the cows."

"What type of game Rhoda?" asked Herbie.

"You might call it an adult game that you'll learn about when you are in your teens. That's all I will say." They all smiled at each other, half knowing what she meant.

THE BOYS would often walk down to Ben's restaurant across the road from Wyman United Church on Main Road. They all had their twenty-five cent allowance and spent part of it on a five cent bottle of coke, but never threw the bottle away because they'd get two cents if they returned it. They'd also buy a five cent box of cracker jacks and sometimes waste a nickel in the pinball machine before returning home and dropping what was left into their piggy banks. But while at Ben's they'd stand outside and observe the 'Rocks' – a motorcycle gang in black leather jackets and Harley Davidson motorcycles. A fellow named Sport Seguin seemed to be the leader, or at least the most respected.

"WHEN'S YOUR MOTHER EXPECTING," asked his girlfriend Kathy Stewart at the end of the school day in early September 1956. Herbie would turn eleven at the end of the month.

"Expecting what?" asked Herbie.

"Expecting the baby, stupid" she laughed. "Didn't you notice?"

"My mother is having a baby?"

Kathy nodded, and laughed as he jumped on his bicycle and sped off towards home at full speed. Once he arrived he burst through the back door and found his mom at the kitchen counter preparing some food.

"Are you expecting a baby Mom!" he exclaimed.

Betty held her maternity suit tight around her stomach and said, "Yes Herbie, the baby is inside my tummy."

"What's it going to be, a boy or a girl?"

"Only God knows Herbie. We will know after he or she comes out. Then my tummy will shrink back to normal size."

Sure enough on 5th November 1956 a baby boy was born. They named him Walter after Charlie's father. Walter, however, was born with a defect – a clubbed foot. So about a week after his birth the hospital surgeons performed an operation in which they broke Walter's little ankle and reset the bone. They then applied a cast which stretched up beyond the knee.

The cast remained affixed for about two months, but they were allowed to take Walter home after the operation. When friends and neighbours dropped by to see the new-born baby Betty didn't tell them about the cast, and when they reached under the blanket to touch him they would quickly withdraw their hand and exclaim, "What's that?!"

After family members had recovered from laughing, they'd tell them.

Baby Walter's granddad never saw his newly born namesake. He passed away two weeks after his birth. Charles went to Moose Jaw for the funeral, but returned two weeks later confident that his mother could take charge of the business.

"HERBIE, PLEASE REMAIN SEATED after classes for a few minutes" whispered Mrs Mclean after walking down to his desk. She was his Grade 6 teacher and it was a week before the 1956/57 school year was to end. When all his classmates had departed Mrs McLean walked down the aisle and sat at the desk in the next row adjacent to Herbie's. Herbie just stared at her half-knowing what she was about to say.

"Herbie," she said, "I have already talked to your mother about this and we both agree. I won't be able to promote you this year. You'll have to repeat Grade six."

"But why Mrs McLean?" asked Herbie.

"It's because your marks aren't high enough. Having been born on 28th September you are the youngest student in the class. If you were born on 1st October you'd be in Grade 5 right now. It takes time for a brain to develop and maybe yours hasn't developed as fast as the other kids. But look on the positive side Herbie, next year you'll be the oldest but not by much and you'll probably get the highest Grades. Anyway, the decision is final … You can carry on now."

On Friday 7th June Mrs. McLean passed out the enveloped report cards. Herbie looked at his teacher and she noticed the hope in his eyes. She simply gave him a slight but pitiful negative nod. Herbie didn't open his envelop, but listened to the other children yelling

'Yahoo' and other such words of celebration. When his girlfriend Kathy looked his way she noticed he hadn't opened his envelop yet and wondered why; she also noticed he didn't come to the bicycle rack where his friends were waiting for him to find out if he passed.

Herbie was too ashamed to face his friends who he knew would be waiting. So he stood by the window on the second floor and peaked around the frame at his friends. When they all had given up waiting for him, he went down, mounted his bicycle and went home.

Another disappointment was awaiting him during the summer of 1957. It was announced that the construction of the new public school named Mount Pleasant built on Blankenship's fields where the boys used to play was complete. He would have to repeat Grade six at that school. Kathy and many other friends would still go to his former school. He never saw Kathy or his other friends again.

"HELLO, MY NAME is Miss Simon," said Herbie's new Grade 6 teacher. "Some of you – especially the boys – may remember me as Rhoda Simon from Simon's farm. I graduated from Hudson High School and went to teachers college, and now I am no longer Rhoda. I am now *Miss* Simon, and that is what you will call me. Do all of you understand?

All of the kids in her class were smiling and she took that as an affirmative answer, so she said, "Now, let's start our lessons."

The joy of having Miss Simon as his new Grade 6 teacher was a compensating factor to the shame of his failure and repeating it in a new school far away from his friends and girlfriend until ...

"WE'RE MOVING BACK to Ontario" kids, said Charles with Betty by his side.

"Why Dad? Hudson is such a nice town," asked David.

"I've been offered a position as president of a company called 'Ontario Marine and Dredging'. It's owned by a man named Sid Byrd and they build docks and break-waters, and dredge harbours in towns all around the Great Lakes in southern Ontario. David, you're old enough so I'll be able to give you summer jobs if you wish. When you get older Herbie that'll apply to you as well."

Charles hired Allied Van Lines, and after all their belongings were safely in the truck the family hopped into their newly purchased 1957 Chrysler and drove away. Friends of Betty, Charlie and the kids waved them good bye.

❄❄❄❄

"THAT LOCKET IS BEAUTIFUL" said Annie Hall, the principal of Clarkson Public School on the day Betty took Herbie there to register. She added, "My mother had one just like it but lost it in India before she moved to Barnstaple in England in 1916 during World War I."

She picked up a framed faded photograph on her desk and passed it to Betty saying, "Here is a photo of my mother wearing it in her younger days. May I please have a closer look at it?"

Betty unhooked the locket and passed it over while saying "You mentioned your mother lost it in India. When my father-in-law passed away my husband and mother-in-law were going through his belongings and found it in a small box. He spent time in India after World War I and found it while living in a Himalayan foothills town.

"What was the name of the town," Mrs Elliot?

"All I can remember is that it started with the letter 'D'; It was something like Darsala"

"Could it have been Dharamsala?"

"Yes; yes, that's it," replied Betty.

"That's where my mother lost hers when a beggar woman snatched it from her neck."

She turned it over and said, "There's a faint engraving on the back. You can just make out part of the first initial. It looks like a 'W'. My grandmother's name was Winifred Sinclair.

"You must keep it Miss Hall. It's a family heirloom to you and it should be yours," said Betty.

"No Mrs. Elliot; like the children say, '*Finders keepers; losers weepers*'."

"I insist Miss Hall."

"And so do I. Now about this handsome boy; please pass me his last report card."

Betty passed over Herbie's last report card saying, "As you notice, he's repeating Grade six."

"Before we spoke about the locket, however, you said your son's name was 'Herbie', but I see the report is in the name of 'Herbert'." She turned to Herbie and asked, "What would you like your teachers to call you, Herb or Herbert?"

"Herbie," he said.

Miss Hall turned to Betty. "Herbie is what he has been called all his life – even by his school teachers in Quebec. Please allow him to be called that name."

"All right. You can leave now Mrs. Elliot; "Herbie please follow me up to your new class."

"Before you leave Miss Hall I want you to know my father – Joseph Benning – was also from Barnstaple."

Miss Hall smacked her forehead and said, "He could have been a close friend of my mother. Do you mind remaining here in my office until I get back?"

"Not at all Miss Hall."

Miss Annie Hall escorted Herbie up two flights of stairs to the third floor. She knocked on the door and entered before the teacher opened it. She said, "Mr. Harrison, this is Herbie Elliot. His last school was located in Quebec and he'll be joining your class today.

Mr. Harrison showed Herbie where to sit and passed him the text books needed for the lessons of the day.

Miss Hall hustled back down to her office where Betty was waiting. After a fifteen minute conversation they agreed that Joseph Benning – Betty's father – had been a close friend of her mother, Wilma Hall. Annie told Betty she had been the flower girl at her parent's marriage and that when she arrived in Canada they knocked on the door of a house they thought belonged to Mr. Benning, but he and Mabel had moved to another house and the current owner didn't know their new address.

"Miss Hall," said Betty, "I'll bring Dad to meet you here some day after school hours if you wish, or perhaps I could let you know when he's in Clarkson next and you could come to the house. He's in his early eighties now."

"That would certainly please me Mrs. Elliot."

"I'm absolutely certain it would please him as well Miss Hall."

After the short conversation Betty walked home.

At recess time all the boys from the Clarkson Road South area introduced themselves to Herbie. There were Terry Smith, Dan Fountain, Brian Skelton, David Shrimpton and David Potts. Most of their fathers worked at the British American (BA)[1] oil refinery at the end of Clarkson Road South and lived on Marigold Crescent in houses actually owned by BA. The company had also set up a playing field with a skating rink and a shack for the kids to change from winter boots to skates. There was also a baseball diamond.

Herbie became instant friends with Terry Smith, Dan Fountain, David Potts and a girl named Harriett Irwin – nicknamed Pixie or Pix.

"SHE'S THE RIGHTFUL OWNER Betty," said Charles after she had told him about the locket.

"I believed that too Chuck, but she wouldn't take it back even when I insisted."

"I have an idea how we can get it back to her without her being able to refuse" said Charles. "Please call Herbie to the dining room."

Betty did so and when he arrived Charles asked, "Herbie, does Miss Hall, your principal, ever leave her office?"

"Yes Dad, when she's not doing principal work she teaches Grade 8."

"Thanks Herbie. You can go back and watch TV now."

Herbie walked away with a puzzled look on his face thinking, *"Why would I be asked such a strange question*?"

Three weeks later, before Herbie was about to leave for school, Betty passed him an envelope and said, "Herbie, sometime during classes ask your teacher if you may be excused to go to the washroom. But instead of the washroom run down to Miss Hall's office and place this envelope on her desk. Keep it in your pocket so your teacher won't see it." She passed an envelope to her son.

"But Mom, there's nothing written on it, and what's the bump inside?"

"I'll explain when you get home Herbie, but make sure you don't get caught. She won't punish you if she catches you though; I can promise you that."

"When Herbie arrived home for lunch he said, "I did it Mom. Now what was in the envelope?"

"I'll explain to the whole family tonight at supper. It's a long story."

OVER THE CHRISTMAS and New Year holidays of 1957-58 the whole Elliot family set out for Daytona Beach, Florida. Betty and David, who by then was seventeen and had a driver's licence, shared the driving while Charlie sat in the front seat drinking beer, and at one point smoking a big fat twelve-inch long Cuban cigar.

When they stopped for gas in North Carolina Charles went around to the back to use the toilet, or perhaps to release some of the beer from his bladder. When he returned he said, "Follow me kids."

When they got to the back of the gas station Charles pointed at three doors. Each had a sign on it indicating 'Men', 'Women', and 'Colored'. The image of those three doors would remain in Herbie's head for the remainder of his days.

"A SWIMMING POOL – YAHOO," all the kids in the Elliot family exclaimed. In the spring of 1958, Charles had hired a contractor to build an in-ground swimming pool in the back yard. There'd be a shallow and deep end with a diving board as well. Once completed the Elliot family became the most popular in the vicinity of Clarkson Rd. South. Charles was a very benevolent man and allowed all kids access to the pool. Sometimes there were as many as fifty children romping around and having fun in that cement pond; and that with no lifeguard. There was only one restriction. Sunday evenings were reserved for the family. Everyone respected that rule.

"A SUMMER JOB? Yes Dad I'd like one, but I'm only 12 years old," said Herbie.

"Good Herbie, your age won't pose a problem. The company is building a new dock at HMCS York on the Toronto lakefront. We need tonnes of gravel to fill in behind the dock. That gravel will come from 'Monarch Sand & Gravel' located on Highway 27 north of Cooksville. Your job will be the company inspector at the pit. You will ensure the weight of gravel on each dump truck is properly marked on the invoice, or bill. You will earn 50 cents an hour. Does that sound good to you?"

"Fantastic Dad! Will David be working at the construction site as well?"

"Yes, he'll be receiving each truck and signing the bills as being received. He'll be doing other tasks between truck arrivals."

Herbie's dad carried on. "You'll start on the first Monday after the end of the school year; that's about two week from now. Your mom will drive you up to the gravel pit the first day and leave you there after she's satisfied you are comfortable with how the scales work. You'll get a ride to the QEW[2] in the last truck of the day, and from there you'll have to hitchhike to the top of Clarkson Rd North and walk home. The next morning and the remainder of the summer you'll have to get up early, walk to the QEW and then hitchhike all the way to work. Do you understand?"

"Yup."

Herbie passed Grade 6 with above average marks, and at 6:45 am on 9th June 1958 Herbie stuck his head into his mom and dad's bedroom and said, "Come on Mom I don't wanna be late on my first day."

"Five minutes Herbie." He could hear the water running from the bathroom sink.

Ten minutes later she walked out the front door and found Herbie sitting in the passenger seat of the family's second car. She climbed into the driver's seat and they were away. It only took them fifty-five minutes to reach the gravel pit in the early rush hour traffic.

About 10 miles north of Cooksville there was a large sign on the edge of the two lane highway marked 'Monarch Sand and Gravel' with an arrow pointing to the left. They turned onto the gravel road and two minutes later walked into the weigh-scale shed where they met the man in charge; Mr. Smith.

"The first truck of the day is being loaded as we speak," said Mr. Smith. "Lean forward sonny and look out the window. The truck will stop on that platform…Each truck has its actual weight printed on its side. Now look at this apparatus in front of you. There is a long measuring bar that ends between upper and lower balancing points. And there is a shorter measuring bar on top of it. The balancing weights are both at the left of the bars. Are you with me so far; what's your name again?"

"Herbie Elliot, and yes Mr. Smith I understand so far."

"Good. The top scale is to subtract the weight of the truck. Then you adjust the weights on the lower bar until it is balanced between the two points. After that you note the weight and write in on the invoice, sign it and give it to the driver.

Betty smiled.

The first truck-full of gravel arrived and stopped on the platform. Mr. Smith went through the manoeuvres explaining everything as he went. The driver was standing there watching. When finished he got Herbie to sign the invoice and pass it to the driver. When the next truck arrived he said, "Your turn Herbie. Show *us* how to do it."

Herbie carried out the manoeuvres flawlessly, while explaining what he was doing with each move."

When Herbie had successfully completed the weighing of the second truck on his own Betty said, "I'll be off now Herbie. Mr. Smith please inform all your drivers that if they are the last of the day, to drive Herbie down to the QEW and drop him there."

"Already done Mrs. Elliot."

"Thank you and nice meeting you Sir." She smiled and said, "Bye Herbie, and no sleeping on the job," before climbing back into the car and driving away.

Herbie was on his own knowing full well this was the most important responsibility he had ever been entrusted to do. Before that moment the highest had been making his bed every morning.

On his drive to the QEW one late afternoon in the middle of the summer the driver was a foreigner. He didn't have an Italian accent and he had a tanned completion. He thought he may be a Paki[3]. While driving, the man spoke of all the financial difficulties his family was going through. Herbie didn't believe a word of it, but knew he would soon ask him to be dishonest and give him a thousand pounds extra on the bills. When the man told him he had a pretty daughter his age he'd like him to meet that confirmed it in Herbie's mind. He was trying to bribe him.

The next day when that driver entered the scale shack to ensure the weight was calculated correctly he passed Herbie an Oh Henry chocolate bar. Herbie gave him fifty extra pounds, which would only make up the cost of the ten cent treat. The driver walked away grumbling, while Herbie hoped the man was never the last truck of the day again. He knew he should have reported the man to his father but didn't, for the man's sake because he had a family to feed, and besides his dad would have scolded him for taking the treat in the first place.

Herbie's summer job lasted six five-day weeks. He worked for eight hours a day and at fifty cents an hour earned $120. His dad brought him home his pay cheque the evening after his last day on the job. Since Herbie didn't have a bank account his mom walked him up to the Canadian Imperial Bank of Commerce to co-sign his cheque. He told her that he wanted it all in one-dollar notes. Betty, knowing he wanted to show off to his friends, complied. Once at home he stashed all the money in the very back of the top drawer of his bedroom dresser. He put two dollars in his pocket.

"WHAT DO YOU WANT TO BE when you grow up?" asked Mr Haslett, of each member of Herbie's Grade 7 class on the first day of the 1958/59 school year." Herbie's closest friends all had different answers.

David Shrimpton wanted to be a doctor; Brian Skelton a lawyer; Dan Fountain a farmer; Terry Smith a soldier;" while Harriett Irwin wanted to be a nurse.

When it was Herbie's turn he proudly said, "A dump truck driver." His whole class burst out laughing while Herbie just smiled. Of course his aspirations were spawned by the dump truck rides after work during his summer job. While leaving the class for recess that morning Mr. Haslett took him aside and suggested he set higher aspirations in life. Herbie never forgot those few words.

All the kids liked Mr. Haslett.

In late October Herbie's brother David found Herbie's money stash and leaned out the upstairs window. Herbie was playing in the backyard.

David yelled, "Hey Herbie; look what I found," while holding the money in his hand.

Herbie cried out, "That's mine, give it back."

"Ok," said David and tossed about $100 into the breeze, amongst the autumn leaves that were still falling.

Herbie knew exactly how much money he had and managed to retrieve every single dollar.

"ANOTHER SUMMER JOB? Yes Dad I would. Will I be weighing trucks again this summer?"

"No Herbie; you'll be a 'gofer' on a construction site."

"A gofer Dad; what's that?"

"*Go for* a pipe wrench; *go for* a crow bar; *go for* some water ... Do you get it now Herbie?"

"Yes Dad I get it, but I thought that guy was called a 'bum boy'."

"Some call it that, but there are evil meanings to that term as well Herbie and I won't explain them. You'll have a guardian while there. The fellows call him Nug. He's a Japanese Canadian whose family emigrated from Japan to Canada about twenty years before the last World War. You and Nug will share the same room in a boarding house just across the road from the job site."

"Where is the construction site located Dad?" asked Herbie.

"Oh, it's at a place called 'Perch Creek' located on the southern shore of Lake Huron, near Sarnia. One of the company executives will be driving there to check on progress shortly after your summer vacation starts and you'll get a drive up with him."

"That's quite far from here. Does it mean I'll be up there all summer Dad?"

"No Herbie. Nug lives with his elderly mother in New Toronto and he'll be driving home each weekend to check on her. He'll drop you off here at home on Friday evenings and pick you up on Sunday afternoons."

"I can't wait Dad, thanks."

Herbie was promoted at the end of the 1958/59 school year; this time with average grades except for art where he topped the class.

On Monday 6th June the company executive picked Herbie up at the house and drove him to Perch Creek. The trip took about five hours. Once there he stopped the car just before the bridge over the creek and they walked to the centre. They looked down at the job site while the man explained things that were going on below them.

"OK Herbie, we're building two wooden walls that will stretch out into the lake. As you can see the channel walls are being built with downward facing thick pieces of wood called piles."

"What's happening now?" asked Herbie.

"The crane has claws on the end of the cables. It is scooping up earth from the bottom, and depositing each load into that rectangular boat with the four square holes on top. The bottoms of the holes are closed right now, but the tug boat will tow the dump scow – that's what it's called – about a mile out into the lake and a man on the scow will pull a leaver at each hole and dump the load. It's an easy job for the man on the scow until the return trip. While returning he has to close each hole by using a crank mechanism and it takes a great deal of strength. You look like a strong lad and I think the foreman Ernie Porter may give you that job."

"How do they construct the sides of the canal?" asked Herbie.

"You'll see when you start tomorrow Herbie. I've got to go down and speak with Ernie now. Come along and I'll introduce you to him. After we speak I'll be driving back to Toronto this evening and you'll be on your own." He looked at his watch. "It's close to quitting time, so if you wait for that Japanese guy Nug," he pointed at him, "he'll take you across the road and settle you in. Your rucksack is in the back seat so run back and fetch it."

Herbie retrieved his bags, and he and the company man climbed down the bank and walked over to the foreman. After introductions the two men spoke and Herbie sat on a platform and observed. Nug saw him and came over to welcome him. He said, "Quitin time will be in about 45 minutes so just sit here and I'll walk you across the road and introduce you to Bernice and Stan who own the boarding house, a few small cabins and the docks on the river bank where sporting fishermen from Sarnia park their boats during the week."

"Ok Mr. Nug."

"Thanks for the respect Herbie, but just call me Nug."

"Alright Nug."

At 5 pm Nug walked over and as they walked across the road said, "You and I will be sharing the same bedroom. It opens to the living room. Stan works in the day at the oil refinery in Sarnia and arrives home at around 5:45 pm. Supper is at 6 o'clock. Another company labourer who sleeps in one of the cabins will eat with us. We'll have enough time to meet Bernice and then I'll show you the room where you can drop your bag on your bed. We're allowed to watch TV at night but Bernice controls the channel switch; whatever she wants to watch, we watch or go to our room, or for a walk."

Bernice was a pretty woman about thirty-five years of age; Stan was tall, slim and muscular, and around forty. They appeared to like Herbie because they both gave him a warm welcome.

While in the bedroom Nug explained that in boarding houses there was no menu; what the landlady wanted to cook, everybody had to take it or leave it. That was the same as a family meal with which all people were familiar. That evening they had roast beef, mashed potatoes, carrots and Brussels sprouts. It was delicious, as were all meals during the summer.

That evening Bernice wanted to watch the CBC Television reports about the ongoing investigation of a man called Steven Truscott who was accused of murdering a girl named Lynne Harper. Nug and Herbie watched as well, however, Herbie would have preferred to watch the sitcom *'The Adventures of Ozzie and Harriet'* on American Broadcasting Corporation.[4]

At 7 am the next morning Nug and Herbie got up, took turns in the bathroom, had breakfast and walked across the road to the job site at seven forty-five. As other labourers and the crane operator arrived Nug introduced them to Herbie.

Sure enough, as the company executive had predicted, Herbie was given the job as the dumper on the dump scow. On the first journey into Lake Huron to dump the load, another labourer joined him and taught him how to release the apparatus that opened the doors at the bottom of the square holes. He released the first one and told Herbie to do the same with the other three. On the way out into the lake they had simply sat with their legs dangling over the stern of the scow.

The hard work, however, started on the return trip. Herbie watched the labourer close the doors on the bottom by the use of a crank mechanism. Basically, he inserted a specially-built bar into a gear box and used his arms and strong back to crank the gear until the bar was at deck level. Then he did it again, and again several more times until the doors were closed. He then went to the next box and said, "Your turn Herbie."

Herbie discovered this was no job for weaklings, but he smiled at the other labourer when he had finished; he also realised he'd build up a lot of muscle while doing that job. The labourer said, "I'll tell Ernie you're fit and strong enough to handle the job. Now come ashore because while the crane fills the next load you will be told to do other things."

This was when Herbie really experienced the 'gofer' part of the job his dad had mentioned. In fact, once he was asked if he could swim, and he confirmed that he could. "Good," said Ernie, "that rope is tangled in something beside the wall. Did you bring your bathing suit with you? If not, you'll have to skinny dip."

"Yup, it's in my bag."

"Then run across the road, pick it up and you can change into it in the tool shed." When Herbie ran off Ernie called after him, "And bring a towel as well."

Herbie ran across the road, burst though the kitchen door and came to an abrupt halt as he entered the living room. Bernice and the handsome Italian grocery delivery man were in a passionate embrace, but released each other when they were seen.

Herbie had just stopped briefly, but slipped into the bedroom, dug out his bathing suit and departed. Herbie didn't mention what he had seen to Nug.

The crew wasn't in the dredging mode at this point so there wasn't a great deal of mud in the water. Ernie pointed at the rope and speculated what had snagged it, while explaining everything to Herbie as he proceeded. When finished he said, "Got it?" and when Herbie nodded he said, "Show us what yer made'a. Off you go."

Herbie dove in to find the rope had tangled around a splinter projecting from one of the wooden piles that had been driven into the bottom by the pile-driver. He unhooked it within the thirty-second oxygen supply in his lungs and arrived at the surface holding the rope. He exhaled deeply while his co-workers clapped hands.

Herbie really enjoyed his summer job of 1959. It was not complete but it ended for Herbie a week before he was about to enter Grade 8 during the first week of September. He hoped his dad would give him another job in the summer of 1960.

## Notes

1. Later Gulf Oil.
2. QEW – Queen Elizabeth Highway; back then was a four lane divided highway – today (2018) an eight lane highway.
3. In 1958 more Pakistanis had immigrated to Canada. Indians came later – most from Punjab.
4. At 14 seasons; running from 1952 to 1966 it held the record for the longest-running prime time comedy in U.S. television history, until it was surpassed by *The Simpsons* in 2003.

# Fourteen

**"BON JOUR, JE M'APPELLE** Mademoiselle Blanchette. Comment vous appelez vous?" Herbie's Grade 8 French teacher pointed at the first student in row one of the classroom. Annie Hall, the principal cum Grade 8 teacher of all other subjects was standing beside her. The kid the French teacher pointed to stared back at her with a blank look on his face, as did all the others as she walked up and down the aisles.

When she repeated the question to Herbie, however, he replied, "Je m'appelle Herbie. Comment allez-vous aujourd'hui Mademoiselle Blanchette?" All of his classmates looked at Herbie, some in amazement, some with smiles on their faces.

Miss Blanchette looked at Herbie wide-eyed and asked, "Herbie, where did you learn to speak French so well?

"I moved here from Quebec just after the start of Grade 6 and in that province English schools start teaching French in Grade 3."

"Oh, that explains it," she replied, "Well done Herbie."

ON A SUNDAY AFTERNOON in the fall of 1959 the family with the exception of David, but including their nanny and granddad were visiting Sheridan Nurseries. Herbie sat in a garden chair in a state of sadness. As he looked down over the rock garden he saw his nanny and granddad walking on a path between the rows of shrubs about 200 yards from where he sat. His granddad was shuffling along, shoulders hunched over, and using a walking cane to help him get along. Herb's nanny was helping him to walk by wrapping her arm around his. Herbie loved his granddad so much, but it was only then he realized Joseph Benning's life was approaching its end.

"GRANDDAD IS DYING Herbie," his mother said around 5th May 1960.

"Yes Mom; I knew this would be coming soon. Is he in hospital?"

"Yes Herbie, one called 'St. Joseph's Hospital' in western Toronto. You can see it up on a hill overlooking the new Gardiner Expressway."

"Can we visit him Mom, just you and me?"

"Yes, we'll run in on Saturday morning, but be forewarned, Nanny may also be there."

"That's OK Mom. Thanks."

On the way to the hospital on Saturday Herbie said, "Last night in bed I was thinking Mom"... His eyes welled up, "that it is perfect my granddad, who seemed to be a saint to me, will die in a hospital named St. Joseph's."

"I never thought of that Herbie, but you're right. You have a powerful mind for a thirteen year old. Don't forget to use that power when you get older."

When Herbie and his mother entered Joseph's room, they found Nanny Benning sitting on one side of the bed holding his hand. Herbie took a seat on the other side and Betty stood at the foot. Herbie took his granddad's other hand and said, "Hi Granddad, it's me Herbie."

Joseph chuckled, "Hello Herbie. My eyes may be closed but I'm not in a coma yet. I know it's you because I recognise your voice and felt the love emitting from your hand." He then asked, "Where are you standing Betty?"

"I'm at the foot of the bed Dad."

Joseph turned his head towards her and said, "Thanks for coming Dear, and for bringing Herbie with you. I love you both so much."

Herbie bowed his head because his eyes were welling up. His Nanny was there, and *'big boys don't cry'*.

"YOU HAVE A NEW sister kids," announced their father on the morning of 18th May 1960. "She was born early this morning at around 1 o'clock."

All kinds of questions followed.

"Is she healthy; how much does she weigh; does she have a clubbed foot: what will we name her?"

After the last question Herbie said, "I say we should name her Josephine, after Granddad. He's in a coma and will die any minute now."

"That's a good idea Herbie. I'll tell your mom that that is your wish and I'm absolutely sure she'll agree," said Charles.

At 5:30 pm the phone rang. Herbie picked it up, "Hello," he said.

"Hello," said the voice on the other end of the line, "May I please speak to Mr. Charles Elliot?"

"He'll be home at 6 pm Sir. May I take your name and number and tell him to call you?"

"No, I'd rather not. I'll call back at 6:30, just to make sure he's home."

At 6:30 pm Charles was standing by the phone hoping that nothing was wrong with Betty or the baby. When it rang he picked it up immediately.

"Hello, Charles Elliot speaking."

"Mr. Elliot my name is Doctor Kalkman. I'm calling from St. Joseph's Hospital. I know your wife has just delivered a baby so I thought it best to call you. Your father-in-law Joseph Benning passed away peacefully four hours ago ... If you intend to visit your wife this evening and if she asks about him, I suggest you simply say 'no change', as the bad news may negatively affect her and thus, the baby at this stage."

"Thanks for informing me, and I'll do as you recommended."

When the call ended, Herbie was standing beside his dad.

"Your Granddad has gone Herbie. That was a doctor from the hospital on the line."

Herbie didn't hear the last few words of what his dad had said, as he was halfway to his bedroom where he bawled his eyes out into his pillow for half an hour. He came up from his basement bedroom of the split-level house and ate supper in silence, after which he retired to his bedroom again.

Charles went down at 7:30 pm and found Herbie leafing through a photo album his mom had given him the day before she left for the hospital. It contained photographs of his granddad at about the age of thirty – he and another man were playing chess; his nanny and granddad's wedding; and those of their early life in Canada. Then there were even a few of himself with his grandparents when he, his mother and brother Lawrence had lived with them before his mother married her second husband who he now called Dad.

"Come to the recreation room Herbie. '*Ozzie and Herriot*' is about to start," said Charles.

"No laughter for me tonight thanks Dad, maybe tomorrow night."

The next morning Herbie's dad passed him an unsealed letter and told him to leave for school early and pass it to Miss Hall before classes.

When Herbie rounded the corner and commenced walking up Clarkson Road he opened the letter and read it.

Dear Miss Hall,

*Herbie's grandfather Joseph Benning passed away last night. I believe you came over to our house a year or two ago and spoke with him and his wife Mabel, and that your mother had been a dear friend of his, and even introduced him to Mabel.*

*Herbie's mother Bettina just gave birth to a baby girl eighteen hours prior to the death of her father, so it is I who write this note. The funeral will be held at Bethel Baptist Church in Leaside at 10 am on Saturday 28th May if you wish to attend. It'll be thirteen days after Herbie's new sister was born so his mother will be able to attend.*

*Warm Regards*

*Charles Elliot*

Herbie stood by and watched her read it. "Oh Herbie," she said, "This makes me feel so sad ... If you'd like to skip classes today, please feel free to go home."

"No Miss Hall; Granddad was old and feeble. His time had come to go to Heaven just like yours and mine will someday. He would want me to carry on, and I *will*.

"Good Herbie, you're a strong boy."

During classes that day Annie didn't ask Herbie any questions, or make any funny remarks as she usually did. She didn't want to evoke laughter for Herbie's sake.

"A STRIPED WHITE and black sports jacket is all I have Mom. Do you think that's alright to wear at a funeral", asked Herbie a couple of days before it was scheduled.

"Good thought Herbie, but your Granddad would love it."

Two days later Herbie's mom and his aunt Molly sat on each side of their grieving mother who was dressed in black from veiled hat to shoes. She wept profusely throughout the service. The families of Betty and Molly flanked the sisters.

Mr. Lewis the minister of Bethel Baptist officiated and a friend of Joseph's read the Eulogy.

Mr. Lewis had been the pastor for as long as Herbie remembered.

Herbie sat in a daze throughout the funeral, but as the family exited the church to their cars, he did notice Miss Hall, his principal and current teacher, watching him. She gave him a weak nod, which he returned.

There must have been a procession of cars following the Hurst to the close by Mount Pleasant Cemetery, but Herbie didn't remember the next day. All he remembered about the whole day was the coffin bearing the man that he loved the most being lowered into a deep dark hole in the ground, and walking down the short mound on which the grave was situated. As he walked away he suffered the strongest headache he had ever experienced due to the holding back of tears. The words *'Big boys don't cry; Big boys don't cry; Big boys don't cry,'* rang through his mind until he reached the car.

After his beloved granddad's passing, Herbie's grand-mother planted another demon in his head. Every time she left the Elliot's house after a visit she would take Herbie aside and say, "Whenever you are thinking of doing something bad, remember, your granddad is watching," and she'd look skyward. She continued to do this until her dying day at age 95. Towards the end, which was in the early 1980s, all she had to do was touch his shoulder and look skyward. She knew he knew what she meant, and he did.

"WHERE TO this summer.Dad?" asked Herbie.

"This year you'll work at a town called Bayfield located on the east coast to Lake Huron, about 15 miles south of Goderich. Nug will be there as will your cousin Bill Carruth. All the regular company employees will stay overnight in Goderich at a small hotel called the Royal and drive to and from the job-site every day. You and Bill will share the same hotel room. Further, Nug will still be driving down to see his mother each weekend so you and Bill can come down with him."

"Is the constructing work similar to what we did last year?"

"Yes and no. Yes, because we'll be building a dock and no because there won't be any dredging.

Again, Herbie really enjoyed his work at Bayfield. Some evenings the fulltime company men would meet in one of the bedrooms of the hotel, and tell dirty jokes, sing songs and drink beer. This was when Herbie at the tender age of 14 experienced drunkenness for the first time in his life. He enjoyed the feeling.

"OH BOY; there's football!" exclaimed Herbie after entering Lorne Park Secondary School located in the town next door to Clarkson. In fact there were two football leagues – Junior and Senior – and they'd play against teams from nearby high schools in Peel County. Boys in Grades 9 and 10 played in the junior league and those in Grades 11, 12 and 13 played in the senior.

"Ok boys, you all know the principles of football from watching the game on TV," or do I need to explain them to any of you?" asked Mr Long the coach on the first afternoon of practice. Nobody raised their hand.

The process of selecting positions took two hours – the full length of the practice time – and Herbie was selected as 'defensive tackle', due to his heft, and muscular arms and legs. He enjoyed this position immensely for the remainder of his high school years.

Herbie liked his French teacher Mr. Mackie and again he excelled in that subject. In public school he paid attention in history lessons because they were about Canada and the United States – General Wolfe; Pierre Radisson; John Cabot; the Hudson Bay Company; Lewis & Clark; the Civil War and such. But in high school the lessons went to other parts of the world – Turkey; the Roman Empire; Great Britain, and Herbie wasn't interested in hearing about these places. Further, he disliked Mr. Fullerton his history teacher.

Herbie didn't have a girl friend in Grade 9, but made many new male friends though including one friendship that ended in the early-1990s.

He passed Grade 9 with high marks in French and art, and marginal marks in the remaining subjects.

"IT'LL BE COLLINGWOOD this summer Herbie. It's located on the south coast of Georgian Bay almost due north of here. Again Nug will be with you, but your cousin Bill won't. The foreman is a man called Moose Hernshaw; 'Moose' because he's big and husky, but he's a good fellow."

"Any dredging and dump scow work this summer Dad?"

"No Herbie, we're just building a wharf along a portion of the waterfront, but there will be steel pile driving. I've told Moose to ensure you are not given the job of interconnecting the steel piles before the driving starts, because it can be rather dangerous, especially on windy days."

Thanks Dad. I'm looking forward to it.

So, on the first Monday after Herbie's 1960/61 Grade 9 school year ended, Nug and his Volkswagen Bug stopped in front of 818 Sunningdale Bend and picked him up. They arrived in Collingwood about four hours later and went to the boarding house where Nug had been living during the week. Herbie got a single room. They arrived after the communal supper had ended so they walked to the local A&W for a burger and root beer.

The next morning when Herbie and Nug arrived at the job site, one of the permanent company men said, "Welcome back Herbie. Last summer we got you drunk. This summer we'll get you laid."

Herbie just smiled when everybody else laughed. He knew it wouldn't happen.

Again Herbie enjoyed his summer job and mixing with the old guys. A couple of times he found himself sitting in a tavern with a group of them. The legal drinking age in Canada was 21 and Herbie was only still 15 years old. On one of those occasions he tried to act indifferent as one of the waiters stared at him from behind the bar. Herbie imagined the waiter was thinking '*he doesn't look as though he's twenty-one*'. But he wasn't challenged.

On the last day of working at Collingwood, Moose took Herbie aside and said, "This will be your last summer of working for Ontario Marine and Dredging. Your Dad told Sid Byrd the owner to 'pound sand up his ass' and walked out."

Herbie knew his father wouldn't have used those words, but also realised what had happened. His dad had quit his job.

It wasn't long, however, before Charles Elliot secured a new position at an American company called Wickstrum Limited. The company was attempting to expand into Canada and Charles took charge of the Canadian office based in Toronto.

One evening his dad took him aside and said, "You'll have to find your own summer jobs from now on, which will be a valuable learning experience for your further employment after your schooling ends."

At this point – 1961 – Herbie's brother David had been married to a young lady named Stephanie and they were parents of a baby boy named Chris; his sister Maggie would to entering Grade 12; and his younger brother Lawrence would enter high school. Herbie's youngest brother Walt would be entering Kindergarten, and his baby sister Josie was still an infant. David supported his family by working in the daytime for a printing company and in evenings pumping gas at the nearby Charlie Brown's service station. He was still only 21 years of age.

Charles Elliot was a man with a great sense of humour. That summer he posted a large sign on the back of the garage which faced the swimming pool. It read, We Don't Swim in Your Toilet. Please Don't Pee in Our Pool. The pool was open to the community every day of the week except Sunday evenings which was reserved for family.

Mr Fullerton, Herbie's history teacher at Lorne Park High School lived two houses down the street from the Elliots. He had two little mischievous boys Charles called the 'scorpions'. Early on a Sunday evening in September 1961, Mr. Fullerton and the scorpions appeared at the side gate to the pool. Herbie and his dad were sitting on lawn chairs talking. When Charles saw them entering the gate he said, "Sorry, the pool in reserved for family on Sunday evenings. Everyone knows and respects that rule."

Mr. Fullerton gave him a rather indignant look and said "Are you telling me this pool is closed?" as though it was a public swimming pool.

Charles simply replied, "Yes, I am."

Fullerton stood there dumbfounded for a moment, and then turned and walked away. Herbie and his dad laughed when they heard the scorpions crying.

Later that autumn Charles walked into the dining room when the family was about to eat. He was holding a fancy box with leather sides and top, and a hinged lid. He said, "I purchased one of King Tut's[1] fingers today kids." None of them knew who King Tut was but the questions were all pretty much the same.

"Can we see it? Please show us Dad."

"Ok; everybody gather around."

When they were all in place he slowly opened the box and there it was. A finger lay on flat white cotton batten; there was royal blue silk on the sides of the box

"May I touch it Dad," asked Maggie.

"Sure, go ahead."

Maggie reached into the box with extended index finger and lightly touched it. The finger immediately sprang up to an erect position. Maggie screamed and everybody laughed. The item was their dad's middle finger which he had inserted through a round hole in the bottom of the box and laid it on flat cotton padding.

LATIN was one of the optional subjects of Grade 10, as was typing. Herbie saw no use in learning Latin and didn't want to study it, but his dad insisted he should. Herbie also chose typing, which his dad described as a 'girls job' and thought it should be closed to boys. Herbie hated Latin and after failing the first set of exams which were held just before the Christmas holidays he said to his Dad, "I want to drop out of Latin."

Charles said, "Well you can't; you'll need it to go to university some day and become a doctor, lawyer or scientist."

"Dad,' said Herbie, "I believe a father should let his kids be what they *are* and not what he wants them to be."

Charles was taken aback by that profound statement from a 16 year old. He gave in saying, "Okay Herb. Go ahead; drop Latin." He had a sad look on his face.

So Herbie said, "Dad, I don't want to be a doctor or lawyer and if it means I won't get a university education without Latin I believe I can make out in life without one."

Typing, on the other hand, was one he enjoyed and learning the craft was advantageous in later life. Herbie also enjoyed the subject of 'Shop' which involved working on wood and steel lathes. Until he began taking 'shop' he didn't know the difference between cross-cut and rip saws. The girls studied 'Home Economics' while the boys were at 'Shop' classes.

Herbie passed Grade 10 with marginal marks in all subjects except typing and shop.

"MORE BRICKS ... more mortar," were the words flung at Herbie at intervals of 5 minutes during his summer job of 1962. He had found a job with a company called 'Pet Construction' and he was a bricklayer's assistant. The company was building a two-story warehouse in New Toronto.

Herbie's job was to mix mortar, pour it into a special wheelbarrow, and run it up ramps of the scaffolding and deposit some onto the pallets of three Italian brick bricklayers. Once that was completed, he'd race back down, throw more dry sand and cement into the mixer, use a hose to add water and let it mix while he loaded another type of wheelbarrow with bricks and run up the ramps again. He'd never done anything as strenuous in all his life and he knew he'd be all muscle by the end of the summer.

Sometimes when he got behind in his work one of the bricklayers would come down and help him. Herbie sat with these fellows, during lunchtimes. While talking he learned those of them who weren't much older than him were just toddlers when their parents emigrated from Italy to Canada after World War II. Benno the oldest, who must have been 10 when his family emigrated, really boosted Herbie's pride when the summer was approaching its end and 'back to school time' was rapidly coming.

He said, "Herbie, other assistants who have come to us during the summer didn't last more than one week before they quit because they couldn't handle the hard work, but you stuck with it and we're all proud of you."

Herbie smiled as the other bricklayers clapped. He told his mom and dad when he got home that night.

"RAM HIM…RAM HIM Len!" A boy hung out of the back window of a new model Dodge Dart and was banging the fenders of Lenny Johnson's 1956 Ford as they raced down the QEW towards home at about midnight on a Saturday in the early spring of 1963.

Every Saturday evening Herbie and his friends drove down to Niagara Falls, NY where the legal drinking age was 18; they were still only 17 but could pass for 18. They would drive across the border check-point and up around the corner to the Rainbow Bar, where the majority of the patrons were under-aged boys from Ontario.

On this particular night, as they were passing through the border check point on their way home, a group of boys in a late model Dodge Dart passing through another check point started yelling vulgar insults at them, which Herbie and his friends hurled back. Those in the other car indicated for Lenny, the driver of the car Herbie and their companions were in to follow them. These boys lived in Niagara Falls, Ontario, but Len the driver didn't follow them, thinking that it might be a set up. He continued driving along the QEW on the way home. His normal homeward bound speed was 80 mph (129 kph).

Since they hadn't followed the Dart, it followed them onto the QEW. The Dart eventually started to pull up beside them in the passing lane; the boys noticed that one was hanging out the back window wielding a tire iron. Len sped up to 95 mph (153 kph). The Dart moved faster and the one with the tire iron started banging the rear fender of Len's car. Just as the tire iron wielding boy was about to smash the driver's window the cry went out to ram him. Rob turned the wheel sharply to the left and his front left fender struck the Dart. He quickly brought the Ford back on course. When the impact of the strike on the Dart's front took effect it caused the rear fender to come to the right and it struck Rob's rear fender. The Dart lost control and ran off the QEW at almost 100 mph (161 kph) and came to an abrupt stop when it hit the four foot high dirt cliff-shaped edge of a farmer's field.

Cars weren't fitted with safety belts in 1963, and for all the boys in Len's car knew, the occupants of the Dart could all have been killed, but they didn't care; they just kept on driving home – laughing all the way.

HERBIE FAILED GRADE 11 miserably. He even had non-passable marks in French and Art. With regard to art, it wasn't due to his skills that caused his failure; it was because he simply wasn't interest in learning about the works and techniques of European masters – Van Gogh; Leonardo da Vinci; Michelangelo; and such. The only thing he liked about high school was playing football.

GEORGE, IT'S BETTY ELLIOT from Hudson speaking."

"Betty, it's nice hearing from you" said George Leonadas. "I had heard through the grapevine that you, Chuck and family moved to the Toronto area. How are things in your family?"

"We're fine George. I was just calling to see if you'd be able to give Herbie a summer job. He's 17 years old now and a strong boy."

"As you know Bet, I was recruited from a company in Montreal back in '56 to be the Vice-President sales for Coca Cola Canada. And, yes, I can give Herbie a job whenever he's ready to show up."

"This is Wednesday, so how about Monday morning. Would that be OK?"

"Perfect Bet. Tell him he'll be a salesman's assistant. Salesmen drive the trucks around town and deliver cases of 24 bottles to stores, restaurants and bars. We pay $100 weekly and there's a commission on the number of cases sold. I'll see he gets a good route – one in the downtown which includes Young Street. Our building is located on the corner of Richmond and Parliament, and he should arrive by 8 o'clock for the morning sales briefing. The sales department is on the second floor and the briefing room is just off the elevators. Any questions Betty?"

"No George; you've explained everything. Thank you so much."

"Don't mention it; and say hello to Charlie for me. Good bye."

"Good bye George, and say hello to Emma and the boys from the Elliot family."

When Herbie arrived home that afternoon his mom asked him if he intended to work for Pet Construction again in the summer. Herbie said, "Well Mom; I enjoyed working with those Italian fellows, but the work was rather strenuous for the amount of pay I earned. I've decided to look for another job."

"How'd you like to work as an assistant salesman on a Coca Cola truck in downtown Toronto?"

"That sounds interesting Mom. Please explain what's involved."

His mom told him she had called Mr. Leonadas and described what she'd been told. Herbie was more than pleased. So at about 7:45 am on Monday morning he stepped off the elevator and walked into the briefing room. He walked up to the man who seemed to be the manager and introduced himself. The manager walked him down the hall and knocked on the door of George Leonadas's office. When they heard him say 'Enter', Herbie walked up to the vice-president with shoulders back and said, "Thanks for the opportunity Sir."

He said, "No need to thank me Herbie. It's nice seeing you again. You can carry on now. Mr. Wilson must get you fitted into a uniform before the briefing."

The uniform was a dark green shirt with a Coke badge on the chest and dark green pants. He rapidly put them on, placed his other pants and shirt into a locker and followed Mr. Wilson back to the briefing room. Most of the briefing was about putting up advertising posters and signs, and ensuring that those already in place were in good condition.

Afterwards, Mr. Wilson introduced Herbie to Don McCray, the driver he'd be working with all summer. They made their way down to the basement to their truck which was loaded with the normal Monday morning load. The night crew at Coke knew the daily requirements of each route. There were about twelve fully loaded trucks, and this was only for the east end of Toronto. There was another plant on the west end. All the trucks drove up a ramp from the basement onto Parliament Street, and to the start of their routes.

While driving to the downtown Don explained a few things along the way. Once finished Don pulled up in front of a variety store and said, "Here's our first stop."

They stopped for lunch at a small restaurant and sat outside on a picnic table to eat a couple of sandwiches. Herbie was the first to emerge and when Don came out he saw Herbie drinking a 7up.

He said, "Herbie if one of the company executives drove by and saw you drinking 7up while wearing a Coke uniform you'd be fired on the spot."

"But I like 7up better."

"That's your prerogative after work, but not in the day while wearing a Coke uniform."

Herbie took a deep swig and placed the half full bottle on a different table.

At the end of the first week Herbie received his $100 cheque. When he asked about the commission he was told it was calculated during the following week and he'd be paid that portion of his salary on the next payday. Herbie was fine with that.

His best friend Wayne Kelly also had a pretty high paying job that summer, so on Friday evenings they would drive up to Wasaga Beach on Georgian Bay and whooped it up all weekend. They'd chase girls, drink bootleg beer, sleep in a small rented cabin and they even went for a swim once. They'd return home on Sunday nights with just enough money in their pockets to sustain life until the next weekend. This continued until the end of the summer.

"I NEED a part-time job Mom and Dad," said Herbie after he started his second year in Grade 11.

"Well you can't get one Herbie," said his dad.

"I have no money. How will I survive? I won't even he able to have a girlfriend."

"Your mom and I watched you all summer and knew this would happen. A summer job is supposed to sustain you for the whole school year. So I'll tell you how you'll survive. You'll stay at home and study!"

That was a hard lump to swallow for a 17 year old, but deep down he knew his dad was doing the right thing and that it was for his own good.

Then, during the first football practice of September 1963 Herbie's coach, Mr. Richardson, walked up to him with a rather sympathetic look on his face.

He took Herbie aside and said, "Herbie, you won't be allowed to play this year."

"Why's that Sir."

"It's because students repeating a Grade aren't allow to play after school-hour sports. That's the rule, and it's been that way for several years."

Herbie walked off the field with a half-broken heart...The next day he walked into the office of Mr. Mumford the LPSS principal and told him he was dropping out of high school. Mr. Mumford asked him why and Herbie replied, "Because I can't play football."

"That's a weak excuse Herbie, but if you're sure you know what it means, here are the papers to fill in and sign." Herbie filled in the papers and walked all the way home. The next morning Herbie stood in front of Mr. Wilson the sales manager at Coke. He asked him for his job back and if possible with Don McCray.

"You quit school Herbie?" asked the manager with a look of dismay on his face.

"Yes Sir, yesterday."

"Are you sure that was a wise decision?"

"Quite sure Sir. My father wanted all his kids to be doctors or lawyers after they left school, but that has never been my intention. I figure I can get a better education doing something more interesting, and I have an idea in my head that I've been toying around with for a few days now, so I may only be with you for a couple of months if that's OK."

"Ok then Herbie. I'll put you back with Don starting from Monday morning. It's Wednesday today so come in tomorrow ready for work and you'll work under another driver until Friday.

On his second week of working at Coke Herbie stopped in Lorne Park and knocked on the door of a girl named Shawna with whom he wanted a date. Her father answered the door, and when Herbie asked speak to his daughter the man's eyes homed in on the Coke badge on Herbie's shirt.

He said, "So you have an after-school job at Coke do you?"

"No Sir, I work for them fulltime," Herbie replied with his chest stuck out.

"In that case I have a few words for you to listen to, so listen hard"... "Are you listening?"

Herbie nodded.

"Ok, you're a high school dropout and that means you're **Fuck All"** ... "You've got **Fuck All...** and you always will have **Fuck All;** so **Fuck OFF!"** The man slammed the door in his face.

Herbie walked back to his car in a rather shocked state of mind. He sat in the driver's seat. While sitting there he didn't think about the girl – she meant nothing to him. He thought about the crude rebuff he had just received from her father. A thought ran threw his mind: *that rude man was correct when he expressed his feelings about high school dropouts*. He began to think of options to prove the man wrong, even if he was a dropout.

And then one evening after working at Coke for two months his father took him aside. He said, "Herbie I've given up on you. The only thing I can suggest is that you join the Army."

Herbie knew that Canada had been in the Cold War for well over ten years. He wanted more action that marching around army bases and practicing for a war he didn't expect would come. He wanted to see far off places. He wanted more excitement and travel. So on Sunday 20th October during supper he informed the family he was going to submit his one month notice to Coke in the morning and apply to join the Royal Canadian Navy on 21st November.

"YOUR NAME IS ELLIOT, but why does your birth certificate say it's Cunningham?" said the young uniformed Leading Seaman (Corporal) at the Royal Canadian Navy (RCN) recruitment centre on Monday morning 21st November.

"Yes, I thought you may ask. It's because my mother divorced my natural father when I was young and when she remarried I took the name of my step-father." Herbie hoped he wouldn't be asked for adoption papers because his parents had never got around to getting that job done.

The fellow simply said, "That explains it." He went on to explain a few things that he could expect to happen. One was to be given a medical; and that would take place in about half an hour.

The sailor said, "If accepted your initial pay will be $98 per month until you have completed basic training when it will be raised to $102 per month."

"Ninety-eight dollars per month!?"

"Don't shoot the messenger Elliot. It's my job to tell you, but tell me, what was the last job you had."

"I was a helper on a Coca Cola truck in downtown Toronto. I earned $100 per week plus commission."

"If you want to throw your life away working at *glorious* jobs like that then Goodbye and Good Luck. But if you want to see far off places, learn a trade, and have plenty of fun while doing it, you are in the right place. Your pay will increase over the years of course as you get promoted."

"Ok, you've made your point. And it stuck deep. Let's get on with it."

Herbie had no worries about passing the medical; after all, a wimpy school chum had passed about four months earlier. The young sailor escorted him to the doctor's waiting room where he waited until another hopeful fellow walked out. He was then told to enter. He went into the examination room and walked out ten minutes later full of confidence.

He walked back to the main lobby and the young man told him he'd be informed of the results on Wednesday and if positive he should report back on Friday the 29th for signing the papers. After that he'd be an Ordinary Seaman in the RCN and report to Union Station in downtown Toronto, board a train to Montreal, meet other sailors coming from points to the west and from the surrounding Quebec area. They'd then board another train to Saint John, New Brunswick where they'd board a ferry across the Bay of Fundy to the town of Digby, Nova Scotia where a Navy bus would be waiting to transport them to HMCS Cornwallis about 10 miles up the coast.

"That'll be a little confusing to a bunch of young fellows," said Herbie.

"Don't worry; I'll be at Union Station to see you off and the others who have just been accepted, and a Petty Officer 1st Class will meet you in Montreal and escort you onwards.

## Notes

1. King Tutankhamen the boy Pharaoh of ancient Egypt.

# Fifteen

**"MOM, DAD, COME QUICK.** President Kennedy has been assassinated!" cried Herbie in the afternoon of $22^{nd}$ November. His mom and dad were both in front of the TV within seconds. The scene kept being repeated as it was beamed in from NBC in Buffalo, New York to their TV antenna on the roof. President Kennedy had been standing in the back of a limousine convertible in Dallas, Texas waving at the cheering crowd one minute, and the next minute he lay dead with security guards trying to revive him. By the time the Elliots were watching it authorities had already arrested the assassin; a man called Lee Harvey Oswald.

All Charlie Elliot could say was, "What is this world coming to?"

Two days later Herbie was watching a live broadcast of Oswald being escorted out of the Dallas courthouse after being officially charged for the Kennedy assassination when a man named Jack Ruby stepped from the crowd and shot him dead.

On Wednesday he received a call from the RCN recruiting office saying that he was medically fit and to report for the signing on Friday.

On Friday he met three other new recruits from the surrounding area – Dennis Timms, Bill Harrison and Mike Angelle, and they all signed the bottom line of the papers. They were now officially members of the Royal Canadian Navy. They were told to report to Union Station on Sunday morning with just a bag small enough for two sets of spare underwear, soap, tooth paste and brush, one towel and shaving gear. They'd be issued naval clothing the day after arrival at Cornwallis.

Herbie's mom drove him to Union Station and the same fellow from the recruiting office saw them off. Sure enough when they arrived in Montreal an announcement came over the broadcast system: All Naval Recruits Report to The Man in a Naval Uniform Under the Clock.

The boys did as instructed and gathered in a group around a man in uniform who they would learn later was a Petty Officer 1st Class (P1). He spoke with a mild voice and told them to form a line in front of him, which they did. He then walked down the line with a clipboard and pen and checked off each name.

"Good," he said with a smile, "everybody showed up. Now follow me to the platform and once told to board the train by the Station Master, take a seat. You'll all have chair seats. I, on the other hand, will be in the car ahead of you in compartment 4c, but don't come wake me up unless it's an emergency."

The train pulled away, arriving at St. John N.B. the next afternoon at 3 pm. The ferry to Digby, N.S. was waiting.

Once they had all disembarked the P1 said, "Follow me," and he walked up the gangway. He stood there until the last of his charges had boarded. He then said, "Ok fellows; you are free to walk around and explore the ferry, but do not under any circumstances enter the bridge or the engine room."

When they arrived at Digby, all the recruits walked down the ferry gangway and boarded a bus that the soft-spoken P1 had indicated. After a twenty minute journey the bus drove through the gates of HMCS Cornwallis and down the road toward the waterfront. When the bus stopped in front of a two-storied building, the soft spoken P1 changed into a raging tyrant.

He yelled at the top of his lungs "*This is joining block where you'll spend the next two* weeks. ***Now run inside and place your belongings on a bunk on the first or second floor and be back standing in front of me in three ranks in three minutes. GO!"***

"What a shock!" they all thought, but ran inside as instructed. Once outside again the P1 selected a fellow who had been a P2 in Sea Cadets and said he'd be temporary Divisional Captain and to march the motley crew down to mess hall for supper.

When they got there, young sailors already under training gathered around them and asked, "Is it was true that President Kennedy had been assassinated; or was it some kind of training hoax?" When told it was true, some had a hard time holding back tears.

After being in joining block for two weeks they moved to another building for further training. Their division was Margaree 4/63; where the '4' indicated the number of divisions that had been assigned as Margaree that year; and the '63' for the year.

Basic training consisted of everything imaginable – from marching, tying boots and shoes the navy way, shooting rifles, to brushing their teeth.

During rifle training one of the trainees made the mistake of calling the weapon a gun.

The instructor said, "This is my rifle" (pointing to it); "This is my gun" (while grabbing his crotch). "One is for shooting…one is for fun." (Laughter).

Halfway through the 14 week training period Herbie approached his divisional P1, He said, "Petty Officer Turpin would you please arrange an appointment with the padre for me?"

"Is there anything I can do for you instead?"

"No Sir; I think this is a matter for the padre to deal with."

Turpin picked up the telephone and got Herbie an appointment the next morning at 10:00.

"HOW MAY I HELP YOU Ordinary Seaman Elliot?" asked the padre the next morning.

"I don't know my natural father Sir. All I know is what my mother told me about him. She said, 'He had been shot down in a bomber during World War II; had parachuted to safety, was captured and put into a POW camp, and was repatriated near the end of the war. He returned to Canada and I was born, but they broke up two years later. I think Air Force headquarters may be able to find his whereabouts. I just want to meet him, nothing else."

The padre asked Herbie his father's name and any other details he'd been told by his mother. Herbie told him all he knew.

Two days later Petty Officer Turpin summoned Herbie. "The padre has some news for you. Go up to his office right away as he won't be around for a week or so, starting tomorrow."

Herbie hustled up to the padre's office. "Your father remained in the RCAF after the war and is currently stationed at headquarters in Ottawa." He gave Herbie the phone number of his father's desk while saying "Your records say you lived in the Toronto area before joining.

Perhaps you could arrange to meet him while on your two weeks of special leave after basic training."

"Thank you Sir. I'll write to my mother and tell her what I've done. She could drive me up to Ottawa and maybe he and I could have lunch together."

"No thanks required Elliot, that's my job – helping others – and it's a good idea to write to your mother to tell her what you've done."

Herbie wrote a letter to his mom that night.

ON 12TH APRIL 1964 Herbie and his mom walked around the corner onto Elgin Street in Ottawa and saw a man in air force uniform standing in front of the Lord Elgin hotel; the agreed upon meeting point.

Bill Cunningham saw them coming and shortened the distance by walking towards them. Herbie noticed the two and a half stripes on the cuffs of his uniform and realized he held the equivalent rank of a Navy Lieutenant Commander, but didn't know the name of the Air Force rank.

When they met, Betty was the first to speak. "Hello Bill, it's nice seeing you again. And this is your son Herbie. As you can see he's grown up and a proud member of the Royal Canadian Navy."

"Hello Betty, it's so nice for me to see you too. Hello Herbie." They all shook hands although Herbie thought his father would rather have hugged his mom by the look on his face.

"I'll be off now to do a little shopping. You two have a nice meal and I'll be back to pick Herbie up in an hour and a half." She turned and walked the hundred feet to the next corner and Bill didn't move until she walked around the corner and was out of sight. Herbie detected a look of sadness in his father's eyes.

Once inside Herbie wished he hadn't worn his uniform, because he thought it may be embarrassing for his father – an officer – to be seen eating with a navy boy of such a low rank in a five star hotel, but he had worn it to show his father he had grown up, and had followed his footprints into the military.

Few words were spoken during the meal, but Herbie was taken aback when his father asked, "Tell me Herbie, what is the purpose of this meeting?"

Herbie lowered his head and in a weak voice said, "I just wanted to meet you Sir. I don't remember you very well, but I think it may have been you who I played peek-a-boo with at the door of 37 Macnaughton when I was a toddler."

"Yes, that was me Herbie," said Bill in a rather sad voice. "Your memory goes back a long way. Is there anything else you remember?"

Herbie sensed relief in the eyes of his father when he said "No Sir."

When Herbie and his father stepped out of the Lord Elgin onto Elgin St., Betty was standing on the sidewalk. They all shook hands and when Herbie and his mom were rounding the corner he took a quick glance back to see his father standing there watching them depart.

He seemed to be sad.

While driving back to Toronto Herbie told his mother about Bill asking the purpose of the meeting. She said "There was never any talk about his father. I'm not sure if he knows who he was or is."

❄❄❄❄

*"HEY YOU COCK-WALLOPER you drank the whole thing!"* cried Scott Hunter, Herbie's best friend. Scott wrapped his fist around the empty beer bottle and smashed the Yank in the side of the head. The blow incited a bar room brawl – Canadian sailors against the Americans– in the 'Horse & Buggy' pub in Hamilton, Bermuda.

The bar had been crowded as a ship of each navy was berthed in Bermuda, and the pub they were in was their favourite – the other that allowed sailors without a suit and tie inside was the Hog Penny on the waterfront road.

Sailors had been standing in a crowd about eight feet deep trying to get served. Herbie and his friend Scott already had bottles of beer in their hands. A Yank who hadn't been served yet asked Scott for a sip of his.

"Sure Mate," said Scott and passed the American his beer. That was when the fun started. The Yank almost fell to the floor due to the force of the blow to the side of his head.

He came back at Scott full of vengeance. Sailors from each ship ended up in a brawl similar to those they had watched on television as boys while enjoying cowboy programs like Wild Bill Hickok on television.

Halfway through the battle both Herbie and Scott found themselves on their hands and knees face-to-face. Herbie cried, *"Let's get the fuck outta here!"*

The room was dimly lit and they crawled to what they thought was the exit door of the bar on the second floor. But they were 180 degrees disoriented; they mistakenly found themselves in the storeroom behind the right-hand end of the bar. When they realized their mistake they weaselled out and jumped up to the elevated area at the far end of the room and plunked themselves down at a table with an American couple from the State of Maine who were on their honeymoon. Both Scott and Herbie laughingly proclaimed, *"We started it! We started it!"* The honeymooners just gawked at the brawl in a sense of shock.

Both sailors laughed when they watched the British-type bobbies haul some of their more violent shipmates to the paddy wagon.

Once all the excitement was over they bid the newlyweds good night and left. When they got out onto the street and were halfway down to the corner, Herbie said, "Damn! We should'a grabbed a bottle of rum while in the storeroom. All three bartenders had jumped over the bar and were trying to break up the fight."

Scott said, "Look." He opened his jumper a little and pulled out the top of a 40 ounce bottle of Bacardi dark. He then laughed while saying, "At least one of us doesn't have shit for brains." Herbie laughed along with his buddy.

He laughed but did say, "Don't even *think* of trying to smuggle that onboard tonight. If caught you'd get 30 days stoppage of leave, or worse.

"So, what should we do with it?"

"Let's just sit on this bench. It's across the road from 'Hog Penny'. The ship is a couple of hundred yards away, with the foc'sile facing us; the gangway is on the quarterdeck so no one will see us. We'll start into the bottle and offer a few wets to our buddies who are on their way back to the ship. But that's only if you promise not to start another brawl."

"I promise."

So they sat and shared the bottle with their shipmates and were more than a little tipsy when it was empty. Herbie, not being a litterbug, dropped the empty into a garbage basket near the bench and he and his buddy walked the remaining hundred yards to the gangway of their ship.

As they crossed the brow the Officer of the Day (OOD) was standing beside the Corporal of the Gangway. Herbie said, "Sir, some of our shipmates were thrown in the clink by the cops this evening."

"No Elliot; the police brought them back to the ship. How did it start in the first place?"

"No idea Sir; it just erupted as though it was seventy-five hungry monkeys fighting over six bananas."

"Monkey's they may have been, but I doubt if bananas was the cause. Now you two drunken fools get below!"

While climbing down the ladder to three-deck, Herbie and Scott laughed all the way to one mess – the messdeck with bunks, lockers and a settee for Sonarmen. All this had happened in the summer of 1965 when the two were stationed on HMCS Kootenay, their second ship together.

"D'YA HEAR THERE this is Captain speaking" blared over the ships' main broadcast on the day before the Kootenay was to enter Halifax after the Bermuda cruise. "Our next cruise will be to Chatham, England to attend 23rd September christening of HMCS Ojibwa, Canada's first Oberon Class submarine. We'll also witness the launching of Canada's next submarine Onondaga from the dry dock. She won't be ready for christening for another year or so. Another will come within two years. We'll sail from Halifax on 12th September. Saguenay and Nipigon will accompany us. After departing Chatham the squadron will drop into Amsterdam, in the Netherlands for a goodwill visit. Until we depart there will be a leave period."

Both Herbie and Scott applied for leave before entering Halifax. When a Leading Seaman (LS) named Murphy learned that Herbie lived in the vicinity of Toronto he asked if they would mind picking up his car at the shore base – HMCS York – his last posting. Herbie said, "Well, I have a Volkswagen and we were planning of taking turns driving that one up and back, but I suppose one of us could drive each car."

"Thanks," said Murph, "here's the name and phone number of the fellow who will give you the keys."

Once alongside and the gangway was open both Herbie and Scott went up to the Fleet Lockers, put on their civies and packed their bags. It was 10 am and they set out immediately in the 1958 Volkswagen Bug Herbie had purchased a week before setting out for Bermuda. They took turns driving and sleeping curled up in the back seat all night, arriving in Clarkson – Herbie's hometown – about 24 hours later. While passing through Toronto they had stopped at HMCS York and picked up Murphy's 1956 Dodge. Scott stayed the night at the Elliot abode and in the morning took the Volkswagen on to Sarnia, near Perch Creek, the place of Herbie's first summer job as a gofer on a construction site.

It was a good leave for Herbie – tooling around Clarkson and Lorne Park, and mixing with old High School friends. Most had graduated by then and some would go on to University in September.

At one point during his leave Herbie was standing in the kitchen and overheard a small confrontation between his mom and dad.

"Bet, would you please ask Herbie to take the Chrysler up to the beer store and buy me another case of beer?"

"He's only 19 Chuck. David's outside by the pool with Steph. He's almost 24 now and well over 21, the legal age."

"You know full well that Herbie's been buying beer since before he joined the navy. He looks to be over 21; one of the permanent employees of Ontario Marine told me he drank beer in taverns when he was as young as fifteen; and further I don't want David to get into the habit."

Betty walked into the kitchen and asked, "Herbie, have you ever bought beer at the Brewer's Retail before?"

"Sure, lots of times Mom, even when I was only seventeen" said Herbie, a little proud of the fact.

"Then would you please..."

"I heard Mom, sure."

Nobody considered Charles Elliot to be an alcoholic, but every Friday the Brewer's Retail delivery truck would stop in front of the house, drop off two cases of 24 Molson Golden at the foot of the driveway and pick up the empties of the previous week. Sometimes Herbie would see his dad drinking a beer before breakfast.

Herbie was back with the beer in about twenty minutes. While driving up and back though some painful thoughts ran through his mind; '*Dad doesn't care if I get into the habit, but is worried that* David *would*'.

SCOTT WAS BACK in front of the Elliot house in the late afternoon of the day before they would set out for Halifax. There was someone with him. Herbie saw them arrive and welcomed them saying to Scott, "And who is this?"

"He's an acquaintance of my family who is also on leave and asked for a lift back to Halifax. I agreed."

"Good," said Herbie after learning the fellow's name was Walt Harris, "Walt you can help with the driving."

"But I don't have a drivers licence," said Walt.

"That's OK, we'll teach you along the way."

After a swim in the pool, a beer each from Herbie's dad, a fine meal and an 'early to bed; early to rise' sleep, they set out eastward at 06:00 the next morning, in order to avoid the Toronto eastbound traffic rush. Scott drove the Volks and Herbie the Dodge. They drove past Montreal where they joined the Trans-Canada Highway which crossed the St Lawrence River at that point.

Scott had been teaching Walt how to shift gears of the Volks along the way and had let him take the wheel on his own a couple of times.

Somewhere about three-quarters of the way between Woodstock and Fredericton, New Brunswick Herbie was driving the Volkswagen ahead of the Dodge, which Scott was driving.

Herbie pulled off the highway and told Scott who had also pulled over that he was dead tired and falling asleep at the wheel.

Scott said, "If we stop for the night we'll be adrift (late) in the morning and be charged."

Walt had been sleeping in the back seat of the Dodge, but when he woke up Herbie said, "How about you Walt. Can you drive the Volks for a while?"

"*Ok*," he said with a note of scepticism.

"Good, the keys are in the ignition."

Herbie curled up in the back seat of the Dodge for a couple of hours of sleep, but within 10 minutes he got a rude awakening.

"Holy fuck Herb he rolled her – two; three."

The Volkswagen bug had rolled three times and Herbie and Scott ran to the wrecked car, which was lying on its side. They laughed when the saw Walt's arm opening the door and seeing it fall back closed again. They helped him out when they arrived at the scene. Now they knew they'd be adrift in the morning.

"What now Herb?" asked Scott.

"I guess we'll have to report it to the closest RCMP station. They're usually situated on the highway, but when we get to the next gas station, we'll ask."

They were fortunate, because within ten minutes they came across a gas station where they were told the closest RCMP cop shop was back in Grand Falls, which was only about a half hour drive in the direction from where they had already travelled.

"Should we go back or just leave it and carry on?" asked Scott.

"If we don't go back they'll track me down by the licence plate number and I'll be charged for leaving the scene of an accident."

The fellow who pumped gas at the service station was wrong. Grand Falls was a fifty minute drive. Once at the police station they walked in and reported the accident. The police wanted to see the scene so off they went back in an easterly direction and stopped when they reached the doomed Volkswagen.

"Who was driving," asked the officer.

"I was," said Herbie, knowing full well he couldn't say Walt who didn't have a licence.

"Looks like a write off to me," said the officer.

"There may be a few salvageable parts, but I don't want it. It's off the highway so would you please call a wrecker in the morning and tell them to take it away?"

"I'll do that, but first I need some information. Please show me your driver's licence and the ownership papers."

While reaching in his pocket for his wallet Herbie said, "Scott, you and Walt go to the wreck and try to open the glove compartment. Then bring all the papers to us."

They did as instructed and passed them to Herbie. He leafed through them and passed the requested papers to the officer, who inspected them and said, "Everything is in order, you boys can carry on now."

About 20 minutes later they saw an all night highway diner. Herbie was driving and pulled in saying, "Let's have a coffee and sandwich."

When they finished their refreshments and were about to take off in the Dodge Herbie said, "Damn! I forgot my ball cap on the table. Walt, would you please run back in and retrieve it?"

"Sure," said Walt as he ran back.

Before he had even reached the door of the diner Herbie had opened the trunk of the Dodge and had thrown Walt's bag onto the pavement. Walt exited empty handed to see the tail-lights of the Dodge driving away.

Scott said, "Yer evil Herb," after which they both laughed for ten minutes.

They had called ahead to tell the ship that they'd had an accident and would be late.

When they arrived in Halifax at 10:30 am they parked the Dodge on Russell St. near the Fleet Lockers where they dumped their bags and changed back into uniform. They walked into HMC Dockyard at 11:20 am and as they approached the Kootenay, Leading Seaman

Murphy was standing near the gangway watching for them. As they were passing the pay phone booths Murph yelled "Which car was it?"

Scott yelled back, "The Dodge."

After crossing the brow, Herbie said, "It's still driveable. You can pick up what's left of it on Russell St., just up from the corner of Barrington. Here are the keys."

"Where's your Volkswagen?"

"We parked that near South Gate."

"I was told that one of the cars was a right-off, but not which one."

"Obviously, the wires got crossed somewhere along the way."

When 'Hands to Dinner' was piped, LS Murphy was fully dressed in uniform and had been given permission from the OOD to proceed ashore for an hour to check his wrecked car.

He arrived back at the ship forty-five minutes later and was furious. He went straight to One Mess where he found Scott and Herbie telling their messmates about the incident. Upon entering the mess he yelled, "You Sons of Bitches, you wrote off the Volkswagen. There's nothing wrong with the Dodge. I gave up my tot just to go up and find a perfectly good Dodge!"

"So we played a joke on you, but that was nothing compared to what we did to the hitch hiker – another Navy guy – who rolled my Volks," and went on to tell him.

Murphy laughed and said, "You guys are bad to the core. And thanks for picking up the Dodge for me," adding, "When you're old enough to draw your tots each of you owe me one."

"HANDS TO STATIONS for leaving harbour." The date was 12th September 1965. All Able Seamen and Ordinary Seamen of the Sonar department ran up to the quarterdeck dressed in their number 3 uniforms. They all wore a knife and spike in a leather sheath on a narrow rope around their waists.

The Kootenay, being the senior of the three ships that would sail away that day, was the first to let go all lines and back out into the centre of the harbour. Once there, she turned sharply to port and pulled away slowly, allowing enough room for the Saguenay and Nipigon to follow. When they were all in the middle of the harbour Kootenay led the way and the other two followed her past downtown Halifax. All seamen on the upper deck stood in a single rank until the ship was well past Georges Island.

The voyage across the Atlantic was uneventful. The Able and Ordinary Seamen stood a three watch system; each watch named after the colours of the Union Jack. On 21st September the three ships entered the English Channel and hugged the coast of England. At 0800 Scott and Herbie were standing at 'Hands Fall In' on the quarterdeck and could see the White Cliffs of Dover on the Port beam.

# Sixteen

**HANDS TO STATIONS** for entering harbour was announced at sixteen hundred and again all the Sonarmen ran up to the quarterdeck. The Kootenay was secured alongside in Chatham by eighteen hundred, with Nipigon and Saguenay alongside her.

It was a Thursday evening and Scott and Herbie, both being tired after standing the middle watch and morning watches ((0000-0400 & 0400-0800) decided to remain onboard that night to catch a good night of shut-eye. They'd take a train to London the next evening. It was only about 40 miles away.

So they boarded a train at 1700 on Friday evening along with many other sailors of surface ships and the submarine – Ojibwa. There were about six stops along the way, and just before the train stopped at each station an elderly gentleman sitting on a stool would announce its name twice over a broadcast system. As they were about to enter a town called Higham, all seamen onboard stuck their heads out the window and yelled, "Who's the most rotten 'Son of a Bitch' in town?

When the old man announced the name Higham with a strong Kent accent it sounded like *"I am; I am."* Some of the insults were much worse than SOB.

Herbie and Scott laughed all the way to the next station; Scott finally said, "We must remember to do that tomorrow."

"I don't think we'll have to remember, with all these others onboard," replied Herbie.

At 1730 they stepped out of Charing Cross Railway Station and found themselves on what was called 'The Mall'. They had heard of a seedy part of London called Soho[1] and decided to go there, so they asked a gentleman who was walking his dog for directions.

"Decent young men like you seem to be should stay away from there. It's full of brothels, dirty bars, foul-mouthed men and women, pimps and pick-pockets."

"This is our first visit to England and you might even want to call us tourists," replied Herbie. "Some of our older shipmates told us to have a look and we'd just like to see it. That's all."

"Then the only advice I can give you is to keep your peckers in your pants. You're headed in the right direction. Ask someone else in about fifteen minutes." He then walked away with his dog in tow.

Herbie thought *'pecker in your pants'* was a rather rude use of words from what seemed to be a gentleman.

Within two minutes the two young sailors found themselves on the south side of a large square with a sign indicating it was 'Trafalgar Square'. There was a tall pillar in the centre with a figure of a man on top.

An educated looking young man was walking in the opposite direction and Herbie excused himself saying, "Excuse me, but do you have time to tell us who that man on the top of the pillar is and why this square is named Trafalgar?"

"Of course, the figure on top is a likeness of Admiral Lord Nelson who commanded the fleet of the Royal Navy in the 1805 Battle of Trafalgar... In essence, twenty-seven British ships under the command of Admiral Nelson aboard his flagship HMS Victory defeated the combined fleet of thirty-three French and Spanish ships in the Atlantic Ocean off the southwest coast of Spain, just west of Cape Trafalgar. The Franco-Spanish fleet lost twentytwo ships and those still afloat were captured. Not a single British vessel was lost. It was the most decisive naval battle of the war, conclusively ending French intentions of invading England in the Napoleonic Wars. Lord Nelson was killed by a sniper's bullet during the battle. His body was brought back to London and was buried at St. Paul's Cathedral."..."If your ship is ever in Portsmouth, HMS Victory is still afloat and open to visitors. Free guided tours are given."

"Thanks for your informative lesson on our British heritage. My grandfather was born in Barnstaple, North Devon and was from a cattle-breeding family. I assume your heritage is British too Scott."

"Yes, many generations ago, but I don't know from which part."

"Would you please direct us to Soho," asked Herbie.

"Yes; do you see that tall building down the way on the other side? You just turn left there and walk for five minutes and you'll be in the heart of it, but be careful."

"Thanks for everything," said Herbie as he and Scott carried on. Within fifteen minutes they were in the thick of it and it was everything the man with the dog had described.

It seemed as though every tenth door had a red light above it and a sign that read 'Model Upstairs' rather than 'Prostitute Upstairs'. With the red light, nobody needed a clarification. They walked into a bar named *'The Cork Screw'*. It was packed with scruffy-looking working class men with greasy coveralls and filthy hands.

The boys sat at a table and asked the waiter for two pints of bitters. They didn't really know what 'bitters' was, but had heard it was a type of beer. They discovered their assumption was correct when the waiter returned with two pints and placed them on the table.

Hookers walked amongst the tables. One stopped at the table of the young Able Seamen[2] and asked, "Are you looking for a little pleasurable fun upstairs tonight fellows? Some clientele of the *Cork Screw* say I'm the best of the lot."

"That may be so Miss, but we won't be one of them, because we won't be putting you to the test." ... "How much do you charge anyway?" asked Herbie with no intention of accepting whatever she offered; "*Granddad is watching – Granddad is watching*".

"Only five pounds," she said.

*"Five pounds?"* exclaimed Herbie. "We're low ranking sailors; not the Admiral of the Fleet. That's way beyond our budgets."

Two Leading Seamen with Nipigon cap tallies walked in and sat at another table. They too ordered beer. Herbie and Scott smiled as one of the Nipigon killicks[3] left with the same hooker who had approached them. He returned to his buddy in 15 minutes with a smile on his face and gave him a 'thumbs up' sign. His friend promptly got up and left with the same 'woman of the night'. She didn't return that evening.

"Maybe she earned enough for a week-long vacation in a single night," said Scott.

They left the *Cork Screw* bar shortly after and checked out a couple of others that were much the same, and departed for Charring Cross railway station at 2200. None of the sailors onboard the train stuck their heads out of the window while passing Higham; most were asleep.

Both Herbie and Scott were in their bunks and asleep by 0015 in the early morning of 23rd September.

'WACKIE WACKIE; Hands to breakfast was piped over the main broadcast at 0700 on Tuesday morning. All crew members climbed from their bunks, wrapped a towel around their waists, donned their flip-flops and headed for the washplaces, where most had a quick shower, and all had a shave and brushed their teeth. They then returned to their mess-decks, dressed, and went for breakfast.

The ships companies of all three surface ships and crew members of Ojibwa were fallen in on the jetty by 1045 on the morning of 23rd September. All were dressed in their number one uniforms with gold-coloured rank badges, trade patches on their upper left arms, and Canada flashes at shoulder level on the tops of their jacket or jumper sleeves – suit jackets for P1s and above, and typical sailor uniforms for P2s and below. All shoes were spit polished for the occasion.

The ceremony went off flawlessly. The last act was to blow the 'still' on the bos'n pipe. All crews came to attention as the Canadian National ensign was raised on staff on the after part of the casing (quarter-deck on surface ships) and the Jack; also the Canadian ensign, was raised on the jack-staff on the bow. Finally the Commissioning Pennant was raised on a small staff on the conning tower at mid ships.

After all ships' companies had returned to their ships, leave was piped. Both Herbie and Scott were on the 1200 train back to London with about a hundred other sailors. There wasn't enough room for either of them to stick their heads out of the window and holler insults to the poor old man at Higham – all windows were occupied by other heads.

"PRIME MINISTER HAROLD WILSON has invited the two of us to tea at 3 pm," said Scott to the bobby standing to the right of the door of 10 Downing Street.

"If he did, he probably meant at his country estate in Kent, because that is where he is at the moment.

"Damn," said Scott, "we should have hopped off the train on the way up from Chatham this morning."

"Get out of here you fools. The prime minister mixes with admirals. He doesn't mix with ordinary seamen."

"The next time I'm talking to our admiral, I'll ask him to give Mr. Wilson a scolding; and by the way, we're not ordinary seamen; we're *Able Seamen*!"

"*I said 'Get out of here*!"

They said "Bye Bye," walked out of Downing Street with smiles on their faces and onto Parliament Street to the point where they had turned right when they had encountered Downing Street. Within five minutes they could see Big Ben – their original destination. As they advanced they could see the British Parliament Buildings attached to the Big Ben fourfaced clock tower.

Scott said, "If anyone ever says something bad about Big Ben we can say, 'At least it's not two-faced like you'."

They went across the road and gazed at the Gothic structure where history had been made when Sir Winston Churchill had made his *'this was their finest hour'* speech in 1940, amongst other historic events like granting independence to India and the creation of Pakistan. Their backs were facing a river. They turned and looked at the small craft passing by in different directions.

A gentleman was walking by and Herbie said, "Excuse me Sir, is that the River Thames?

"No," replied the man while smiling, "it's the Seine."

"Where's the Thames then? I thought it ran through London.

"It's behind you," replied the man and walked away, while Herbie stood there scratching his head.

Scott said, "The man was just pulling your leg. The Seine is in France and runs through Paris."

"He must have thought I was a dumbbell."

"Was he wrong?"

"Let's walk downstream and see Tower Bridge. We'll just hug the bank of the river and I estimate it'll be about a forty-five minute walk." Scott was carrying a tourist guide book of London with a fold out map. "I'm sure you'll recognize it from the movies or pictures you've seen of London."

The walk was shorter than Scott had predicted; it was in sight within fifteen minutes. It was the tallest bridge under which boats or ships with tall masts could advance up the Thames. The others upstream from Tower Bridge were arched and closer to the waterline. London Bridge was one of them, but quite a distance away.

"Let's walk to the centre once we're there," said Herbie.

"OK."

Once in the centre they observed pleasure craft and fishing boats returning to home port as dusk had fallen.

They walked up to SOHO when the street lights came on and into a bar called 'The Wood Eye & Hare Lip Pub'. After the waiter had dropped their pints of bitters at their table Scott asked him, "How on earth did this pub get its name?"

The waiter looked around and said, "It's not too busy yet so I guess I have time to explain...The original owner lost an eye in the First World War. When he returned to Britain he didn't have enough money to purchase a glass eye, so he went to great pains to make himself a round wooden eye. But it was quite noticeable that it was wooden and not glass."

"Yes," said Scott, "but where does the Hare Lip fit into the picture?"

"Wait for it," replied the waiter. "He lived up in Selby in county Yorkshire. On the annual harvest festival weekend, there was a dance in his town. The man went to the dance but none of the women would dance with him and he supposed it was due to his wooden eye.

So he walked around the hall looking for a woman with a facial defect and saw a woman sitting alone. She had a hare lip. The man said to himself *'ah ha, she'll most likely dance with me'* and walked up to her. He said, 'Would you like to dance Miss?' and she exclaimed 'Would I? Would I?' our hero then yelled 'Hare lip! Hare lip!' and walked away"…"And when he came to London he gave the pub its name."[4]

"Ha! Ha!" said Scott, "We've gotta remember that one as a joke at tot time tomorrow."

"I don't start drawing my tot until the 28th but I guess I can sit there and listen while you tell it. The 28th is the day we sail for Amsterdam."

The next day when Scott told the 'wood eye – hare lip' story to their messmates Freddie Molyeneaux said, "That's an old joke I have heard a million times. Either the waiter was spoofing you, or he was told it when he started working there and he believed it."

The Onondaga was launched on 27th September. Herbie was happy to miss it because it meant he didn't have to get all dressed up for the ceremony. He was bosn's mate on the gangway – in other words the Corporal of the Gangway's *gofer*.

The next day, 28th September, was Herbie's 20th birthday. That meant he'd be eligible to draw his first tot (Navy rum). It was also announced that the ship would slip (sail) at 1300; high tide.

At 'Hands to Muster for Grog', all Leading Seamen and below lined up in the flats and the large bucket of rum was placed in front of the Regulating Office. The junior Officer of the Watch and Cox'n[5] stood by while a Storesman dipped a small brass cup large enough to hold 2.5 ounces into the recipient's tot mug. The recipient was required to mix Coke or water into his mug before walking away. If he wanted to drink it straight he had to do so before walking away, as storage of rum was forbidden.

Herbie stood in the line, and when it was his turn he proudly announced "Elliot, 62436-H" (his official number). As the Storesman poured the rum into Herbie's mug the Cox'n, knowing it was his first said, "Happy birthday Elliot and be careful; remember, we sail at 1300."

"Thank you Cox'n. I will."

Herbie, however, wasn't careful. As he sat around the settee with his messmates they all poured a little of their tot into Herbie's mug. Scott, his best friend, acted as his Rum Bos'n. He took a large empty mug around the ship to all mess-decks of other Leading Seamen and below and collected a contribution for Herbie's 20th birthday.

Herbie had changed into his number 3 uniform prior to drawing his tot in case he was rushed when 'Hands to Stations...was piped.

When it *was* announced he was in no condition to work. He arrived at the quarterdeck singing the filthy sailor's song. As soon as Petty Officer Cole the quarterdeck PO saw him he said, "Get that fool outta here"

Scott grabbed Herbie by the arm and said, "You're in no shape to be of assistance today Herbie," but Herbie resisted until he saw PO Cole approaching.

He yelled *"Get below Elliot or I'll charge you – birthday or not."*

Scott took him back to the mess and stuffed him behind the great-coat hanger and out of sight. He said, "Sleep it off Herbie. Don't come out until supper. I'll come for you." He then returned to the quarterdeck. So the squadron sailed out of Chatham and into the English Channel.

At 1645 Scott and a few others dragged Herbie out. He had vomited all over the deck and his uniform. They helped him undress and struggled to get him up to the top bunk (the highest of three). He fell back asleep immediately. His buddies threw his soiled uniform on the winch in the cable deck – the next compartment.

The squadron entered Amsterdam three days later. Herbie didn't know it at the time, but this was where his natural father – William Cunningham – had been repatriated with Canadian troops that had played a crucial role in liberating Amsterdam.

While the quarterdeck party was fallen in prior to entering the final leg of their transit, Herbie asked Buck Taylor[6] who was standing beside him if he knew why Ottawa had so many tulips in the spring.

Buck said, "I guess they just like tulips."

Herbie replied, "Buckie, you don't know your arse from a hole in the ground. One million tulip bulbs have arrived in Ottawa every year since 1947 as a thank you gift to Canadians for giving the Dutch Royal Family refuge during the last war and declaring the hospital room where Princess Margriet was born in 1943, as Netherlands soil."

"Thank you Herbie" said Buck, "now I can ask the same questions and give the same answer to others."

Prior to arrival in Amsterdam it was announced it would be a four-day visit and there'd be 48 hour leave periods for each of the two watches – Port & Starboard. Herbie was on the Port watch and Scot was on the Starboard. The Port watch would be the first. Herbie and two other friends of the Port watch – Brian Jackson and Gerry Dean – went ashore together. They rented a room for one night at the Grand Hotel Krasnapolsky, located in the heart of the city. On the last day of their leave they'd sleep back on board to save the expense of the hotel. After checking in they walked into a side street and entered a pub. They received a warm welcome from both staff and patrons alike.

Of course, it had only been 22 years since Canadian troops had liberated Amsterdam in World War II and the Canada flashes on the boy's shoulders identified their nationality – the Dutch had long memories of the horrors they suffered and the feelings of relief when they saw friendly troops arrive.

All three of the fellows ordered Heineken beer, which elder sailors had told them about. The bartender said, "The first one is on the house."

Ten minutes later everyone in the pub including the bartender cheered. Herbie asked the bartender, "What were you cheering about, what just happened?"

The bartender said, "The toilets are located upstairs. Turn around and you'll see a circular staircase." Herbie and the others turned. "Some patrons choose to slide down the railing and one just did. Everybody likes it when they see it done…and more importantly to me, that staircase brings in more patrons than any other pub on this street."

Herbie, Brian and Gerry all turned to watch for men going upstairs. The bartender noticed and said, "Just carry on as normal. I'll let you know when someone's about to do it."

The fellows turned their heads back towards the bar and engaged in light conversation. A couple of other men accomplished the feat while they chatted. They cheered along with the others when it happened.

Then after Herbie's second Heineken he had to go upstairs to use the toilet. He climbed the circular staircase and did his business. He emerged from the hallway and onto the top of the staircase, and yelled, *"Here I go!"* He then hoisted himself up onto the railing spread his arms for balancing and let gravity take effect. He zipped down the railing and landed in a heap on the floor of the barroom, much to the delight of all patrons.

A few people helped him to get up. Fortunately he hadn't broken any bones, although one elbow hurt. After he sat back down with his two mates he asked the bartender, "Did I do it wrong?"

"Yes, watch the next person do it. He'll use one hand in front to hold the rail and slow down the speed and the other hand behind to keep himself from falling backwards." Sure enough, the bartender was correct. The speed of descent was much slower than Herbie's had been.

While they were drinking their third beer the waiter asked, "Have you visited the red light district yet?"

Herbie said, "No we haven't. Tell us a little more about it."

"It's just one narrow lane lined with women in the windows on both sides. Some sit smiling invitingly at observers; some stroll around in their enclosures while slowly manoeuvring their arms and bodies in sensuous gestures of pleasure. If a customer does enter, the woman simply draws the curtain and they do their business on the bed. Some locals call it a disgusting part of Amsterdam even though it is a great tourist attraction. Some tour busses even stop there for 30 minutes for people to have a look. The women don't even mind being photographed."

"Do you guys wanna have a look?" asked Gerry.

"It sounds as though it's worth a look" said Herbie…"but I ain't gonna lose my virginity to no hooker…I may not be a virgin when I marry, if ever I do, but it won't be no prostitute."

"Where's it located asked Brian?"

"It's down the street that ends at your hotel. So just turn right when you reach that street and walk for about eight blocks. You'll find it on the right – can't miss it."

"Let's have one more," said Gerry, "and head that way."

"Ok," said Herbie, "and before we go I'm going to take another crack at that stairway."

"Fellows, are you off again tomorrow?"

"Yes, tomorrow is the second day of our 48 hour leave period," said Brian.

"Then I propose you take a canal cruise of historic Amsterdam. It'll cost less than 5 dollars, and it will be money well spent. Ask for one that passes Anne Frank House. Afterwards come in here and tell me what you thought of it."

"Thanks Sir," said Herbie, "but before we go, my bladder is full again, so I'll make another attempt at that railing when finished."

So up he went and when finished at the urinal he exited onto the platform before the staircase. He hoisted himself onto the railing, placed his left hand in front and his right hand behind – both holding the railing. He then let himself go; it was almost flawless except for the fact that halfway down he almost lost his balance. Had he, he would have fallen backwards onto the table below. Those who had witnessed his first attempt cheered the loudest.

The bartender had given them directions so the fellows walked the ten blocks down to the red light district. It was everything the bartender had described and even more. Gerry drew the attention of his two mates to a big fat transvestite with a five o'clock shadow sitting on an armchair beside his bed. He smiled at the fellows and pushed his right cheek in and out several times by using his stiff tongue, and afterwards licked his lips. The young men laughed and moved on – *Granddad is watching Herbie.*

The next morning they rose and after breakfast asked the travel desk how they could take a canal cruise; they emphasised the one that passed Anne Frank House. It was only a ten minute taxi ride to the starting point. Once onboard, they marvelled as the canal tourist craft winded its way through a portion of the long waterway. When they passed Anne Frank House the guide told them the diary of Anne Frank was retrieved by a man named Miep Gies in 1945 after the war ended. Mr. Gies gave it to Anne's father, Otto Frank, the family's only known survivor. The book was initially published in the Netherlands under the Dutch name which when translated meant '*The Diary of a Young Girl*'; when published in the mid-fifties in New York, it was renamed '*The Diary of Anne Frank*'.

In the afternoon they took a historical bus tour. As they passed the English Reformed Church the guide told everyone that in fact it was part of the Church of Scotland, and one of the oldest buildings in Amsterdam. It was situated in the Begijnhof, right in the heart of the city. The bus stopped at Waag, built as part of the city's fortifications between 1481 and1494; it was later a weighing house, now a cafe and museum. The guide said there'd be half an hour to walk around to explore, or to have a snack. Coster Diamonds, one of the oldest diamond polishing factories in the Netherlands, was the next major point of interest – not for all people on the bus, but certainly for the three young sailors. Again, the bus stopped and all occupants went inside to watch craftsmen at their machinery.

When the tour ended they went back to the pub with the circular staircase and told the bartender their thoughts about the red light district and how they had spent the remainder of the day. They had a couple more beers and as dusk was turning to night they walked back to the ship.

Upon arrival, Scott was bosn's-mate on the brow. Herbie told him where they had stayed and what they had seen and done; especially emphasizing the bar with the circular staircase.

The morning after the starboard watch returned from their 48 hour leave period the squadron sailed for their home port of Halifax, arriving during the last week of October. There was a two-week Anti-Submarine Warfare (ASW) exercise in November using the Ojibwa in real life conditions. The squadron remained in Halifax and Christmas and New Year's leave started at the end of December. The Port watch got Xmas leave which only lasted a week.

## Notes

1. A fashionable part of London nowadays.
2. Ordinary Seamen were automatically promoted to Able Seamen after 18 months of service.
3. A Leading Seaman's rank badge was a killick – an anchor with two hooks facing outward. Sometimes Leading Seamen were called Hookies.
4. Adopted from an old joke – author unknown.
5. Coxswain– equivalent to Army Regimental Sergeant Major.
6. For some unbeknownst reason, all men whose last name was Taylor were given the nickname of Buck.

# Seventeen

**THE WHOLE CANADIAN FLEET** sailed southward during the second week of January 1966 under the command of the much loved Rear Admiral William Landymore OBE, CD. He was a World War II veteran who, as a junior officer, had survived the sinking of two ships – HMCS Fraser & HMCS Margaree – one due to collision and the other by torpedo. Afterwards, he had advanced through the ranks between the 1950s and 1960s and he was eventually promoted to Rear Admiral[1] and commanded the entire Canadian Fleet – on both the East and West coasts.

The east coast ships and the submarine Ojibwa advanced slowly to various islands in the Caribbean and West Indies. The aircraft carrier HMCS Bonaventure and the tanker Provider berthed in San Juan, Puerto Rico; a deep water port. The Kootenay's port visit was to Kings Town, Saint Vincent an island in the British West Indies. The west coast ships and submarine Grilse passed through the Panama Canal and dispersed to other islands. The main purpose of these visits was to paint the ships, as it was too cold to do so in the Canadian winter.

The Kootenay berthed with its port side to the jetty. Shortly after securing alongside young men and boys dived into the water, swam to the starboard side of the quarterdeck and urged the fellows to throw coins. Once a coin was thrown they'd dive under the surface and rise while holding it above their head in triumph.

Herbie said, "My Mom and Dad had told us kids about this when they returned from their honeymoon cruise to Haiti."

"Your mother and father had children before they married?" asked Scott.

"It's a long story Scott and I'll tell you it some other time and place; now let's throw coins."

The number of coin throwers thinned down to zero after their pockets were empty.

The first day in port was a Saturday and the ship's company (crew) was given leave on arrival. On Sunday there would be leave after cleaning stations were completed and on Monday they'd get down to scraping loose paint off the decks and start painting them plus the ship's sides. Herbie, Scott, Buck Taylor and Dan Boone walked down the gangway and strolled along the road. They only wore their bells and gun-shirts; plus their caps as it was too warm to wear jumpers in the south. This would be the dress code in all ports of the cruise.

The fellows saw two dark overweight resident women walking towards them from the other direction. When they met Scott said, "Hello ladies, where can we find a good bar?"

One replied, "Hail a taxi and we'll take you to one."

Once they were all packed in a taxi and it was advancing down the road they saw a stoker from the Kootenay by the name of Alex Woodcock walking along. Herbie stuck his head out the window and cried, "Hey Woodcock!" Both girls giggled while repeating *'wood cock', 'wood cock'* over and over again.

They arrived at a bar on the other side of the island. It was situated at the top of a 20 yard incline ending at a small beach. They all ordered Budweiser – an American beer. It didn't live up to the standard of Canadian beer, but it served its purpose.

Herbie and Scott had taken their bathing suits and towels in one issue attaché bag in case the bar was at a beach. Since it was, in the late afternoon they went down to the beach for a swim. They went into the shrubbery and changed and took turns guarding their uniforms – the last thing they wanted was to have their wallets and contents of their pockets stolen; especially their identification cards. After an hour of swimming dusk was falling and they returned to the bar.

As they entered the two women they had picked up along the way walked over to them and one asked, "Would the two of you like to go back to the beach and have some fun – if you know what I mean?" Both fellows knew what she *did* mean and declined.

"Let's order two bottles of Bud without glasses and walk down to the beach again. It's a wonderful moonlit night," Herbie said, Scott agreed, so down they went for the second time.

A half hour later when they'd finished their beers and were about to go back up to the bar Scott tapped Herbie on the shoulder and whispered, "Look over there. Buckie is humping one of the bar girls."

Sure enough his silhouette was seen clearly on the side of the slope. Herbie whispered, "Let's go over; sneak up behind him, and steal his pants."

Scott covered his mouth so Buckie wouldn't hear him laughing and when he recovered, crept along the beach parallel to Buckie's position and snuck up behind him, tickled his knackers, grabbed his bells and knickers, and crept back down the slope. They walked back to the path leading to the building. Upon entering the bar Scott walked quickly to the bartender and passed Buck's pants and underwear to him, and told him to make the owner come to him to fetch them.

Ten minutes later Buck walked in, naked from the waist down with the exception for his socks and boots. He yelled, "Where are my pants?"

The girl he was with, who couldn't have been a day older than 18, was walking behind him yelling *"I want my money!"*

Once Buck had finished putting on his knickers and bells all the fellows left the bar and climbed into a waiting taxi. While it was moving away, the poor girl ran beside the car pleading for her money. Herbie yelled, *"Stop this taxi."* The driver jammed on the breaks and the girl was still yelling in the open back window. Herbie then said, "Pay the poor thing Buckie." The others agreed. Buckie begrudgingly reached into his pocket and dug out five dollars, the agreed upon amount and passed it to her.

The girl had the courtesy to say 'Thank you'.

THE NEXT DAY, being Monday, all non-engineering hands got to work painting the upperdeck and ship's sides. While they painted a local band played traditional West Indies music on the jetty near the quarterdeck. When 'Hands to Dinner,' was piped they were served dinner in the main cafeteria. The corporal of the gangway and boatswain's mate watched over the instruments, which had been laid on the jetty. In the afternoon they played for donations. By the end of the week they had earned a good week's pay.

They finished the paint job by Friday and the ship would sail on Sunday morning. On Saturday afternoon Herbie, Scott and Brian Jackson went ashore and told a taxi to take them to a good beach. Thankfully they didn't arrive at the same one where they had stolen Buck's pants.

They did arrive at a beach where they saw a bunch of about fifty black local girls jumping around in a state of excitement. A white British policeman was standing back watching and when they emerged from the taxi they walked over to him. Scott asked, "What are all the jungle-bunnies so excited about?"

"John Lennon and Ringo Starr of the Beatles will be arriving soon. They'll be going over to Young Island for a vacation with their partners or wives," he replied. He then pointed to the island about a quarter of a mile off the coast. Scott and Brian went to the crowd, and tried to get in position for a glimpse of the two superstars of the rock world when they arrived.

*'They won't see a thing,'* thought Herbie. He then assessed the situation and saw a threefoot wide wharf with a motorboat tied up on the right hand side. *'That must be their mode of transportation'.* He then walked onto the wharf and stationed himself halfway between the boat and the shore and watched for the arrival. When they did arrive he saw them approaching the wharf and turned with his back to them pretending he was indifferent. He then felt a tap on his shoulder. He turned. It was John Lennon. He said, "Excuse us please."

Herbie turned around and pretended to be surprised and said, "Yes, certainly John."

"Thank you," said Lennon as he, Ringo and a couple of women followed. Herbie was the closest anyone in the crowd ever got to the two famous rock stars, due to policemen bearing batons clearing the way through the crowd of excited young women.

'*SHELLBACKS* AND *'POLLIWOGS'* were nautical names of those who had or had not crossed the Equator. From the names, it's not hard to recognize which was which.

After leaving the Caribbean, the flotilla formed up and sailed southward. Three days later was the day they would cross the Equator. The shipwrights and bos'ns had created a square canvas tub on the covers of the mortar well and filled it with salt water. Slimy gash from the galley was also inserted and well-mixed in. There was a specially-built chair with a back to rest on, but no back legs hinged up on a lengthwise round pole that stretched across the forward end of the tub.

It was functional at 1000 and after that, all Shellbacks chased the Polliwogs around the ship and dragged them up to the quarterdeck. Then one after one the Polliwogs officially became Shellbacks after being dipped backwards into the slimy water; all were wearing their bathing suits to save having to wash their work clothes afterwards. Once initiated, they began chasing other Polliwogs.

An announcement was made over the ship's main broadcast system: "The Captain will become a Shellback in five minutes." The whole ship's company went up to observe their captain being dipped into the slime, after which he too got into the act. Being inaugurated as an official Shellback he grabbed a young Able Seaman with a dry bathing suit and dragged him to the slime-tub. Laughter and cheering broke out. Everyone liked Captain Pratt.

There was a banyan on the quarterdeck that evening; barbequed hamburgers were served. Fellows from some mess decks had guitars and they played them when members of their mess decks sang. All messes took their turns singing. Great fun was had that evening.

"LOOK, THERE'S SUGARLOAF Mountain," cried Herbie as the flotilla was approaching Rio de Janeiro, "and look at that pinnacle-shaped mountain with what appears to be a statue of a cross on top."

"That's not a cross Herbie," replied Scott, "it's *'Christ the Redeemer'* with arms outstretched."

"Where did you learn all this stuff Scott?"

"Grade 12 that you missed out on attending."

"Go ahead Scott, rub it in. Is Rio the capital of Brazil?"

"No, the capital is Brasilia located to the northeast."

***A portion of the fleet in Rio de Janeiro – Bonaventure on right, three destroyers with three in front of them on left, and two submarines at end of jetty.***

As the fleet entered the port it was strange that one thing in particular caught Herbie's attention. The balconies of almost all residences in ten-story apartment blocks lining the waterfront had laundry hanging from the railings of their balconies. *'I guess it makes sense,'* he thought, *'where else can they dry it?'*

Once all the ships and submarines were berthed in the port, shore leave was granted. It would be a six day visit with every afternoon off. Herbie and his friends wore their bathing suits under their bells and carried their towels. They went to Copacabana beach they had heard so much about. It was wonderful – swimming in the salty water that goes with it. Afterward they sat on the patio of a sidewalk bar. When they ordered a 40 ounce bottle of Bacardi dark rum, the price of $1.50 surprised them. It would have cost a great deal more in Halifax.

A tour was laid on for all Canadian sailors who wanted to see the statue of *'Christ the Redeemer'* up close. They were forewarned there'd be a long climb up a stairway from the train at the base of the pinnacle. Herbie and his friends opted out and continued to go the Copacabana instead.

A MAJOR EMBARASSMENT to Admiral Landymore, Captain Pratt and the Canadian public in general took place while the fleet was in Rio.

One morning a load of newspapers were delivered to the gangway head of each ship of the fleet. The front page featured a picture of two Canadian sailors wearing shaggy blond wigs and acting drunk. The caption below the photo was written in Portuguese but had the English translation below: *'Two Canadian sailors make complete fools of themselves on the streets of Rio'.* The second Officer of the Day was at the gangway when the newspapers arrived and immediately took one up to the Captain's cabin.

When Captain Pratt saw the photo he turned to his steward and said, "Topley, do you recognise the two men in this photo?

"Yes Sir," said Topley, "they are Able Seamen Elliot and Hunter; both Sonarmen on the Kootenay."

The captain took the speaker of the ship's broadcast system located in his cabin and piped, "The weapon's officer is requested to the captain's cabin."

The operations officer arrived before the weapons officer and passed a message to his captain. It read, "The captain on whose ship those two sailors on the front page of the newspaper are on is to report to Admiral Landymore on the Bonaventure with an explanation of the circumstances as soon as possible."

After the weapons officer arrived, both Elliot and Hunter were piped to the captain's cabin. They both arrived at the same time and were told to enter."

Captain Pratt showed the lads the newspaper and said, "The admiral is furious and has ordered me to report to him with an explanation. What have you got to say for yourselves?"

Herbie spoke first. "Well Sir; Hunter and I were walking down a street yesterday morning minding our own business when a fellow holding a camera walked up to us. He passed us those wigs, and asked us to put them on and wrap our arms around each other's shoulders. He said he'd take a picture of us, and send it to us in the morning. Thinking it was harmless we complied. But after we passed the wigs back to him he ran off saying, *'I am from the communist newspaper'*. We chased him with intentions of opening his camera and destroying the film reel, but when we were within yards of catching him he jumped into the back seat of a waiting car and it sped off."

The captain said, "That picture is not only on the cover of one newspaper in Rio, but on the cover of all major newspapers in Canada ... You both can leave now."

Commander Pratt then walked rapidly down the gangway of Kootenay and a hundred yards or so to the Bonaventure. He reported to the Admiral who was waiting impatiently. Pratt explained what he had been told by the two culprits and the admiral seemed to be satisfied saying, "They were victims of Communist trickery. No charges are to be laid against the lads"... "Now I must send a message to Paul Hellyer.[2] He's been hounding me every hour since the news broke in Canada. He will then pass it on to Prime Minister Pearson."

THE FLEET SAILED from Rio de Janeiro on Sunday morning. As the Kootenay passed the two major attractions of the port Herbie said to Scott, "I wish I had taken that tour to 'Christ the Redeemer' statue, especially since my granddad had taught me everything – from birth to death – of Jesus Christ."

Scott didn't reply.

It took the fleet five days to reach Buenos Aires, Argentina. The Bonaventure and Provider berthed to the deep water port of Montevideo, Uruguay. Buenos Aires was a boring port for young sailors and Herbie and his pals simply went bar-hopping. The only great laughter Herbie and the others really got was a night when they were in a bar with a mixed male/female toilet.

Halfway through the evening Buckie said, "I've gotta drop a leak," and walked into the toilet.

When he emerged, the whole front of his uniform was soaking wet.

His friends all enquired, "What in the devil happened to you?"

"I don't know," replied Buck, "When I entered, another man was using the toilet so I used the urinal. When finished, for some strange reason the flusher was a step lever of the floor. I stepped on it and a fountain of water shot up and drenched me.

"Take us all in and show us so we understand."

Buck took them back and showed them. Norm Powell said, "That thing is a bidet for women to clean their pussies you idiot." They all laughed at poor Buckie again.

SANTOS, BRAZIL was Kootenay's next port. She and two other ships from the fleet visited Santos after leaving Buenos Aires. The remaining ships visited other ports along the coast of Brazil. Le Guaira, the seaport of the Venezuelan capital Caracas, high in the hills, would be the last foreign port of the historic voyage.

In Santos there wasn't much to see or do, but there was a wonderful beach similar to Copacabana. That's where Herbie and his chums went every day. On the first evening, after their daytime swimming, they sat at a patio bar and ordered a 40 ounce bottle of Bacardi dark. The price was $1.50; the same as in Rio.

On the second night at the same bar, however, when they ordered their rum the waiter rather sheepishly said, "I'm sorry, but last night we made a mistake. The price is supposed to be $3.00." These were innocent young Canadians who were used to fair play and honesty.

They had never heard the term 'Third World'. Cheating to them meant peaking while playing hide and seek.

They simply said, "Set 'em up!" Either the waiter pocketed the extra buck fifty or gave it to his head waiter nobody knew. But anyway...That night there was a table next to them where four men and one woman sat chatting and laughing. It wasn't long before the woman walked the short distance to the table of the fellows and said, "Would you like to join us," in perfect English. They boys moved their chairs around the large round table and as it just so happened, Herbie sat beside the woman. She introduced herself as 'Diva Porshat de Assis', an English teacher from Brasilia spending time in Santos during her summer vacation. She was staying with one of the men.

By the gestures and tones of speech of the men it didn't take long for Herbie to suspect something strange about the men. Then it dawned on him. He leaned over to Scott and whispered, "They're all queers." (In the sixties the word 'Gay' meant happy.)

"Don't you mean 'homos'?" asked Scott.

"I'm not talking about milk types Scott. I'm talking about these men."

"Where have you been all your life Herb?…"Homo is also short for 'homosexual' and yes, I suspect they are; but 'queers' is the most popular word used by sailors."

So 'They're all queers,*'* was passed around to the others one by one. And it didn't take long before their suspicions were realized when one of the men asked, "Which one of you has the longest penis?" Brian Jackson, for some strange reason pointed to Herbie. Actually, he should have pointed to Scott who had the longest.

The man asked "How long is it?"

Herbie played along anyway and held his hand up about a yard higher than his crotch.

"How do you masturbate?" asked the man.

Again he played along by wrapping his hands around an imaginary fence post, and stroked it up and down a few times. Laughter erupted from all.

Herbie didn't notice a man sitting directly opposite him give Diva a weak nod.

When the bar was closing and the boys were getting ready to leave, Diva asked Herbie, "Would you like to spend the night with me? I'm staying with that fellow." She pointed at the man who had previously given her the unnoticed nod.

Herbie said, "Yes I would," and turned to his companions saying, "I'll see you guys in the morning."

*"WHY ARE YOU BACK so early Herbie?* What happened?" cried Scott as he was climbing into his bunk and saw Herbie climbing up the ladder into one mess.

The others heard the commotion and gathered around, as did all friends who knew nothing of what had taken place on their evening sortie.

Herbie cried, **"She was a wooden duck...a wooden duck!"**

"What the hell do you mean by 'wooden duck', Herbie?"

"You know, those things hunters put in ponds to attract real ducks."

"Those are called 'decoys', you dummy."

"Wooden duck; decoy; who cares...Scott, brief the other guys on what took place until I left with that woman and the milkman."

"Homo," said Scott

"Whatever, tell 'em!"

Scott briefed the others and when finished said, "Now tell all of us what happened next, and why you are back so early."

Herbie explained: "So the man drove me and Diva to his residence, and I followed Diva into her bedroom. She said, 'He has a young male 'keep' in his own bedroom'."

"We undressed and I lay on the bed first, but when Diva still had her panties and bra on she said, 'I must go to the toilet,' and left the room. Seconds later the *hoe-moe* entered the room, stark naked. He wasted no time in walking to the bed and lunging at my doniker. But I fought the good fight which ended with a guy lying on the floor writhing and crying after a swift kick to the knackers.

I dressed so quickly I didn't even put on my socks or undies. Look, they're stuffed in my cap. I ran from the apartment. I hustled to the street and hailed a taxi. Now, here I am."

All his friends laughed heartily and the next day it didn't take long before the story made its way around the whole lower decks. Even some of the officers heard it. The Weapons Officer asked if he'd be going back for more that night as he passed him in the flats.

The next evening Scott asked Herbie, "The same place tonight Herb?"

"No fuckin' way!"

That night was uneventful except that the bar they chose had a Brazilian band that mostly sang Beatles songs and American rock & roll music.

The ship sailed the next morning.

THE NIGHT PRIOR to entering Le Guaira, the seaport of Caracas, Captain Pratt addressed the ships company. His message was straight and to the point. "This is to inform all of you that 20 percent of the members of the ships company will be confined to ship when we arrive in port tomorrow because they are under treatment for gonorrhoea, and the majority of them are married. These people will be able to go ashore upon return home, because it will be cleared by then. However, since there's a 30 day confinement to ship period anyone who gets infected here in Venezuela will have to wait 2 weeks before being allowed ashore in Halifax. So for *God's sake*, remember your marriage vows."

The Executive Officer was the next to speak. He said, "We've been informed that the streets of Le Guaira are not entirely safe, so those remaining here for shore leave are advised to go ashore in groups; not singly. And if you choose to be such men as Captain Pratt just referred to; there are complimentary condoms available with the quartermaster as always." He paused for a moment before adding, "Further, there are buses laid on to take crew members of the fleet up the hills to the Caracas Sports Club, where they can take advantage of the swimming pool and other outside sporting facilities. Complimentary soft drinks will be served from the pool-side bar. There are outside washrooms and changing rooms available. The main club building is only for the use of members and officers."

"I don't know about you fellers, but I'm going up to Caracas Sports Club on one of the buses," said Herbie. "I've missed swimming in an outside pool since I joined, and I've had enough bar-hopping for this cruise"... "What about you guys?" he asked.

"Well, I came from a family of a working man who arrived home from work in coveralls every night. He supported my mother and seven kids so we didn't have the luxury of a backyard pool like you did Herbie," said Scott, "but I'm with you on that one."

All of their other friends agreed, but then started asking Herbie about his family life such as: how big was the pool; did it have a diving board; with wealth like that, why are you in the navy and not in university?

"Can we just drop the subject?" Herbie eventually said with a slight edge to his voice. They did.

Upon arrival the next morning sure enough eight buses were lined up on the jetty waiting to take loads of matelows up to the Caracas Sports Club. When secured alongside, Herbie and his pals rushed down to one mess and changed into their number two uniforms. Then they grabbed their bathing suits and towels and rushed to the brow where they had to line up in front of the Officer of the Day and ask, "Permission to go ashore Sir?" Once granted they ran to one of the busses. When the bus was fully loaded it pulled away.

After leaving the level ground of the port they started their climb upwards into the mountains. Venezuela was the richest country in

South America in the 1960s due to the oil in Lake Maracaibo. The road was thus wide and pothole free.

Herbie and most of his friends had never been driven up mountains; let alone seen one. The scenery was beautiful with green leafed trees, valleys with miniature lakes or ponds, far off mountain tops, plus small villages on narrow roadways here and there. The drive, at only 45 minutes, was too short for most of them; the bus soon entered the outskirts of the capital. Mountains could still be seen over the roof-tops, but the scenery was not the same.

They soon turned left and passed through the gated entrance of the club and all passengers were directed to the pool and sports area. Besides the pool there were badminton, tennis and volleyball courts. They spent most of their time swimming and sun-bathing, or sitting around tables sheltered from the sun by umbrellas and telling jokes.

On the first day Buckie pulled a 40 ounce bottle of rum he had smuggled onboard while in Santos and shared it with his buddies, who mixed it with the complimentary coke.

The next morning as Herbie was walking past the regulating office he heard the Cox'n yelling at an Able Seaman Storesman named Paul Bremner. He yelled, "Where were you last evening when 'Men under punishment to muster; Reg office flats,' was piped?"

"I was ashore Cox'n."

"Who gave you permission to go ashore?"

"Sub Lieutenant McNair, the Second Officer of the Day."

"The circumstances?"

"Well Cox'n; I lined up with the others to request permission to go ashore and he granted it"

"You pulled a 'swifty' on that young Sub Lieutenant. Your punishment was due to end the day before we sail Bremner, but I'm extending it by one day; so I hope you enjoyed yourself yesterday, because it was your last shore leave in this port."..."Further, I have a mind to formally charge you but I won't because it would get your victim, the incident Subbie[3] in the shit with the Executive Officer. Now get out of my sight."

Herbie and his friends continued to go to the Caracas Sports Club for the remainder of their visit to Le Guaira. The fleet sailed after the six-day visit and entered Halifax ten days later.

❄❄❄❄

"STOP IN THE NAME of the law," cried Herbie as he donned a policeman's cap and ran behind a cap-less Halifax cop chasing a black fellow northward on Gottingen St. The policeman finally gave up the chase and turned around to see Herbie wearing his cap.

Herbie stopped, removed the cap, and held it out saying, "Is this yours?"

The policeman said, "I thought *he* had it," and grabbed Herbie by the scruff of the neck and said, "You're under arrest!"

"What for? I found your cap and gave it back to you didn't I?"

"Drunkenness in a public place," replied the cop. He then started walking him back to the scene of the scuffle that had caused the cap to land at Herbie's feet. Other policemen were there including the dreaded Sgt. Bishop.

As they approached the scene of the fight, Herbie jerked his strong right arm up and released the cops grasp. He then started running southward past the dying down scuffle, while the original cop ran back to his Sergeant and told him what just had happened.

Herbie was almost up to Cogswell St. when they set out on the chase in a squad car. Sgt. Bishop was sitting in the front passenger seat. He saw Herbie turn right on Cogswell and as they turned they just caught a glimpse of him turning right again onto Creighton St. The squad car was on Creighton St. when Herbie thought, *'I can't outrun them,'* so he ran between two houses, but came upon a six-foot high picket fence. On his first attempt to scale it he fell backwards, but one picket ended up under his uniform piercing the jumper, thus hanging him there. He managed to hoist himself up enough to release the picket, but by then Sgt. Bishop was upon him. He gave Herbie two powerful blows in the face before calmness came into the episode.

They drove Herbie up to the *'Cop Shop'* and threw him into the bullpen with that evening's batch of new drunks; one scruffy guy called out, "Welcome to my second home young feller." Herbie gave him a nod of acknowledgment and sat down on a bench beside a sad-looking sailor, the only other one in uniform that night.

They sat in silence for a few minutes before Herbie nudged the other fellow's arm and asked, "How did you end up here tonight?"

The fellow answered, and after he had finished asked, "And how about you?"

"My friend Scott and I went to the Derby, had a little more than a little too many drafts, and then went to the Carpenters Hall for dancing. When it ended we walked onto Gottingen St. with intentions of returning to the ship. But a fight broke out between about six black guys from Creighton St. and the same number of white guys. We just stood there watching, but during the fight the cops showed up and entered the battle. One of their caps fell off and landed at my feet. I quickly bent down, picked it up and stuffed it into my jumper. My buddy said, 'What a trophy; let's get outta here', so we continued walking back to the ship. Then I saw a cap-less cop chasing a black guy..."

When Herbie finished his story Rob, the other fellow, said, "Yah, that Sgt. Bishop is a mean sucker. By the looks of it now, you'll have a shiner in the morning."

That night they both slept on the floor of vacant side-cells reserved for violent offenders.

Herbie and his new friend paid the $7.75 fine for 'Drunkenness in a Public Place' the next morning and they were escorted to a Shore Patrol paddy wagon where their custodians drove them back to their respective ships. When they arrived at the foot of the gangway of Kootenay the Petty Officer in charge took him to the Officer of the Day and reported the incident.

It wasn't long before Herbie was piped to the Coxn's office. When he arrived, the Coxn, after scolding him said, "You'll go in front of the X.O. the next time he holds defaulters."

Herbie said, "But..."

"But what?"

"On civie-street you can only be charged once for the same misdemeanour."

"This is the Navy sonny boy, the *Royal Canadian* Navy, and not civie-street. Get used to it or you won't last long." ... "How long have you got to go before your three years run out?"

Herbie said "This is April," and started counting silently on his fingers, '*June, July, August, September, October, November*', and continued, "six months."

"Yer a good man Elliot, think twice about getting out, consider signing on and making a career of the Navy."

"Thanks Cox'n I'll do that."

"ARE YOU SIGNING ON Scott?" asked Herbie..."It's June now but our three years end in November," he added.

"I don't think so Herb. It's not that I dislike the navy, but I've got Rose my high school sweetheart waiting for me and I think we'll be married by the end of the summer of '67"..."What about you; gunna sign on?"

"I too have my girlfriend Marilyn here in Halifax; or I should say Dartmouth. She's a nice young woman and I see possibilities. Then there's that sign-on bonus they just implemented; $400 if you sign on for four years and $200 for two years. I think I'll sign on for four more years. Besides I've got no hope occupation-wise on the outside, and I also like life in the navy. I think they implemented that sign-on bonus because they were losing too many possibly good men after their initial 3-year engagement. If I sign on now, I'll immediately be posted to another ship. So I'm going to milk the system for all it's worth and take advantage of this time in Halifax to get more familiar with Marilyn, and then sign on around the first of November."

All members of HMCS Kootenay who were due for release within the following few months were posted ashore to HMCS Stadacona in June 1966. Herbie was temporarily stationed at CFS Shelburne a naval station located on the south shore of Nova Scotia, equipped with an array of hydrophones that stretched out into the Atlantic. Acoustic operators mostly Wrens would listen for Soviet submarines patrolling the coast.

Herbie made two new friends while in Shelburne; Wayne Brown and Loggie McLean.

"WHERE DO I SIGN?" asked Herbie with a smile on his face.

The P1 Bos'n with World War II and Korean War medal stripes on his uniform jacket pointed at the document on the desk and said, "On the bottom line of course; just like you did three years ago, or have you forgotten already?" ... "All legal and binding documents you sign in life are done so on the bottom line. Anything below your signature isn't worth the paper it's written on, and that includes your marriage certificate. Got it?"

"Got it," said Herbie as he hesitated for five seconds before scribbling his signature on the document. The date was 3rd October 1966.

## Notes

1. Army equivalent Major General.
2. Minister of National Defence.
3. Short form of Sub Lieutenant.

# Eighteen

**AFTER SIGNING ON** for another four years in October, Herbie Eliott was immediately posted to HMCS New Waterford, an old Second World War frigate. It had much less comfortable living conditions than those of his previous ship – the Kootenay – but at least it had adjustable punkalouvres; circular swivelling things in the ventilation trunking that one could open and close or move about like an eyeball, thus pointing the direction of the air conditioning to or from a man's head.

Thankfully, New Waterford set sail on its final cruise in mid-October. They paid a short uneventful four day visit to Plymouth, England and on the return trip stopped for one night at the Azores for fuel. No shore leave was granted in the Azores because it had a bad reputation as a port where venereal disease ran rampant. When they arrived the whores waved at sailors invitingly from outside the guarded gate of the dockyard, only one hundred yards from the gangway. Some even lifted their dresses to waist level. The ship sailed the next morning.

Since the New Waterford was going to be decommissioned shortly after it arrived in Halifax, posting messages for the crew started arriving from Maritime Command on the return to Halifax. Herbie would be posted to HMCS Fraser two weeks after New Waterford's return. Those two weeks were spent de-storing the ship.

During the first three years of his naval career Herbie seldom frequented the Fleet Club – the mess for Leading Seaman and below – at the shore base HMCS Stadacona. He did, however, like to attend the Sunday afternoon hootenannies where a disc jockey played rock & roll and soul music for dancing. The music would simply blare from the amplifiers.

One Sunday afternoon in December he and a couple of other fellows from his new ship the Fraser went to the Fleet Club to attend the weekly hootenanny. As they entered they spotted a shipmate named Loggie McLean sitting alone at a table. They plunked themselves down with him. Herbie sat beside Loggie. Soon some women Loggie knew walked in and joined them. Everybody danced and drank beer, simply having a whale of a time.

At about mid-afternoon Loggie leaned over towards Herbie and said, "I've gotta have a dump," and walked toward the lobby where the toilets were located.

About fifteen minutes later Herbie and his friends noticed a scuffle had erupted in the lobby, but paid no attention because scuffles were common. They did, however, notice that Loggie did not return to the table that afternoon and wondered if he was involved.

The next morning Herbie was Bos'ns Mate at the brow when a Shore Patrol paddy wagon stopped on the jetty near the foot of the gangway. The Petty Officer in charge got out and opened the back doors. Much to Herbie's surprise Loggie stepped out.

The Petty Officer walked Loggie up the gangway and asked to speak to the Cox'n. The Corporal of the Gangway dialled the number of the Cox'ns office, after which the Petty Officer escorted Loggie below decks.

Herbie was bewildered, *'What had Loggie done,'* he wondered; *'was he involved in that* scuffle *at the hootenanny yesterday*'?

Ten minutes later the Shore Petrol PO departed.

After being relieved as Bos'ns Mate Herbie went down to the main cafeteria for lunch. He saw Loggie and asked him what had happened. Loggie's explanation almost broke Herbie up; it was that hilarious.

Loggie explained: "I had been going to the Fleet Club every night for the past few weeks. Last week the men's heads was under repair and since women rarely frequent the club during the week they stuck a 'Men's' sign on the women's washroom door."

"So yesterday when I had to have a crunch I mistakenly walked into the women's toilet, not noticing the men's sign had been removed. I entered a cubicle, pulled down my pants to floor level and sat down. Then, wouldn't you know it, two women walked it. I heard them gossiping. That was when I realised my mistake. So I climbed up onto the toilet seat with my pants still down at ankle level in case one of them needed to use the other cubicle and noticed my legs and pants. And one did enter the next door cubicle. Just as she started to piss, I lost my balance and fell to the floor. That was when the fun began. The woman started screaming while I tried to explain my mistake, but when they saw me pulling up my pants and zipping up they started yelling '*Pervert'*. So I hurled insults back at them. Soon the manager burst in, and again I tried to explain my mistake, but those damn women kept on screaming 'pervert'. It was quite extreme when the manager called the Shore Patrol. I spent the night in cells and here I am. The Coxn says I'll go up in front of the XO as a defaulter next week."

After defaulters the following week when Herbie asked Loggie what punishment he got. Loggie said, "After my explanation the XO was laughing so hard he almost pissed his drawers. He finally gained enough composure to say 'Case dismissed, now get out of here you clown'."

ALL OPERATIONAL EAST COAST ships of the fleet sailed south to the Caribbean for the annual Maple Spring exercises. The ports for the Fraser would be San Juan, Puerto Rico, St. Thomas of the US Virgin Islands, and St. Lucia of the British West Indies. Between port visits they'd carry out Anti-Submarine Warfare exercises.

On the way southward the ships encountered a gale that lasted three days, and being at sea in rough weather often resulted in a lad experiencing sea sickness. On the third evening of the gale Herbie and his shipmates were sitting at the settee in four mess and knowing Lou Dawson was prone to seasickness Herb asked him how he was making out.

Lou said, "Early on during in my navy days I learned the upper deck was the best place to be during really rough weather. A fellow rarely feels the effects of seasickness in the open air. Still, one can't remain up top forever, so a return to the smelly, oily lower decks is inevitable."

"Today, with the wind a-howlin' and the seas in a great state of unrest, I finally had to yield to fatigue and venture below. As I made my way forward on the Burma Road[1], I met Mike Boyer. He was surprisingly chipper, considering the fact that he was as prone to the effects of heavy weather as I, so I asked him how he was handling this particular storm."

"Mike told me he'd just come from the galley, where he'd asked one of the cooks for something to eat that would stay down. The cook, Jim Cummings, told him there wasn't much on hand at the moment, but on the spur of the moment, he gave him a package of frozen strawberries. Mike said he had basically swallowed them frozen."

"Well I thought; if it can work for Mike, it can work for Lou, so I went to the galley and asked if there were any more. Sure enough, there were lots in the freezer. Following the leader, I downed the entire package of frozen berries. They didn't stay down long. After a quick trip to the heads for an up-chuck, I went back out onto the Burma Road and again bumped into Mike. Needless to say, I gave him a 'what-for' about the berry theory. I said, 'I thought you said they helped you get over your seasickness'!"

"Mike said, 'I didn't tell you they stopped me from being seasick. I just wanted something in my stomach, 'cause I hadn't eaten for days and the strawberries, even frozen, went down pretty good. The trouble is; they came back up almost right away. The best part is: they tasted almost as good coming back up as they did going down – and they were thawed by then'!"

Four days after the gale the fleet pulled into San Juan. This was Herbie's first visit to San Juan and after leave was piped, Mike Hershel, one of his messmates said, "Let's go to the 'Black Angus'."

"What's that?" enquired Herbie.

"It's a scruffy bar not far from the dockyard where hookers are plentiful. They sit at the bar and smile invitingly at the room full of sex-starved sailors. Some walk around between the tables."

"Ok," said Herbie, "but for me it will only be for the drinking and fun; no hookers for this cat."

Herbie and Mike were early arrivals and were thus able to find an unoccupied table. By the end of the night the place was standing room only. Herbie watched as sailors departed with hookers and returned fifteen minutes later with a 'shit-eating' grin on their faces. One hooker walked past Herbie and Mike's table and smiled at them. Her slightly tanned Latino face was simply beautiful; her long black hair hung to her waist; her hips seemed to be those of a mandarin and her calves were sinuous. Herbie was tempted but refrained when those troublesome words of his grandmother; *'Granddad is watching; Granddad is watching'* entered his mind.

After four days in San Juan the flotilla sailed in order to carry out Anti Submarine Warfare (ASW) exercises, but returned to the same port two weeks later. Again it was the 'Black Angus' where all the lower deckers headed.

The next port for the Fraser was Charlotte Amalie of St. Thomas in the U.S. Virgin Indies. She and another ship from the squadron visited that port while others visited different islands in the Caribbean. There weren't any 'dives' like the Black Angus in Charlotte Amalie so Herbie and his pals satisfied themselves by swimming at a beach in the afternoon and sitting at patio bars drinking rum and coke in the evenings. Upon departure more ASW exercises followed.

The final port of the cruise for the Fraser was Castries the sea port and capital of St. Lucia located in the British West Indies. It was a great port – lots of slummy joints to hang out in, and plenty of up-market ones as well. Besides the drinking establishments, there were beaches, mountains, and an abundance of friendly people. St Lucia is also a stop off point for pleasure cruise liners, although sometimes they drop in just after sunrise and sail again to the next port before sunset of the same day.

To Herbie's mind, St. Lucia seemed to be more developed than its neighbour St. Vincent, the port he entered in 1965 – the one where he had had a very short exchange of words with John Lennon of the Beatles.

One evening a messmate named Eddie Whitaker climbed down the ladder to the Sonarmen messdeck and said, "You'll never guess what happened to me today."

Herbie and the others said, "Then tell us!"

"You might say I became a reluctant stowaway," said Eddie. "I was ashore souvenir shopping with a couple of stokers. After our shopping spree we sat down on the patio of the closest bar, an establishment called 'The Jolly Pirate's Den', and ordered rum 'n coke all around. At about 12:30 three British women in their mid-forties also sat down at a table on the patio near to ours and ordered fancy drinks. It wasn't long before both groups – the thrillseeking tourists and the love-sick sailors – merged into one group."

"The women were all passengers on a cruise ship that had pulled in earlier this morning. As it so happened there were three women and three guys, and it wasn't long before we had paired up. I paired with a chubby little one who was the most jovial of the lot. After several drinks my lady asked if I'd like to have a tour of her ship. Sensing that she had ulterior motives I said, 'Sure. Let's go'. We left the others behind, as the other women weren't too keen on the idea. You couldn't blame them; the stokers were engaged in an ongoing farting contest."

"As we approached the cruise liner the woman said, 'Just walk up the gangway as if you own the ship. Nobody will stop us. If they do, I'll tell them I'm just going to show you around the upper deck.' So that's what we did, and although there was a hand manning the gangway head, we passed by without being challenged."

"As we walked around the upper deck; I, being a sailor, explained the usage of several deck fittings to my companion. The tour only lasted about ten minutes before she said, 'And would you like to see the cabins'? I, of course, said 'Alright'."

"Her cabin was single occupancy and was located on the after quarter of the ship on the starboard side. It contained a large double bed, a desk and an easy chair, and there was a separate shower enclosure. A large porthole allowed the afternoon sun to cast a beam on the deck."

"We don't need a detailed description of the cabin Eddie;" exclaimed Herbie, "get on with the interesting part – why you became a reluctant stowaway!"

"OK. Within five minutes of entering, both of us were lying naked on the bed. We engaged in heavy-duty romancing until around 4 pm when we both dozed off."

"We were rudely awakened by the sound of the ship's horn. I glanced up at the porthole and saw that dusk was falling. I jumped to my feet and looked out of the closed porthole. The ship was moving! In fact, it was in open water about a nautical mile outside the port. When I heard a toot-toot of a smaller vessel I opened the porthole and looked downwards where I saw a boat was alongside the starboard quarter, and about to pick up the Castries harbour pilot. I leaned out and yelled, *"HOLD THAT BOAT!"* The boat captain looked up and gave me the thumbs up sign."

"With that, I grabbed my pants, pulled them on and ran out into the passageway while doing up my belt and throwing on my gun shirt. I slapped on my cap and carried my shoes and socks in my hand. My gun shirt wasn't tucked in. My afternoon lover was in the same state of disarray as she ran after me shouting, *'I love you! I love you'!"*

"I ran out onto the quarterdeck; my lover in my wake. I climbed down the accommodation ladder, and jumped into the waiting pilot boat. The woman remained at the top of the ladder blowing me kisses and yelling 'I love you' as the boat pulled away."

"Of course, the episode didn't go unnoticed by other passengers on the upper deck. I looked up and saw a whole gaggle of them at the guardrail laughing. I gave them a deep bow from the stern of the pilot boat as it pulled away; they all applauded."

"As the *'I love you'* words faded away in the distance I turned around and 'mooned' the remaining passengers on the quarterdeck. I could hear their laughter."

THE FRASER VISITED Expo 67 in the summer of 1967. It was a gigantic trade fair held in Montreal to commemorate the hundredth year of Canadian Confederation. There were pavilions from all provinces of Canada and those of several foreign nations. There was also a fairway with rides and what-not. Most naval ships of the fleet dropped in to Expo for a week and visitors were allowed to tour the upper decks. Part of Herb's family – his Mom and Dad, his sister Josie, and brothers Walter and Lawrence – drove from Toronto to visit him, his ship and Expo 67. Being family of a crew member they were allowed to be escorted below decks and view the living conditions. Upon seeing Herbie's bunk, the upper-most of three, his little seven year old sister Josie said, "You sleep way up there?"

"Yes Dear."

"What happens if you have to pee in the middle of the night?"

"I climb down and go to the heads."

"You pee on the other guy's *heads*?"

"No, no Dear; 'heads' is what we call toilets in the Navy."

"Why do they call it that? I think if they were going to call them after parts of the body then *'bums'* or *'weenies'* would be better names?" (Laughter).

"It goes back to the early days of navy ships. Have you ever seen pictures of wooden ships with sails?"

"Yes, last year in school."

Well, on many of those ships there was a carved wooden figurehead on the bow, or in other words, the pointed end."

Herb saw his dad standing by smiling as his seven year old daughter interrogated her twenty-one year old brother like a pro. "Dad between taking slugs of your beer on the way home, please explain to Josie what a figurehead is." (Laughter) "Mom does most of the family long haul driving anyhow."

"So Josie, the toilet on those ships was right up at the bow where the figurehead was located, and that is why navy toilets are called 'heads' to this very day."

President Charles de Gaulle of France paid an official visit to Canada in July 1967. His first stop was Montreal to visit Expo 67 and then he would visit Ottawa to meet Prime Minister Lester B. Pearson. While in Montreal he caused a major diplomatic incident when he addressed a crowd from the top of the stairs of the Montreal Town Hall. At the end of his speech he uttered, "Vive Montréal! Vive le Québec!" ("Long live Montreal, Long live Quebec!"). He then added

"Vive le Québec libre!" ("Long live free Quebec!"); with particular emphasis on the word 'libre'. This went down well with those in the crowd who had been demanding a breakaway from Canada, thus making Quebec a republic. Lester Pearson was furious and refused to meet de Gaulle after his controversial statement.[2]

IN THE FALL OF 1967 Fraser and a couple of other ships were on a cruise to Europe – Portsmouth, England; Brest, France; and Oslo, Norway. One Saturday afternoon while in Portsmouth, Herbie saw Ron McIntosh, a messmate approaching him in the flats and said, "Let's go to the 'Golden Fleece'."

"What's that?"

"The older guys tell me it's a great pub for sailors. They say it's one of the toughest pubs in Portsmouth and a favourite for British and Canadian sailors. They say there is sawdust on the floor often damp with rough scrumpy; it has bloodstains on the ceiling; there are a few tables with melamine tops and short stools dotted around, which often are thrown around. Most sailors simply call it 'the Fleece'; everybody who has ever been to Portsmouth calls it that."

"What's scrumpy?" asked Ron.

"I asked Freddie Molyneaux the same question when the Kootenay was in Chatham for the christening of the Ojibwa in 1965. Apparently its strong cider made in western England."…"So, do you want to join me on a visit to the Fleece?"

"Sure, I see you're already dressed for going ashore. Wait for me on the quarterdeck while I change. I'll only be ten minutes."

Fifteen minutes later as they were walking towards the main gate of HM Royal Dockyard, they passed HMS Victory – the flagship of Admiral Lord Nelson during the Battle of Trafalgar. A line of about eight people were waiting to be escorted on a guided tour.

Herbie said, "I'm going to tour the Victory tomorrow afternoon. Wanna join me?"

"Sounds like time well spent; sure," said Ron.

They exited the dockyard and hailed a taxi. Herbie simply said, "Take us to the Fleece." The driver knew exactly what he meant.

To their delight, when they entered, there was a wedding reception in progress. A young Royal Navy Able Seaman had just married one of the tarts that frequented the place. It wasn't a closed affair as all patrons were welcome, provided they paid for their own drinks – a wedding reception 'on the cheap' if you will.

It was a great afternoon; everybody was happy; the bridesmaids passed out sausage rolls while guys and gals danced to tunes blaring out of the jukebox; everyone was guzzling down the pints – great fun indeed! At one point, the drunken bride danced on a table top. That was when Jean Paul Lavois tapped the bridesgroom on the shoulder and asked, "May I kiss the bride?"

"Sure Mate," said the groom.

With that, Jean Paul lifted the brides wedding gown – she was still dancing on the table top – and kissed her on the panty clad place where the legs meet the torso!

Did this start a brawl? On the contrary! The drunken groom burst into hearty laughter and did the same, much to the amusement of all onlookers.

At one point during the afternoon, as the celebration continued, all patrons exited to the sidewalk to cheer on their favourite of two bridesmaids engaged in a drunken fistfight as a British sailor took bets on the outcome.

The next afternoon as Herbie and Ron were about to cross the brow and proceed to HMS Victory, a little blue paddy wagon pulled up at the foot of the gangway. Herbie and Ron remained on the quarterdeck to see what was going on.

The paddy wagon had a metal cab and lower portion of the back. But there was a lacquer coated wicker cage wherein culprits were confined.

The British Leading Seaman walked up the gangway and saw a man who he thought may be the Cox'n. He asked, "Excuse me; are you the Cox'n?"

"Yes I am," said Chief Petty Officer Sykes. Who have you got and what have they done?"

"I don't know their names but since they have Fraser cap tallies I brought them here. They must have drunk too much rum at tot time and were walking towards the dockyard gate yelling vulgarities and making obscene gestures at all females they encountered. We were called and they're in the back of our vehicle."

"Bring 'em up."

The Leading Seaman walked back down the gangway and opened the back of the paddy wagon. Able Seaman Jean Marc Pitre, a Steward emerged and walked up the gangway with his head bowed in shame. The Cox'n said, "Don't even think of going ashore again today Pitre."

Able Seaman Bluette another Steward was in a fighting mood. He put up a physical struggle while cursing everyone in sight. The Leading Seaman looked up at the quarterdeck as if seeking instructions. The Cox'n yelled, "Take him away!" With that, they threw him back in the paddy wagon with great difficulty.

Once that was accomplished, the Leading Seaman went back up to the quarterdeck to ask a few questions, such as, "What's his name and rank."

While he was up asking questions, Bluette began to bash the top of his head against the lacquer coated wicker roof of the paddy wagon. Soon a crack appeared. Then the top of his head could be seen, similar to the chick breaking out of an eggshell. Eventually, his whole head was sticking out the top of the vehicle, with verbal insults against the Cox'n spewing from the mouth. If that wasn't enough, he worked his fist up through the hole and started shaking it at the Cox'n while saying something rather more offending than, "Cox'n, you rotten SOB!"

Once the Shore Patrol guy had completed his paperwork, he simply ambled down the gangway, got back into the paddy wagon and drove away, with the offending head still sticking out the top. What a comical sight! Even the Cox'n – the recipient of the verbal abuse – roared his guts out in laughter.

The next day when they delivered Bluette back to the ship, he had scratches all over his neck, face and right arm, as a result of being dragged back through the hole against the grain of the wicker. Needless to say, he was embarrassed and full of remorse. The story being rather funny, the Captain only gave the apologetic offender a severe reprimand at the defaulters' table.

Once the drama was over Ron and Herbie walked the 500 yards to HMS Victory where they were given a guided tour along with a couple of shipmates and three civilians.

They were walked around the upper deck and the open-air bridge where Admiral Nelson had been shot by a sniper. Once below decks they encountered a stall with hay on the deck and were told "This is the place where he died."

Nelson's death bed was on the uppermost of three gun decks. The guide stopped at one gun and asked, "Has anyone heard the expression 'cold enough to freeze the balls off a brass monkey' and thought it was a vulgar statement?"

Two of the females raised her hands. One said, "I have, but I think you are about to set me straight."

"Yes I am," said the guide. "Look at those cannon balls stacked in a pyramid...If at sea the pitching and rolling of the ship would cause the pyramid to fall and cannon balls would roll all over the deck. Now look at the edge of the pyramid. That brass ring is there to prevent the pyramid from falling apart. The ring is called a 'monkey'...Now, brass contracts faster than lead when it's extremely cold, so the theory is that if it was freezing cold the monkey would contract far enough to make the balls fall all over the place; hence the saying, 'Cold enough to freeze the balls off a brass monkey'."

"That's interesting. The next time I hear a guy say it in mixed company and the women cringe I'll explain what you told us today."

"I'VE NEVER SEEN AN ISLAND off the coast of Plymouth before Sir," said Mike Keith to the Officer of the Watch."

Mike and Herbie had just come off watch in the Sonar Control Room and were taking in fresh air on the bridge before going below for breakfast. The OOW raised his binoculars and said, "Neither have I Keith."

It was then that an emergency message was received; the Kootenay had suffered an explosion in the engine room during full power trials. The island Mike thought he had seen was, in fact, smoke. The distressed Kootenay was about eight nautical miles east of the ships of the first and fifth squadrons, the aircraft carrier Bonaventure and the tanker Provider. All ships revved up their engines and raced towards the Kootenay.

It was 23rd October 1969 and thus a little nippy in the open air, but Mike and Herbie went up to the flag deck to watch what would happen next. When the Fraser got close enough, they observed the Kootenay travelling in large circles. Crew members were standing on the upper deck – some with only towels wrapped around their torsos since they were having a shower when the explosion occurred. Helicopters from the Bonaventure were carrying netted sacks containing cans full of fire-fighting foam, because those of the Kootenay were stored below decks and inaccessible. Eventually, the fire was extinguished and the doomed ship was escorted back into Plymouth, the port they had exited the day before.

A couple of months after the fleet's return to Halifax, Herbie encountered Douglas Moore, a Leading Seaman he knew to have been on the Kootenay on that fateful day.

"Are you up to telling me about what you experienced during the Kootenay disaster Doug?"

Douglas said, "I'll do my best but forgive me if I break down in tears and have to drop it halfway through."..."I was part of Squadron staff and it was just a fluke that I had just gone on watch in the Ops Room. My watch started at 0750 and at approximately 0825 we heard a lot of commotion. No one on watch in the Operations Room knew what had happened. Some people left and went to the bridge."

"Eventually there were only three of us left in the Ops Room and after a short time we could smell smoke. Kind of made us think it was an exercise like having the Sea Training Team onboard. About 20 minutes later I remember saying to the two Radar Plotters 'we'd better get the hell out of here' and we all headed for daylight."

"I cannot remember where the plotters went but I went to the bridge. I can still see the Engineering Officer (EO) in his white coveralls, or should I say 'soot covered' coveralls. He was reporting to the Commanding Officer, Cdr. Norton."

"The thing that I shall always remember about that is when he saluted the C.O. the skin from his hand and arm was hanging down a good six inches. It was kind of eerie and I remember wondering how he ever managed to muster up the courage to make it to the bridge and make his report. I found out later he and two others were hit with a fire ball of extreme heat. One other person was on the fo'c'sle. The sailors there were holding this individual down. He was screaming "throw me over – throw me over". I later found out it was Able Seaman Dinger Bell, a stoker."

"Shortly after witnessing the EO make his report I left the bridge and went out onto the flag deck. I couldn't believe what I was seeing – the black thick smoke was billowing out of the stacks. I thought for sure we were going to sink or blow up. Lots of different things started to happen in order to put the fire out, however I remained in the bridge area as I was on watch until I was ordered to proceed to the fo'c'sle to help unload cans of fire fighting foam being delivered by helicopters from the Bonaventure. There was a helicopter fore and aft unloading, two more waiting, and two others back at the Bonnie loading. It was a steady stream."

"It took quite a while to put out the fire because they could not reach the shut off valves but finally in the end they were shut off. The fire was finally put out and we headed back into Plymouth."

"There were nine deaths concerning the incident – eight on the ship and one who later passed away on the Bonaventure from smoke inhalation."

'Once we were in port I was part of the cleaning crew – scrubbing down bulkheads,[3] etc. I was also part of the crew who went into the Engine Room to help carry out the stokers who had perished. I cannot shake that part from my head."

"The Squadron Commander eventually sent his staff home, but before departing I ended up being part of the funeral service."

"Until I leave this earth I will never forget it. If I hadn't just gone on watch I may have been caught on the Burma Road or in the main cafeteria and part of the events I saw unfolding before me. I consider myself very very lucky to be a Kootenay Survivor."[4]

UPON ARRIVAL BACK IN Halifax Herbie was delighted to learn his best friend Scott Hunter had married Rosie and had re-engaged. He was posted to HMCS Saguenay – a river class destroyer similar to the Kootenay.

## Notes

1. Main passageway running the length of the ship.
2. A Quebec independence referendum was held in 1980. The question was 'should Quebec remain a part of Canada or become a sovereign nation?.' The majority voted to remain as part of Canada.
3. walls.
4. From an e-book coordinated by the author where retired RCN members were asked to submit their stories.

# Nineteen

**ON 1ST NOVEMBER 1968** the Royal Canadian Navy, the Canadian Army and the Royal Canadian Air Force were unified into the Canadian Armed Forces (CAF); and later simply the Canadian Forces (CF). Unification caused a vicious argument between Paul Hellyer, the Minister of National Defence and Rear Admiral William Landymore resulting in the latter being forced to resign.

One benefit of unification was that sailors were then allowed to proceed ashore in mufti (civilian clothing). Before unification they had to wear uniforms ashore and if they wished could change into civilian clothing at the Fleet Locker Club where they rented lockers for their civies. Another benefit was that a member was automatically promoted to Leading Seaman after completing four years of service. These people became known as 'Hellyer Hookies' (after Paul Hellyer the minister and the hook shaped anchor of the rank badge). Herbie was promoted to Leading Seaman, thus becoming a Hellyer Hookie.

On the down side all forces – the Army, Navy and Air Force discarded their traditional uniforms and were issued green ones topped off with a beret. Further, the naval tradition of serving tots of rum at 12:00 daily was discontinued, but bars were established in the Main Cafeteria for Leading Seamen and below, and the Chief's and Petty Officer's mess; these served hard liquor while in port. Beer machines were also installed and open at sea, but woe betide anyone who was found drunk on duty.

IN EARLY 1970, Herbie was posted ashore to the Fleet Maintenance Group, where he assisted naval technicians of all weapons trades. Herbie worked for Petty Officer Doug Wright and Leading Seaman Cye Farr – a five foot five inch tall thin little Newfoundlander who was cursed with the affliction of stuttering profusely. Both Cye and Doug were Weapons Surfacemen.

One day Doug told Herbie a story about Cye:

*On the night before the ship Cye was serving on returned to Halifax after a multi-foreign port trip, a message was received that his father had died. The next morning when the ship arrived alongside Cye was standing at the gangway – duty free bottle of rum in hand*[1] *– and ready to race to the train station and catch one to North Sydney, Nova Scotia from where he'd catch a ferry to Port aux Basques, Newfoundland; only a hundred miles from his home town. He knew the train schedule and only had half an hour to get to the railway station to buy a ticket. He made it in time.*

*While on the train he started into his duty free bottle of rum and before he reached North Sydney it was empty. He purchased another in North Sydney and by the time he reached home was dead drunk.*

*He entered the house, and knowing he was drunk just sat on the sofa and said nothing. His mother and siblings attributed his silence to sorrow.*

*The funeral was held in the afternoon of his arrival. It was drizzling rain. After the ceremony when the coffin was to be lowered into the ground his mother wanted the family to stand at the edge of the grave. Cye, however, was reluctant. He knew he was drunk and he stood on the pile of earth which would be shovelled back into the grave afterwards. Finally he relented to his mother's pleading and took the few steps forward to stand by the family.*

*That was when the fun began. He slipped on the mud and fell between the edge of the grave and the coffin, and landed at the bottom of the dark hole. He then started yelling, "Wr-wrong guy; wr-wrong guy!" After his brothers rescued him, his mother was not at all impressed.*

*When he returned to the ship after his compassionate leave and told his story to his shipmates he said, "The only one who wo-would of g-got a l-laugh out of it wo-would have b-been the old m-man, b-but he was six f-feet under."*

HERBIE WAS POSTED to HMCS Saguenay in October 1971. He would be sailing with his best friend Scott Hunter again.

In the spring of 1972 the Saguenay set out on a cruise as part the Standing Naval Force Atlantic (commonly abbreviated to SNFL); NATO's standing naval maritime immediate reaction force.

SNFL consists of four to six destroyers or frigates, with the Royal Canadian Navy, the German Navy, the Royal Netherlands Navy, and the United States Navy each contributing one ship on a permanent basis. These are joined periodically by ships from the navies of Belgium, Denmark, Norway, or Portugal. The force operates, trains and exercises as a group, providing day-to-day verification of current NATO maritime procedures, tactics and effectiveness.

Most SNFL exercises were carried out in the eastern Atlantic, but the one the Saguenay was about to embark on would be held on the western Atlantic, the Caribbean and the Gulf of Mexico. Ports would be: San Juan Rico; New Orleans, Mississippi; Norfolk, Virginia; New York City and Halifax. Ships from non-permanent SNFL members would be two destroyers – one from Denmark and one from Portugal.

The ships from across the pond (Atlantic) arrived in Halifax on 1st April and they set sail six days later. They conducted exercises on the way southward and between all ports. The first port being San Juan, lower deck sailors from all ships headed to the Black Angus. Herbie, didn't want to go there, but since Scott hadn't experienced the joint he reluctantly took him, after reminding him he was now a married man, and Scott promising to respect his marriage vows.

The SNFL fleet sailed from San Juan and conducted exercises in the Gulf of Mexico before travelling the 180 miles from Pilottown up the Mississippi Delta to New Orleans. Personnel on the upperdeck stood by the guardrails and regarded the unspoiled beauty of the greenery along shoreline; they even saw the occasional alligator.

Once the ship berthed in New Orleans, Herbie said, "Scott, let's round up Steve and Dudley, and go to the French quarter. There must be a few good bars there."

"What's the French quarter?"

"I've been told the Quarter, as locals call it, is a part of town with old French architecture and a reflection of the diminished French influence after the Louisiana Purchase."

"Sounds good to me Herb," said Scott, "I'll go and round up Steve and Dudley."

Once out on the street Steve hailed down a taxi. When they were all inside Herbie said, 'Take us to the 'Quarter'."

"The taxi sped off and ten minutes later stopped. The driver said, "This is Bourbon Street in the heart of New Orleans' oldest neighbourhood of the French Quarter. What do you intend to do?"

"Bar-hopping of course," said Dudley.

"There are a lot of up market bars where a suit and tie is required to gain entry, but there are many more where patrons in plain clothing like you fellers are wearing are welcome."

After paying the driver and climbing out of the cab, the fellows strolled up the street looking at the mixture of French, Spanish and Victorian style architecture.

They entered a slummy-looking joint where Blues and Soul music echoed off the walls. They ordered four bottles of Budweiser beer and listened to blues songs by Muddy Waters, B.B. King and many others, which blared from the amplifiers as the disc jockey placed vinyl records on his player.

The fellows frequented the same bar every evening of their five-day visit. They did, however, take bus tours on two occasions. One tour was to the battlefield where Col. Andrew Jackson – nickname Hickory – and his troops had defeated the British in the 1814 'Battle of New Orleans'.

THE SNFL SQUADRON conducted exercises en route to Norfolk. Once there the American Admiralty thought it would be a good idea to host parties for the three rank levels of the visiting ships: the Leading Seamen and below; the Chiefs and Petty Officers; and the Officers. The reason given was that since American crew members had been hosted on the other ships – all of which had bars – and there was no alcohol on the U.S. ships, it was payback time. The party for the lower deckers was hosted on a large park within the confines of the base. Free beer was readily available.

Once the party was underway, crew members pretty well stuck together in groups, but there was some intermingling between different nationalities. As the party was winding down buses appeared. Scott said, "Hey Herb, let's stage a fake fist fight between the two of us, but you're a better boxer than me so no head blows."

"Ok," said Herbie.

So the duo started throwing body punches at each other while uttering fake profanities. Their shipmates saw it and ran to break up the fight. They were successful. Both Herbie and Scott threw their arms around each other's shoulders and started walking towards the busses.

On the way Scott said, "You're my best friend Herb and if anyone says anything against you I'll rip his head off."

"The same with me Scott"

As they approached the first bus it was half full and a long line was at the door waiting to enter. Herbie said, "We'll never get on this bus, let's try the next." But as they were passing the first bus, a steward from the Saguenay stuck his head out the back window and yelled, "Hey Eliott, you old cock jaw."

With that Scott cried out, "Don't call my best friend a cock jaw," and climbed up and through the window by using the back wheel as a step. He then started to lay a beating on the steward.

While he was doing so, a black American intervened and hollered, "Leave that poor boy alone." Scott then turned his fury to the American and shouted, "Back of the bus nigger!" He then turned and dived back out the window as if he was diving into a swimming pool.

This didn't go unobserved by his Canadian shipmates in the line waiting to board the bus. Gary Peverell cried out, "Hey, those black guys threw Scott out the back window."

They then surged ahead to take revenge. This eventually ended up as a brawl – Canadians against Americans – all around the bus. At one point Scott and Herbie found themselves facing each other, but on their knees. Scott said, "Let's get the fuck out of here"; just as one of them had said five years earlier at the barroom brawl at the Horse & Buggy bar in Bermuda. This was the second brawl the duo had provoked.

As they walked away, Herbie asked, "I heard you yell something at that black guy but couldn't make it out. What did you say that provoked them?"

"I said, "Back of the bus nigger."

"Oh Scott, how could you? That was the most racist thing you could have said. That man is of a race that has been oppressed by whites for hundreds of years. I was taught as a child that the Lord said 'All men are created equal' but when my family drove to Florida in 1957 I saw three toilet doors in the back of a gas station; one said 'Men', one said 'Women', and the other said 'Colored'. They should hate us, but there he was trying to save a white guy you were beating the shit out of. He's a good man."

"I'm sorry Herb."

"You don't owe me an apology you owe that black fellow one."

As they reached the sidewalk of the road leading back to the ship, three black fellows were waiting. One was the guy Scott had insulted and slugged. Once they came face to face the fellow said, "Hey buddy, that 'N' word and 'back of the bus' died in this part of the U.S. shortly after Brother Martin and Senator Kennedy were assassinated in 1968."

He then shortened the distance as if he was going to slug Scott, but instead said, "The Lord said turn the other cheek, so here is mine"; he turned he head and said, "Go ahead hit it again."

Scott said, "What's your first name?"

"Henry. Why?"

"Henry that was a racist remark I uttered in anger, and I assure you it does not reflect my true feelings about men of your race.... Please accept my sincere apology." He stretched out his hand. Henry clasped Scott's hand and shook it.

IN THE EVENING PRIOR to entering New York Herbie suggested to Scott, Steve and Dudley that on the first afternoon they go to 'Irish Town', one of the several ethnic areas of the city. They all thought it would be a good idea.

When leave was granted the next afternoon they all climbed into a taxi and Scott said, "Take us to a good bar in Irish Town." After a rather long taxi ride, the foursome sat on stools at a bar named 'Paddy's Pub' located on West 38th Street in the heart of Irish Town. Besides the four of them, there was one other patron in the establishment – a fat old floozy. She had grey hair covered with a kerchief, and wore bright red lipstick. She was also sitting at the bar, but separated on the right of the fellows by two stools. She struck up a conversation with Dudley, who was the closest.

The conversation revealed the fact that they were Cana-dian sailors. This caught the attention of the bartender – Paddy himself. Paddy owned and operated the bar bearing his name. He ambled over, leaned against his side of the bar and said, "I've never had the pleasure of hosting Canadian sailors, but I've been told y'all are great drinkers." Scott said, "You heard right!" The remainder gave enthusiastic affirmative responses.

Paddy said, "Then I suggest you drink Irish whiskey."

The boys said, "OK, Set 'em up!"

With that, Paddy poured four shots of Irish whiskey and placed them in front of them while saying, "Don't drink them yet." He then said, "I'll also pour you four large mugs of Irish beer." He proceeded to set them in front of each of the boys while saying, "When I say 'Go' you all knock back your shot and then chase it with a mouthful or two of beer." The four shots and four glasses of beer were on the bar. He asked, "Are you ready?"

“Ready,” they exclaimed!

“Ok, Go!”

They all had their fingers wrapped around the shot glasses. At the ‘Go’ they simultaneously knocked back the shots; slammed the empty glasses back onto the bar; grabbed the beers; threw a big slug down their throats; and slammed the glasses back on the bar. The actions were all in unison. On completion they all uttered a sigh of satisfaction– ahhh!

“How was that?” Paddy asked

They all said, “Smooooth; awesome.”

“Again?” asked Paddy.

“Set ‘em up,”

Paddy set them up and they all did it again ... and again… and then again at intervals of about one minute. On the fourth go, the real fun began.

Herbie couldn’t keep the fourth shot down. It got into his gut alright, but while the others were chasing their whiskey he vomited into his beer glass, but none of the others noticed the fact because their eyes were facing the ceiling. He slammed his glass full of vomit on the bar at the same time as the others slammed down their empty beer glasses.

Herbie was sitting beside Steve. He nudged him and said, “If you’re so good, drink this!” Steve thought it was just beer, so without even looking he grabbed it and drank it in one go. When he slammed down the glass Herbie laughed and said, “That was my puke!”

Steve swished the remnants around in his mouth a few times. Then, upon realizing it was true, he gave Herb a horrified look and promptly turned and to his right and puked his guts out all over Dudley. Dudley ended up with Steve’s lunch, Irish whiskies and beers all over his shirt and pants. The remainder of them, including Paddy and the floozy roared with laughter.

Poor Dudley. While he was in the heads cleaning up Paddy – still laughing – said, “That was the best show we’ve had in here for ages.”

When Dudley emerged from the heads, his front was all wet, but the evidence of being barfed upon was gone. The boys paid up, thanked Paddy, said goodbye to the floozy and carried on.

On the way out Paddy yelled, “Y’all come again now; ya hear! Ha. Ha.”

UPON ARRIVAL BACK in Halifax in the last week of July the Saguenay remained part of the SNFL fleet until the Restigouche sailed away with the other ships five days later.

Scott was Herbie's best man when the latter married his long-term girlfriend Marilyn on 20th August 1970. On 1st September 1971 their first child was born – a girl who they named Anne. She would be the eldest of four siblings – three girls and one boy by the summer of 1979.

## Notes

1. When a ship had visited a foreign port sailors were allowed to purchase a 40 ounce bottle of rum for five dollars upon return to home port.

# TWENTY

**HERBERT ELLIOT HAD JOINED** the Royal Canadian Navy as an Ordinary Seaman in 1963 and years later when 1988 rolled around he was a Petty Officer 1st Class, and it was time to seek a new career. While in the navy he had served on thirteen of Her Majesty's Canadian Ships and visited twenty far off lands located on the shores of the North and South Atlantic, and the Arctic Oceans, the Caribbean, and Baltic Seas, and the Gulf of Mexico. During this time cannons roared but only in practice; they were at war, but this was the so called Cold War, with the adversary being the Soviet Union.

Much of this period was served while young American men of Herbert's generation were fighting a brutal but unwinnable war in Vietnam. Most Canadian sailors liked the 1969 patriotic country music song *'Okie from Muskogee'* sung by Merle Haggard and the peace song *'Where have all the Roses Gone'*, sung by Joan Baez. Most Canadian sailors were at sea during much of the Vietnam War; for that reason few were aware of the riot outside the Democrat National Convention held in Chicago in 1970. All saw the photo of the naked Vietnamese girl running toward the cameraman with arms out-stretched, but few saw the photo of the American GI blowing the brains out of a Viet Cong soldier at close range, or the film clip of an Afro-American war protester carrying a sign which read, 'Vietnamese Don't Call Me Nigger. Very few knew about the shootings of protesting students at Kent State University; let alone the significance of the phrase 'Pentagon Papers, or the word 'Watergate' which had caused President Richard Nixon of USA to resign before he was impeached.

After the Americans met with Viet Cong leaders in 1975 to negotiate their departure from Vietnam, almost no one realized that the return of seven US prisoners of war had cost the country 58,000 lives.[1]

HERBERT HAD KEPT in touch with his natural father, Bill Cunningham by back and forth letters and personal visits over the years while he was still in active service. Bill had retired, and in his father's latest letter he had encouraged him to drop down to Carrying Place near Base Trenton with his family while on vacation.

But disaster struck the Elliot family in late November of 1986 when Herbert confessed to his wife Marilyn that he had fallen in love with another woman and wanted to be with her. This caused the breakup of himself from Marilyn and their four young children; three girls and one boy. The night he walked out the back door of their house to his car with his bags packed, and his wife and children sitting in the dining room watching was sadder to Herbert than the day he watched his grandfather's coffin being lowered into a deep dark hole in the ground at Mount Pleasant Cemetery in Toronto, but sadly he kept walking with *Granddad is watching; Granddad is watching* ringing in his ears.

By 1988 Herbert had found the support payments for his family were simply too much to bear. He needed a job that paid as much as the navy and then let his pension take care of support; hence his 1988 release from the navy, when he could have remained for thirty-five years or more if still physically and mentally fit. Upon retirement he tried to put aside his childhood name 'Herbie' and introduced himself as 'Herbert'.

By January 1989 he had secured a job as an instructor by a defence contractor based in Montreal. While working for that company he met many former navy men who he knew. This was when he realized the name 'Herbie' would be hard to shake off.

He worked for that company for three years until he decided to go into business by himself in a completely different field and he gave the company one-month notice. Two months later his former manager phoned him, "How are things going with your new business plan Herb?" he asked.

"Not as well as expected John." What he was ashamed to say he had been living on stale Christmas cake and tea for the past two weeks.

"Do you want your old job back?"

"No John. I'm determined to make it on my own in business."

"How about coming back as a contractor? Contracting is a business."

"Now you're talking;...sixty-five dollars per hour."

John said, "Are you out of your mind?"

"Then make it forty-five and we have a deal."

"Done," said John.

"I'm not finished yet," said Herb, "plus $100 per month for living expenses; a car – I'll pay the gas – and one trip home to Halifax per month at company expense for family contact."

"Done," said John, "unless you want a Caribbean cruise when the contract ends."

"Out of the question?"

"Fuck off; ha ha!"

The negotiated price for his expertise was over twice that of his former pay ($18.50 per hour); and the extras made it almost three times more.

Herb said, "Ok John, today is Wednesday. I'll drive to Montreal and report for work on Monday."

A few months later in the duration of his contract Herb was asked if he could find subject-matter experts of other occupations (naval trades). He found four former navy personnel of other trades and paid them $25 per hour; just over half of what the company paid him for their services, however they received the same perks. Herb banked close to $200,000 for that contract before it ended more than a year later. He then farmed his Anti-Submarine Warfare (ASW) expertise out to other defence contractors.

IN 1994 HERB RECEIVED a phone call from his mother. She told him his dad (Charles Eliott) was in hospital and dying. All family members would individually be given private time with him at his bedside the following Saturday afternoon.

During Herb's private time he thanked his father for taking him and his brother Lawrence into his heart and for treating them as equals even though they were in fact his step-sons. His father and mother had always been great travellers.

His dad was a great believer and said, "I'm really looking forward to my forthcoming trip to Heaven. I wonder if my mother, father and sister will be there to greet me at the grates.

Herb suggested, "Maybe your first wife Marnie too."

"Yes Herbie, who knows, her too".

Later he spoke of a place he had always wanted to visit – a place in India called Dharamsala high in the Himalayan foothills.

His own father Walter Elliot had lived there for two or three years after World War I. His father had spoken of the church, the Hindu temple and Panditji, the village potters and dhobis, the views of the majestic Himalayas. This fascinated Herb; he pulled a little notepad from his pocket and wrote the word 'Dharamsala'.

After all family members had spoken to their father the doctor walked into the waiting room and addressed the family saying, "I can keep Mr. Elliot alive for another six months with a simple procedure, but this hospital is here to save lives not to prolong them. He will therefore have to go home, and I warn you in advance, towards the end it will be messy and painful ... So what should I do?"

Herb stepped in saying, "Doctor you will agree that Dad is still of sound mind."

"Yes he is," said the doctor.

"Then this should be his decision." Betty and Herb's siblings all agreed.

As the doctor was about to walk to Charles's room. Herb called after him, "And don't tell him you told us first."

The doctor returned in ten minutes and said "He chose the quick route." All family members knew he would.

Charles Elliot passed away peacefully on 24th June 1994 with his wife Betty at his bedside holding his hand. Herbert was chosen by his mother and siblings to be the orator of the eulogy at the 'celebration of life'; he adlibbed the speech.

❄❄❄❄

IN 1998 AT AGE 79 Betty Elliot married James Simpson the widower of a long time dear friend named Heather Simpson, who lived in Orillia, Ontario. At the time Betty had been living in an apartment with her younger sister Molly London, whose husband Bill had also passed away.

Before Jim proposed to Betty he said, "It's possible for a person to love two people – mother and son for instance. While I always loved Heather with all my heart, I have also loved you for a long-long time; even before you married Charlie back in the early 50s."

Betty was shocked. "I never detected it."

After a long pause Jimmy carried on ... "Bettina Elliot, will you be my lawful wedded wife?"

"Yes I will James Simpson."

For their honeymoon they chose to drive around the entire coastline of the United States and back across southern Canada in Jimmy's large Lincoln. Betty did all the driving.

Theirs was a rather short marriage; Jimmy passed away in 2005 with Betty at his bedside holding his hand.

❄❄❄❄

**"GO TO HIM MY CHILD."** Betty Simpson was sitting in her bedroom by herself praying. In her prayer she had said, 'Dear Lord please tell me what to do'. And that was when the words broke out loud and clear. She jumped up and looked all around; had someone been looking over her shoulder at the letter she had been reading? No; she was alone. That was when she realized the Lord had spoken His answer.

The letter was from Bill Cunningham and read:

Dear Betty,

Please come to see me in Kincardine. I can't come to you in Orillia because my wife Mary has dementia and needs constant care.

Betty some unanswered questions leading up to our 1948 breakup need to be addressed. Both your mother and father are long gone and I can now speak freely about one in particular. I currently have prostate cancer and also wear a pace-maker. I fear my time on this earth is limited. Please come soon. The address is 960 Park Place Rd.

Love

Bill

It was a Friday afternoon when she received the letter. Due to the 'Please come soon' segment, she could almost hear the urgency in his voice speaking; and the words from God was also a strong motivator. She therefore rose early on Saturday morning, had breakfast and was on the road by 9 am. Her big Lincoln pulled into Bill's driveway at 12:15 pm and she saw a feeble old man sitting on a rocking chair on the porch, seemingly waiting for her. He rose and started walking toward her, but Betty – an old woman herself – almost ran to him and threw her arms around him. Both stood there weeping for about what seemed to be an eternity, but was only about a minute. They released each other and walked hand in hand into the house.

Bill pointed and said, "Sit in that armchair Bet while I fetch tea. Would you like a cuppa?"

Betty said, "Yes please Bill, only milk, no sugar. But you forgot to introduce me to your wife Mary."

"As I told you in the letter Bet; Mary has dementia, an offshoot of Alzheimer's disease. She just looks straight ahead and doesn't respond to me, our daughter Susanne or our grand children." He departed toward the kitchen to fetch tea and returned three minutes later with two cups and a few biscuits on a tray.

Bill sat in another armchair only two feet away from Betty's. After five minutes Bill asked, "Are you ready for the first torpedo that led to our break up?"

"Shoot," said Betty

"Ok; when I returned from the war early I knocked on the door of 37 Macnaughton to ask for you. Your mother said, 'She's on a Great Lakes boat cruise with Chris Stensson, and grinned'." That grin added insult to injury; I've never forgotten it.

"That ***BITCH"***, cried Betty! Chris and I were on the same boat, but we were ***not*** *with* each other; I was a waitress in the main dining room and he played in the orchestra. After hours when all the guests had departed, the musicians, food and beverage manager and waitresses would sit around tables and tell jokes or talk about the war etc. but Chris and I were definitely not *with* each other, like that bitch implied...but there must be more to the story as to why you came back from the war as a different man than the one who left; for instance being locked up in solitary confinement over two years.

"Let's start from the beginning," said Bill. "Mary and I returned to that little village in Belgium and to the house where we were hidden in the attic. Mrs. Knaaper was there and she told us her husband was the collaborator who had turned us in to the Gestapo. She then pointed to the mantel and I saw the straw-stuffed horse you gave me for luck. I told Mary my mother had given it to me."

"When I asked how she knew about her husband she told me of some clues she noticed on the night of the arrest and when he started arriving home with food that settled it in her mind. She told me she ate the food only to stay alive long enough to turn him in when it all ended; always wondering how many other victims were captured due to his traitorous actions. And she did turn him in. He was beaten to death like all the known male collaborators in the town square on one given day. All the women who had slept with Germans had their hair shaved off and their heads painted orange."

"Wow," said Betty

Bill carried on, "Since we were captured by the Gestapo we were dropped off at one of their stalags. It was a rectangular shaped concrete building with one door on each end. When they were escorting me to my cell I noticed about twenty-five cell doors on each side of a long hallway. Once inside, they opened two cell doors, and pushed each of us into one. The door to the hallway was heavy steel with a two by six inch hinged steel window for them to look in and check on us. There was another door at the outer side of the cell. It was hinged from the inside and had no window. We found out later this door was to an eight by eight square foot barbed wire chicken coup type enclosure. We were let out for half an hour once a day for fresh air, but never two prisoners at the same time. There was a 40 watt light bulb in the ceiling of our cells to provide light in the day. It was turned off in the evening."

"Talk about cruelty," said Betty.

"Inside the cell there was a water bucket and metal cup for drinking and another for toiletry but there was no tissue. If we wanted to wipe our rectums after defecation we had to use our fingers and clean them with water in the same bucket. At least they had a fortunate Jew come in to change the foul water daily; I say fortunate because at least he escaped the gas chambers."

"We had three foot high beds with a thin three inch thick straw-filled mattress, but no pillow. They threw in a thin wool blanket for warmth in winter; it didn't help very much. There was no fan to ease the extreme heat caused by the sun shining down on the roof in summer."

"We were fed a metal bowl of a porridge-based slop with bits of protein and other vitamins and minerals mixed in; twice a day – one at 8 am and the next at 8 pm.

He paused when he saw tears running down Betty's cheeks. "I think you have heard enough for today Bet. You can stay the night and we can address another issue this evening after supper, and then return to the story tomorrow morning."

"Good idea Bill.

AFTER SUPPER Bill said, "I'm so glad Herbie, as a young sailor, took the initiative to see the base chaplain and ask him to find my whereabouts. We kept in touch over the years and he came down to visit us in Carrying Place on several occasions. What caused his divorce?"

Betty said with a chuckle, "I'm so glad my mother passed on before it happened, so I wouldn't have to hear those dreadful words once again."

"What dreadful words Bet?"

She smiled and said, *"Like father; like son!"*

"Oh no!" cried Bill ... he looked at Betty's smiling face and then they both broke out in laughter.

"Betty, you always insisted that Lawrence was my son, but how could that be so? We hadn't made love since about Remembrance Day, and he was born in the third week of September 1948."

"You've forgotten Bill. Don't you remember that birthday party we attended at the mess in mid-January? We came home a little tipsy and made love."

Bill closed his eyes and searched his memory. Then he sprang to a straight sit up position, "Yes...Yes; now I remember and that must have caused the pregnancy."

Betty just nodded her head.

"Oh Betty, I'm so ashamed of myself. You must bring him up next weekend."

"I'll do that Bill, it will relieve him of pain and you of shame. I can assure you though he had a wonderful step-father who accepted both he and Herbie into his heart ... Lawrence too is on his second marriage. The cause is rather complicated for my small brain; all I can say though is to best of my knowledge it wasn't another *'Like Father, Like Son'* episode."

"Thank God for small mercies," said Bill.

There was a knock on the door and Bill's daughter walked in. She was surprised to see her father talking to a woman she didn't know. Bill said, "Susanne, this is Betty Simpson, my first wife. I sent her a letter last week and asked her to come because there were some things she didn't know about that caused our 1948 break-up."

"It's a pleasure meeting you Mrs. Simpson. I've come to take Mother to bed."

"Please simply call me Betty, Susanne, and it's a pleasure to meet you too."

After Susanne had departed Betty said, "Bill, Herbie told me you also had an adopted son. I think he said his name was Sammy. Where does he live and what does he do?

"We lost him about twenty years ago Betty."

"Do you mean he died?"

"Yes Bet, he died."

Oh no! What was the cause?"

"Sammy was a high spirited boy when he came into our lives. Once he reached adulthood he also became a little reckless. ... He and his wife Fiona were in Florida on vacation. One afternoon they were on a beach and Fiona asked him to run and fetch her a bottle of Coke. So he ran towards the stores on the other side of the street, but being reckless he jumped over a yellow plastic warning strip that said, 'DO NOT CROSS'. He was barefooted at the time and seared the bottoms of his feet on freshly lain asphalt. An ambulance was called, but the asphalt entered his blood stream. It had reached his heart and he died before the ambulance reached the hospital."

"The family must have taken the tragedy hard."

"Very hard Bet."

THE NEXT MORNING after breakfast Betty and Bill sat in the same armchairs. Bill started; "The next part is not as gruesome as yesterday Bet."

"I'm glad to hear that," she said.

"We worked out a code to communicate from cell-to-cell. It wasn't Morse code but a separate one we worked out together. We tapped it on the water pipe running between the cells. We discovered there were RAF and American airmen prisoners. We had to be extremely cautious because there was always a lower ranking Gestapo soldier sitting at one end of the cell block. One American was caught tapping on the pipe to the other cells when that soldier looked through the viewing window of his cell door. That soldier reported what he had seen to his officer. The next thing we heard was some loud yelling, presumably in the American's cell. He must have been stripped naked and given forty lashes. I counted each lash, but the American refused to cry out in pain. The officer kept crying out orders to the soldier; probably telling him to beat harder, but still no cries of pain, which must have infuriated our captors.

"But as you told us after you returned, you jumped from a cattle car a few months after D-Day, made your way to Amsterdam and were repatriated, and that's all that matters; except for the fact you weren't allowed to rejoin your squadron and fight to the finish."

"Yes Bet; that was the straw that broke the camel's back. I wanted so much to rejoin the fight."..."And I now realize that upon return I was suffering from 'Post Traumatic Stress Disorder', which wasn't recognized until the 1980s, due to what I had gone through and the thoughts of the one I loved so much having an affair with her first cousin."

"In around 1952 an article in the *Toronto Star* caught my attention. The title of it read, 'German WW2 Prisons of War in USA'. A picture showed five German prisoners leaning on the fence of a farm; they were all smiling. As I read the accompanying article I was filled with mixed emotions – envy; jealousy; and anger. According to the story, these prisoners were transported across the Atlantic to fill the void in the farmlands which was caused when American boys joined the forces to fight."

"They weren't paid, but were housed in comfortable barracks and well fed. Those who the authorities considered trustworthy were allowed to go to town unaccompanied, with a curfew set at 11 pm. Some had American girlfriends. After the war ended and Germans were allowed to emigrate they returned to the US and married those girlfriends."

Betty left for home at 1pm with a promise to come back the next weekend and to bring Lawrence along. Before she left however, she said "Lawrence also has prostate cancer and is undergoing chemotherapy, which has to be carried out at the same time each day. For that reason he may only be able to come up for a brief period on his own before or after his treatment time."

"I can live with that," said Bill.

WHEN BETTY ARRIVED on the following Saturday she said, "Lawrence's chemo appointment is at a rather incon-venient time; 2 pm. We can expect him around four and if you have another room, he can stay the night and depart at around 11 am on Sunday. That'll give you time to get familiar."

"Perfect Bet…Let's sit down again; there's so much more I need to say."

After taking seats in the same arm chairs Bill continued, "Betty, I have never stopped loving you. I kept track of everywhere you lived over the years."

"How did you manage to do that Bill?"

"Through the grapevine Bet. For instance I know you married Charles Elliot in 1953 and shortly after moved to Hudson, Quebec, then Clarkson, Ontario. When I was Prime Minister Lester Pearson's personal pilot, whenever we overflew Clarkson I'd look down and said to myself *'She lives right down there'*."

He continued, "I know that Charles was a wonderful man as was Jimmy Simpson. Remember, he and your best friend Heather got engaged before Jim joined the Army when war was declared. They decided to wait for his safe return until they married.

I ran into them by chance at a conference held at 'The Canadian Legion of the British Empire Service League – now the Royal Canadian Legion – in Trenton in around 1955. I took Heather aside and told her how much I missed you and that I wanted to meet up with you; even if it was in old age, to clarify some things that led to our 1948 divorce, but I couldn't while your parents were still alive.

She informed me of addresses of all the places you lived over the years.

"But how did you know I married Jimmy? Heather had passed away.

"She must have told her daughter Dianne to carry on the correspondences after she passed on."

"She *is* a wonderful step-daughter," said Betty. "She's been taking such good care of me ever since Jimmy passed away."

Lawrence arrived right on time at 4 pm. Again there was a tearful hug. Father and son sat in the same armchairs earlier occupied by Betty and Bill and got to know each other. Betty sat on the sofa and added inputs when she thought it necessary; for instance what a great athlete Lawrence was in his high school days. The conversation continued over supper and to 10 pm until they all retired for the night.

At 1 pm on Sunday afternoon Lawrence and Betty drove away in different directions – Betty towards Orillia and Lawrence towards his house north of Burlington.

Betty promised to return the following weekend.

ON THEIR THIRD WEEKEND together Betty said, "Bill, here's an interesting coincidence Herbie once told me about...Back in the year 2000 he was driving back to his home in Ottawa from a contract he had completed on the west coast navy base and stopped in Regina for the night. The day before his arrival there had been an event called the 'Millennium Symposium on Science, Society & Human Rights'."

"The next morning he walked into the dining room of the hotel where he was staying. All tables were occupied since there were so many people who had attended the symposium staying there. He saw a table occupied by only one person, so he walked over, introduced himself and asked the gentleman if he could join him."

"The gentleman introduced himself as Major General retired something or other and said, 'Please do'. By the look of his tanned complexion and his accent Herb assessed he was from India."

"Herb asked the general if he was in town for the Symposium and he replied, 'Yes indeed. I was one of the keynote speakers. My topic was 'The Demographic Dynamic of the 21st Century', or something like it."

"Herb told the general he was also a retired military man; a sailor, but a noncommissioned officer, but both his natural father and also his step-father had been officers. He told him his step-father was an army engineer during World War II, but retired when it ended, but his natural father – an air force forward gunner cum bomb aimer had remained in the air force after the war ended. He added you had once been Prime Minister Lester B. Pearson's personal pilot, and towards the end of your career you commanded a UN Peace Keeping contingent in Gaza."

"The general said, 'That was a joint Canada/India contingent and I was there. What was your father's name?'

"When Herb said, 'William Cunningham' the general replied 'I remember him, but your father didn't command that contingent; he was stationed with the RCAF in – I forget the name', but it was down close to the western side of the border of Egypt and Gaza."

"Herb asked if he knew you personally and the general said, 'Oh, I crossed paths with him in the UNEF headquarters where I was stationed, and exchanged a few words with him when headquarters staff went down to the place where the RCAF was stationed for Canada's Centennial celebration on 1st July 1967'."

"Herbie told the general that he intended to visit a Himalayan foothill town called Dharamsala someday, as his step-grandfather had stayed there for a few years after World War I.

"They exchanged business cards and the general told Herbie, if he did visit Dharamsala he'd have to land at Indira Gandhi International Airport in New Delhi. He advised him to stay a few days; give him a call or send him an email and they could meet at the Foreign Correspondent's Club. He also said, Delhi was worth exploring and then there was the Taj Mahal, which is India's greatest tourist attraction only 200 km to the south.

"That was indeed an interesting coincidence Bet," said Bill..."The place he mentioned was Rafah and it was just inside Gaza about

6 km from the coast of the Mediterranean. I retired shortly after I returned home."

Betty and Bill had spent three wonderful weekends together until...

"DAD HAD A HEART ATTACK," said Susanne as Betty picked up her ringing phone on Friday 21st November 2008.

"Oh no!" cried Betty. "Is he in hospital?"

"Yes," said Susanne, "He's in Kincardine and District General on Golf Links Road. If you plan to come, just ask anyone on the street for directions; it's well known."

"Thanks Susanne, I'm on my way."

William Cunningham died peacefully on Monday 24th November 2008 with his former wife Betty Simpson at his bedside holding his hand. He was in his 88th year.

Herbert could not attend his father's funeral as he was working on a contract at the naval base in Portsmouth and wouldn't have made it home in time. His daughter Wendy, a sergeant in the Royal Canadian Regiment accompanied her grandmother to the funeral. Wendy was dressed in her full dress uniform and when the military taps were played as the coffin was lowered into the grave she stood at attention and saluted.

Wendy had served in combat in Afghanistan and also on several UN peace keeping missions. At the celebration of life in the mess that followed the funeral several old veterans approached her and asked if all her medals were for merit or actual combat. Wendy explained the significance of each.

While she was serving in Afghanistan she lost nine fellow infanteers[2], including her Regimental Sergeant Major. Herbert wrote the following poem while she was there:

## Wendy Please be Careful

There's a girl I love who's in harm's way.
That girl is Corporal Wendy.
She's a pretty thing as some might say,
And leader - firm and friendly.

She broke the mould at an early age.
Now she strives to do her best.
I was proud then but more at this stage,
As she wears protective vest.

She has helped to enforce freedom earned,
In those war-torn lands afar.
She will employ many lessons learned,
As she serves in Kandahar

I've watched her grow from a little girl,
To a soldier strong and true.
She now stands proud as colours unfurl,
In a land where terror grew.

The Taliban are a deadly foe,
As they brawl in Allah's name.
While cause is wrong and forces grow,
Allah *negates* their foul game.

We dispatch our young to fight our wars.
The mission is still undone.
We'd welcome them back on friendly shores.
Of course *they* won't cut and run.

Look, a dog's corpse on the road ahead.
It could be a booby trap!
They'll try anything; they want her dead,
But that's not in her road map.

You're at the front of the War on Terror.
Oh Wendy please be careful.
Stick to the book, no trial and error.
Your Daddy's ever prayerful.

SHORTLY AFTER WILLIAM Cunningham's passing Betty sold the house in Orillia and moved in with her daughter Margaret Watson in Calgary Alberta. Margaret had also been widowed when a few years earlier her husband Ronald had passed away.

❄❄❄❄

"IF THE TOP OF YOUR HEAD was a forest Mom a wood-pecker would have to pack a lunch," said Herb who was visiting his mother and two sisters – Margaret and Josephine – in Calgary. He had just entered the living room and approached his mother from behind. She was sitting in an easy chair and he started massaging the top of her head, but when he looked down and saw her thinning hair he made the outrageous statement. Needless to say it brought laughter to all present in the room including Betty, the target of the ridicule.

Shortly after her arrival in Calgary, Betty learned that Bill had thought of her in his will. The will predated his 'come to me in Kincardine' letter. He left her $25,000. She promptly sent both Herbert and Lawrence a cheque for $10,000 each. She kept five thousand for herself.

After living with her daughter Margaret for a year and a half Betty chose to move into a luxury retirement home called 'Amica at Aspen Woods'. After all, she could afford it, with Jimmy's pension and life insurance, and Charles's life insurance, plus her Old Age Security (pension) from the government rolling in monthly.

Herb visited his mom at Amica in 2010 and found she had made another close friend; a man simply known to the family as 'Bob'; a tall slim 95 year old. At first the two sat alone at a two-person table in the dining room, but Bob's son thought his father may fall in love with Betty and marry her, thus reducing his inheritance. He put a stop to their sit-together dining. They then sat at tables with others, but every lunch time whoever arrived at the door to the dining room first would wait for the other.

One day during his visit Herb asked Bob, "Are you a war veteran Bob?"

"Yes," he said, "the Royal Canadian Navy."

"Oh; I served twenty-five years in the navy, but all 'Cold War'. What class of ship did you serve on Bob?"

"Just one of those little corvettes," said Bob.

"Canada built 132 corvettes for the war Bob and they were the backbone of the fleet. They may have been small but they were heavily armed and escorted all troop and cargo ships across the Atlantic to serve the war effort. So please don't describe your contribution to the war as *'just'* again."

"Yes," said Bob, "my last ship was HMCS Sackville and we did sink a couple of German U-boats."

"The Sackville you say; she is the last Canadian World War II ship still floating and is the 'Naval Memorial'. She is berthed at Historic Properties on the Halifax waterfront every summer and is open for people to take tours."

"Interesting," said Bob.

CRASH; BANG. "OH NO," cried Betty Simpson as she lay on the floor moaning.

"Nanny; Nanny, I told you to wait until I came out of the toilet and I'd help you get into your wheelchair," cried Herb's daughter Anne who was visiting her grandmother at Amica.

"I think I have broken my hip," said Betty in a more calm tone.

Under normal circumstances, when Betty was to get into her wheelchair, she'd press a button by her bedside and an attendant would come to her room and lend assistance. Betty, however, being a proud woman thought this totally unnecessary, but she was obviously wrong. She had attempted the task while Anne was in the toilet.

Anne promptly pressed the button and phoned reception. She told the attendant what had just happened. Soon a wheeled stretcher arrived at her door. They wheeled her down to the lobby and Amica's ambulance was waiting at the door. Anne jumped into the back portion of the ambulance and consoled her moaning grandmother. Upon arrival at the hospital emergency room the doctors where waiting and confirmed Betty's fears. She had broken her hip. She remained in that hospital for six weeks.

Anne had to return to her place of employment in Nova Scotia shortly after the accident, but one of Betty's daughters, either Margaret or Josephine, visited her every day.

Upon release, Amica officials said they had no facilities to take care of a person in Betty's condition; she'd have to move to another home. Her daughters found one and took her there. Betty was 91 years old at the time.

One day when both daughters were present she said to them, "Girls I know my time in this world is limited. My younger sister Molly died at age 89 and my mother lived till 95. When I go I don't want a gloomy old funeral. I want you to celebrate my life. Tell stories; make the attendees laugh. Have a good time. And when I am on my death bed with no hope of recovery *do not* allow anyone to stick a needle into me to keep me alive. Just let me die in peace."

Both daughters agreed.

IN 2014 HERB VISITED his elderly mother for her 92nd birthday, as did her youngest son Walter. Of course Margaret and Josephine were also present.

"Let's go to Lake Louise" said Margaret. "It's only an hour and a half drive."

"OK," said Betty, so off they drove.

Lake Louise, named 'Lake of the Little Fishes' by the Stoney Nakota First Nations people, is a glacial lake within Banff National Park in Alberta.

It is named after the Princess Louise Caroline Alberta (1848–1939), the fourth daughter of Queen Victoria and the wife of the Marquess of Lorne, who was the Governor General of Canada from 1878 to 1883.

The emerald colour of the water comes from rock flour carried into the lake by meltwater from the glaciers that overlook the lake.

Members of the family wheeled Betty around the paved area in front of the Fairmont Chateau in her wheelchair. A passerby took a picture of the group with Herb's camera. This was Herb's first visit to Lake Louise and he was mesmerized by the emerald coloured lake with the glaciered peaks in the background; he had a hard time taking his eyes off them.

Later the group went into the Chateau for lunch. Once seated Margaret excused herself as if she had to go to the toilet; but instead she went to the head waiter and told him about the ninety-second birthday party and ordered a birthday cake. After the main course the head waiter whispered something to neighbouring tables.

When the cake arrived the family and all surrounding tables sang 'Happy Birthday to you'.

HERB OPENED HIS EMAIL on 7th November 2014. There was one from his sister Margaret saying, "The doctors say Mom has three days at best to live and advised anyone who wants to say their final farewell to come soon."

When Herb arrived he saw the skeleton of the woman he had only seen five months earlier. She looked horrible. He was the last of his siblings to arrive. He threw himself onto the bed beside her, took her hand and spoke loudly into her left ear; loudly because she wasn't wearing her hearing aids. He said, "It's Herbie Mom. I'm here. We're all here now. You can leave us whenever you're ready." Once finished he felt a slight squeeze of his hand. He wept shamelessly.

Members of the family rarely left their mother. Sometimes one or two of the siblings would sleep on wheeled stretchers in the hallway.

At approximately 10 am on 10$^{th}$ November 2014, Betty went into the death breathing mode. The nurses elevated the back of her bed to a 45 degree angle and laid Betty in that position. When asked how long the death breathing would last the nurses said, "Anywhere up to sixteen hours."

Josephine was constantly taking her mother's pulse and at precisely 19:22 she said "She is gone."

All her children gathered around their deceased mother and bawled their eyes out.

A couple of days later while Margaret and Josephine were arranging the celebration of life, Herb found himself sitting alone with his three brothers – David, Lawrence and Walter. He said, "Fellows we all remember our alone time with Dad when he was on his death bed back in 1994."

"Yes," they said.

"Well in my private time, Dad said there had always been a place he wanted to visit, but hadn't had the time. It was a place in India called Dharamsala in the Himalayan foothills; a place where our grandfather on Dad's side of the family had lived for a few years after the First World War." He went on to tell them all the things his dad had mentioned and then asked, "Would guys like to accompany me on a trip to Dharamsala?"

David was the first to answer. He said, "I have just had to re-invent my print factory to keep up with my competition. Ask me again in a couple of years Herb. The idea sounds intriguing, but I have too many debts at the moment."

Walter declined too saying, "I have just erected another building for my business and am also financially strapped at the moment. But like David said, ask me in a couple of years because the idea certainly does interest me as well."

Lawrence said, Emma and I are saving up for a trip to Paris. I think another costly trip would be a little too soon, even if in a couple of years from now.

TWO IDENTICAL CELEBRATIONS of life were held – one in a funeral home in Calgary and one in the Mississauga Golf and Country Club near Clarkson, where one of David's sons was a member. The one in Mississauga had the most attendees; many old friends from their neighbourhood were present. This may have been because the obituary in the *Globe and Mail* started with the words 'Bettina Elliot/Simpson at Herb's suggestion.

Once everyone was seated Josephine took the floor. She stated, "Folks we are here to celebrate the life of Bettina Simpson; known to most of you as Betty Elliot. When Mom entered her nineties she stated to us that her days on this earth were limited, she wouldn't live forever. She then stated she didn't want a gloomy old funeral when she died. She wanted a celebration – laughter and fun for all. So this may be a little untraditional from what you are used to. Now let's get the religious part behind us with Mom's favourite hymn. The speakers rang out with *'How Great Thou Art'*.

After the hymn Herbert took the podium. He said, "Hello Folks, I am Herbert Elliot, better known to most of you as 'Herbie'. I was Mom's first born and am the third oldest of the Elliot brood. 'First born and third oldest you ask; how could that be?' Well, you see, ours was a typical 'yours, mine and ours' family. Let's start with Mom. I was born in 1945 and my brother Lawrence was born in 1948, but Mom divorced my natural father shortly afterwards. Then she married the late Charles Elliot, a widower with two children of his own – David born in 1940 and Margaret born in 1943. That accounts for the 'yours and mine'. The 'ours' came in 1956 with the birth of Walter – the namesake of his grandfather – and again in 1960 with Josephine; who as it happened, is the namesake of our beloved grandfather Joseph Benning who passed away only eighteen hours after her birth."

He went on to introduce his adult daughters Anne, Denise, and Wendy; and explained his navy son Edward was not present because he was on an 'Emergency Responders' course in Halifax after the recent Jihadist attack at the Canadian Parliament buildings, and could not be spared. He also introduced his nine year old granddaughter Abigail and twenty-six year old grandson Brandon.

After the introductions he told funny stories about his mother, including the one about *'a woodpecker would have to pack a lunch'* which got a great laugh. He ended by singing the last few lines of Kris Kristofferson's song 'Loving Her':

*Coming close together with a feeling that I've never known before, in my time; in my time,*
*She weren't ashamed to be a woman or afraid to be a friend.*
*I don't know the answer to the easy way she opened every door in my mind; in my mind,*
*But dreaming was as easy as believing it was never gonna end;*
*And loving her was easier than anything I'll ever do again.*[3]

Herb walked back to his seat with a tear in his eye. The attendees clapped.

His sister Josephine's story outdid the woodpecker story by two to one. After reintroducing herself she said, "Once when I was about five I was attempting to skip on the front porch and when I messed up I exclaimed, '*Jesus*!'. Mom was in the kitchen and overheard. She came to the door and said, 'We don't use that word when we make mistakes Dear,' and went back inside. I messed up again and said, '*Jesus*'. Mom came to the door again and said, 'The next time I hear that word you'll get the wooden spoon'. I messed up again, and again said '*Jesus*'. She was at the door in a flash wielding the wooden spoon. I then looked up with innocent eyes and sang, '*...loves me this I know; for the Bible tells me so*'. That broke up the house.

After all siblings had finished their stories the six-some took centre stage in front of the attendees. Margaret was the orator. She said, "This is the story of the crooked mouth family that Mom used to tell...I am the mother and I talk out of the left side of my mouth; Herbie is the father and he talks out of the right side of his mouth. Walter a dump truck driver talks upward. Josephine a cotton picker speaks downward, and Lawrence a common labourer speaks every which way. David, the only one of the family who speaks normally has a university education."

She went on, "Now, the crooked mouth family had been sitting around a candle reading verses from the Holy Bible. Once finished it was time to blow out the candle. In pantomime Mama tried, but she blew out of the left side of her mouth and the candle was still burning. She passed it to Papa and said, 'Here Pop give it a try', but no results. The candle was consecutively passed around with no results until David got his chance. He had the straight mouth and blew the candle out with no problem. Then Papa exclaimed, 'Now you kids see why I'd been telling you all these years about the value of getting a university education'."

As a closing of the celebration David and Josephine took centre stage. Josephine asked, "Has anyone ever heard that laughter is contagious?" Most of the attendees nodded their heads.

Then the two of them started with small giggles. They increased the intensity of their giggles to slight laughter, then to all-out laughter. From the beginning some of the attendees started laughing. By the time the skit ended the whole auditorium was roaring in deep laughter.

David then announced, "That ends the celebration of life for our dear Mother. I do think she would be happy with the results. Now please join the family for tea, coffee or cocktails in the bar."

One old friend of the family named Ruth told Herb, "That was the best celebration of life I have ever attended, and I have attended far too many in my day."

# Notes

1. Shortly after the American departure the Viet Cong overran Saigon and by 1996, Vietnam was a prospering communist member of the Association of Southeast Asian Nations (ASEAN).
2. A new word created after women were allowed to serve in combat.
3. https://youtube.com/watch?v=HCgnRWVvU8.

# Twenty one

**"ARE YOU READY BROTHERS?"** ask Herb in a conference call to his brothers David and Walter in June 2018.

"Ready for what?" asked Walt.

"Remember three and a half years ago just after Mom passed away I mentioned a place in India called Dharamsala where our grandfather on Dad's side of the family, Walter Elliot had spent time after World War I? Dad told me he had always wanted to visit that place. I asked you fellows if you'd like to join me on a visit, but neither of you could at the time due to your businesses. You both said, 'Ask me again in a few years,' so here I am asking again."

He continued, "As you both know I've been living in a boarding house on my old age pension and half my military pension and my Canada Pension Plan money for quite a while now, but I have saved $10,000 from my contracting days to spend on the trip.

"Why half your military pension Herb?" asked Walt.

"Because Marylyn gets the other half by the laws of the land; so are you guys still with me or do I go alone?"

"I'm ready" said David,

"Me too," said Walter. "When do you suppose is the best time?"

"I'd suggest the end of August as it starts to cool down by then. We could stay for a month or so, and return before the foothills get too cold. While in Delhi we could also visit the Taj Mahal. And there's a retired Indian major general I met in Calgary about six years ago. He told me to give him a call if I ever visited New Delhi."

Walter interjected saying, "Who'll be the coordinator?"

"Ok," said David, "Herb you come up to Burlington in mid-August and stay with me and Walter you can simply come to my place on the day of departure. The coordinator in my office will arrange the flight."

Everything was arranged; the threesome departed from Toronto at 10:45 pm on KLM on 28th August 2018. They arrived in Amsterdam at 11:55 am the next day. After a 2.5 hour layover they boarded another KLM flight to Delhi arriving at 1 am on 30th August.

There was, however, a problem. During the flight across the Atlantic Herb had no problem urinating; nor were there problems at Amsterdam airport. But during the long flight from Amsterdam to Delhi – made longer due to the fact they were flying in the same direction the earth rotates– Herb could not urinate, no matter how hard he tried. He really felt the urge, but when he went to the toilet at mid-ships of the jumbo jet, nothing would come out. It was very painful.

He reported the situation to his two brothers and both agreed this seemed to be serious. As soon as they arrived at Indira Gandhi International Airport in New Delhi and had gone through customs, and collected their baggage they stepped outside and went to the UBER taxi stand. David said, "Take us to emergency at the closest hospital."

Off the driver sped. Then Walter saw a sign on top of a building saying lgna Hospital.[1] It was at quite a distance away and the traffic was heavy so Walter had time to look them up on Google search using his smart phone. He said "It seems to be a good one; they have multiple branches throughout the city." He said to the driver, "Take us to Igna Hospital Emergency entrance."

David paid the taxi and was astonished the bill was only the equivalent of three Canadian dollars.

The three brothers walked directly into emergency and told the doctor on duty Herb's problem. The doctor and his assistant stuck a thin tube up Herbert's penis and into his bladder. The thin tube was attached to a larger tube with a bag on the end. Herb cried, "Success," as his bladder drained into the bag. He then asked the doctor, "Can we go now?"

The doctor replied, "You *can*, but I wouldn't advise it.

"Why's that?"

"This is a symptom of prostate cancer. I'd like to admit you and when our technicians arrive in the morning, put you through a series of tests including a CT scan. What is your nationality?"

Walter stepped into the conversation saying, "We're Canadians and have just arrived from the airport." He turned to Herb and asked, "Do you have a provincial medical insurance plan in Canada?"

"No," said Herb, "I just thought it would be a waste of money."

'You dumb fuck; our grandfather died of prostate cancer; your natural father had it but a heart attack took him first, and your only natural brother Lawrence had it, but survived thanks to his OHIP (Ontario Health Insurance Plan). Couldn't you see the handwriting on the wall? No need to answer."

He then turned to the doctor and asked, "Is there a good hotel in the vicinity?"

"Yes," said the doctor, "There's a Radisson Blu not far from here."

Walt then turned to David and said, "Let's escort Herb up to his room and make sure he's settled in properly and then go to the Radisson for the night. We can come back at around 10 am and see how things are going."

"Ok Walt, everything you've said so far makes sense to me."

The doctor said, "I'd advise the two of you to book about a week at the Radisson. This may take time, especially if an operation is required."

After Herb was settled in the three brothers had some alone time in the hospital room. David said, "Do you think it's advisable to have an operation here in India? Do they have all the capabilities of Canadian hospitals?"

Herb said, "I've done my research. You both are carrying laptops in your carry-on baggage. Check the website of Indian tourism. You will find a tab marked 'medical tourism'. Hundreds of westerners with no medical insurance come to India annually for professional treatment, including operations. India is just as equipped as hospitals in the West."

"Ok Herb," said David, "I'll take your word for it." The two able bodied brothers said 'good bye' to their ailing brother and departed.

By the time David and Walter arrived at 10 am they were told the CT Scan had already been carried out, and their greatest fears had proved correct. The doctor showed the brothers the negatives. Herbert Elliot had prostate cancer. The operation was scheduled for 5th September – four days from the present date.

On 5th September Herbert was wheeled to the operating theatre. After the doctor injected him to put him to sleep he said a childhood bedtime prayer his grandfather taught him as a little boy, *"Now I lay me down to sleep; I pray the Lord my soul to keep. If I should die before I wake take me to heaven for goodness sake."*[2] He then drifted off to sleep.

❄❄❄❄

"HELLO, HERBERT ELLIOT, we've been waiting for you."

"I'm not sure if I know you. Have we met before, and what do you mean by *we've*? Who are you talking about?"

"My name is Peter; most folks call me Saint Peter. Look to your left."

Herbert said, "Oh I get it; the halo should have been a dead giveaway." He then looked to his left and said, "Wow, are all those pearls on that gate real or fake?"

"They are all real Herbert, there is nothing fake in *this* world."

Saint Peter then took Herbert's hand and said, "Let's walk through the Pearly Gates and into the reception hall."

They walked through the gates. Once through Herb saw a long line of people standing across the hall, and two figures standing out front; the two out front were his mother and his granddad. Saint Peter released Herb's hand and walked back through the gate. Herb ran to his mother and threw his arms around her. Tears rolled down his cheeks as he said, "Mom, Mom I have missed you so much since you left us"..."By the way; you held the hands of three former husbands when they died. Which one do you sleep with?"

His Mom laughed and said, "We alternate, but the one I was married to the longest gets the lion's share...I was married to Bill seven years, so he gets seven nights. I was married to Jimmy for six years so he gets six nights; and I was married to Chuck for forty-one years so he gets that number of nights. They worked it out on their own with...I can't say above because we are *already* above, but I can say with a little coaching."

After some laughter Herb then turned to his granddad threw his arms around him and said, "Granddad; Granddad; you have been on my mind ever since you sadly departed in 1960. I had a photograph of you by my bedside for the past 30 years."

"I have a question Granddad," but he hesitated.

"Go ahead Herbie. Spit it out."

Herb asked, "Granddad, have you been watching me all these years?"

His granddad looked down and said with a chuckle, "That's a marble floor Herbie not a glass window, but who told you I've been watching you?"

Herb smiled and said, "Take a guess Granddad." He continued, "Thank goodness you haven't because during my life on Earth

Granddad I did some things that would have disappointed you, but I have always believed in God Almighty and that is why I am here with you at this moment."

They both escorted Herbie to the others waiting. They started in the centre. "Nanny, Nanny, I see you are holding my father Bill Cunningham's hand," he said as he threw his arms around her."

"Yes Herbie," she replied, "All is forgiven here in Heaven."

He stepped to his left and hugged his natural father William Cunningham. He said, "Father, I'm so glad you sent a letter to Mom in your final weeks and tied up loose ends. Mom told me all about your encounters."

Bill said, "Herbie; I'm so happy to see you too. I'm glad you came in this direction upon departure from Earth. They say the other direction is mighty hot." They both laughed.

Bill was holding his mother's left hand. Herb stepped to the left and saw Granma Cunningham. He threw his arms around her and said, "Granma, it's so nice to see you again. The last time I saw you was when Mom married Charles Elliot and we moved to Hudson."

She said, "That's alright Herbie. Your father briefed me on your progress from boyhood to manhood after you contacted him in 1964."

"Did you finally tell Bill who his father was Granma? Yes Herbie, I did. He was..."

Herbie cut her short saying, "I don't want to know Granma. I'm just happy you told him."

They then moved back to the centre and saw his nanny holding the hand of his dad – Charlie Elliot. He said, "Nanny, you didn't approve of the fact that Dad drank so much beer in your presence; sometime even before breakfast, but I see you have accepted him now."

"Yes Herbie," she said, "all of that is forgotten now, and apart from the beer drinking he was a loving husband for your mother and a wonderful father for all of you."

Herb then threw his arms around his dad Charles Elliot and said, "Dad, Walter, David and I were on our way to Dharamsala that your father Walter Elliot told you about, but signs of prostate cancer appeared in my innards when we arrived in New Delhi. I must have passed away while under the scalpel."

His dad said, "I died from that disease too Herb, so David and Walter are also at risk."

Herb carried on, 'I see you have your arm around the shoulder of Jimmy Simpson. He loved Mom like you did Dad and took such good care of her during their short marriage."

Herb then hesitated while in front of Jimmy; he didn't know whether to shake his hand or give him a hug, because he never got ot know him well. He chose the latter.

There was a man standing beside Jimmy. He looked familiar but Herbert couldn't put his finger on who he was. Then it struck him like a lightning bolt. "Scott; Scott! You were my best friend until your wife Rose emailed saying you passed away. It came in the same month as my dear mother died. Your passing was a double whammy for me, a best friend and a mother dying within a few weeks of each other."

"Hi Herbie," said Scott. "I've been waiting for you. We'll be sharing the same quarters."

"I hope it's not racks (bunks) such as those on the Kootenay and Saguenay."

"No Herb," said Scott, "they're more like the double bedroom Captain's cabin. And there are even provisions for old matelows to make their accommodation pitch and roll as if they were at sea."

"Wow, I can't wait to experience that again."

"It's a fantastic feeling."

"Come, I'd like to introduce you to my family, including both of my fathers."

"You had two fathers Herb?"

"It's a long story Scott. I'll tell it to you some other time."

"You told me that the last time I asked you dunder-head."

"Ok; tonight."

## Notes

1. Totally fictitious name.
2. Author unknown.

# Epilogue

*The book you have just finished reading is factual fiction, which I described in the Preface. My epilogue, however, is all fact.*

Beauty; Recovery; Fun; Health; Summit Views; Red Wine; Solitude; Happiness; No Reason; Starry Skies; Restoration; Greener Planet; The Unknown; Serenity; Family Time; Wander; Peace of Mind; Escape; Inspiration; Balance; Green Tea – Yes, I've seen, done, missed, drank or wished for all of the above.

But, one evening a while back, I sat on the living room sofa in my Indian home staring at the book case against the wall in silent reflection. I had just been reading some of the poems in Robert Service's little book 'Songs of a Sourdough' and the words of the last verse of *'The Men That Don't Fit In'* haunted me:

*He has failed, he has failed; he has missed his chance;*
*He has just done things by half.*
*Life's been a jolly good joke on him,*
*And now is the time to laugh.*
*Ha, ha! He is one of the Legion Lost;*
*He was never meant to win;*
*He's a rolling stone, and it's bred in the bone;*
*He's a man who won't fit in.*

I asked myself *'have I failed; have I missed my chance; have I just done things by half?'* Oprah Winfrey once said: "*Think like a queen. A queen is not afraid to fail. Failure is another stepping-stone to greatness.*"

I'm not 'Bill Gates', one of the wealthiest of people in the world by any means, but I don't believe wealth is the only sign of success. Sometimes wealth can lead to sadness. Take a look at Donald Trump for goodness sake, the multi-billionaire and currently (*or previously*

*I hope*) the forty-fifth President of the United States of America. If he's not sad, in my opinion he's the saddest example of the leader of the world's mightiest nation I have seen in my lifetime. *I* am not a wealthy man by any means, but at least I am free.

I do admit I have a few skeletons in my closet, but I *am,* however, the father of four adults – two of whom have followed their father's footsteps into the military, and the other two are in administrative or supervisory roles in civilian life. And then there are four charming granddaughters, and an adult grandson making his own way in finding his proper niche in life. All of the above I love so much I would gladly give the last drop of my lifeblood to protect from harm.

Further, I have a beautiful Anglo-Indian wife for whom I'd also die. She loves me and that love is mutual. She constantly tries to keep me physically fit and encourages me to develop my mind. She often chastises me for not knowing what is going on around me as far as our publishing house business is concerned. She is correct. I simply do not have a business-oriented mind. I am more of the creative type. I am, however, an accomplished proofreader, editor, photographer and travel writer.

On the one hand I believe my predilection to be liked by those around me is one of my weaknesses, however, this does not bother me – it is simply a part of me and I know not how it was implanted into my being. On the other hand, I suppose it's better than having a predilection to be disliked by those around me.

While some of my Canadian friends think I am off my rocker, I am a staunch believer that 'Global Warming' is real. Bob Dylan won a Nobel Prize for his song 'Blowin in the Wind'. Within that song were the words...*'How many years can a mountain exist, before it is washed to the sea? How many times can a man turn his head and pretend that he just doesn't see'.* I believe that we have passed the point of no return – time is not running out...time has run out. An environmentalist friend of mine who lives in Delhi convinced me of this fact as he was keynote speaker in conferences I have been invited to attend in recent years, and in articles he contributes to our magazine on bilateral relations and current affairs.

I have travelled in my lifetime; mostly on business but often on pleasure. As I write these words I have visited 62 countries and in doing so I have developed the skill of travel-writing.

As Willie Nelson sang in his song 'My Heroes Have Always Been Cowboys,' I regret the fact that *'While picking up hookers instead of my pen, I let the words of my youth fade away'.* Well, as a youth I did *not* pick up hookers, but sadly neither did I pick up my pen. It's too late now to capture the words of my youth as they faded away more than sixty years ago and cannot be revived. Am I using too many quotations of others in my epilogue? I don't care...It's mine.

But I do have recent memories – mostly travel-related: I've walked through lush green forests of Canada, and jungles and savannahs of Africa. I've strode upon the deserts of Africa and Asia. I've gazed in awe at the glaciered peaks of the Rocky Mountains, the Swiss Alps and the Majestic Himalayas. I've seen Victoria Falls from both sides (Zimbabwe and Zambia). I've sat quietly with the 'Gorillas of the Mist' in Uganda. I've almost been a lion's lunch in Serengeti, and I've been chased away by an angry female elephant protective of her young. I've laid my eyes on the sources of the White and Blue Niles, their confluence on the Sudanese plains and the mouth of the Nile system at the Alexandria delta. I've walked amongst the great pyramids, and I've taken an overnight cruise boat trip up the Nile to Luxor and entered the three magnificent tombs of Abu Simbel. I've visited the monolithic rock churches at Lalibela in Christian northern Ethiopia, and have sat and conversed with the cave-dwellers of Sof Omar in Islamic southern Ethiopia. I have drifted past the Ghats of Varanasi – a city that predates the long gone Babylon – and watched the Hindu pandits wave flaming torches while chanting at the Holy Ganga, while the funeral pyres blazed one hundred metres downstream. I've walked up the *'Way of the Cross'* in central Jerusalem and stood in front of da Vinci's original *'Last Supper'* in Milan. I've admired the paintings of the masters of a bygone era in the State Hermitage Museum at St. Petersburg, Russia; I've sailed on several oceans and seas. I've stood on the Great Wall of China, and I have *Watched–the–Sun*–go–down–on–Galway–Bay.

Those listed above represent the most memorable, however there were many more. I have described most of my experiences and adventures in detail in travel stories I have written for client organisations – most of which were/are on contract for Delhi-based foreign diplomatic missions and Indian missions abroad. I also write investment promotion and bilateral relations articles for the aforementioned publications.

In my Preface I mentioned that halfway through the writing of this book signs of prostate cancer started to appear. After a biopsy they were confirmed. I was forced to stow my laptop at Chapter 10 while an operation was conducted, but a month later I picked it up again and continued writing.

So I don't think I have failed; I don't think I have missed my chance; I don't think I have just done things by half. I do hope this book will reinforce the fact...While on the subject of 'fact', I must mention all facts in this book are true – even though some of the characters and circumstances are fictional (factual fiction if you will). I researched everything that may not have been invented, used or existed, at the period (date) I am at in the book; such as Lee Enfield rifles used by British soldiers during WWI. I visited company websites and those of museums, and of course the Canadian and British Army, Navy and Air Force history websites. All Canadians know our country became a dominion in 1867, and most know Newfoundland and Labrador joined Confederation in 1949, but how many can tell me off the tops of their heads the year in which they became a Dominion? I discovered the fact by researching the website of the (now) Province of Newfoundland and Labrador. I even had email conversations with Barnstaple Municipality representatives in North Devon and Salvation Army headquarters in London; both in England; and the World War II Liberation Museum in Amsterdam.

It took me two years to write this book so stand by for the next one somewhere around 2020. And guess what; I already have the title in mind.

**William Hawke**
New Delhi
William.Hawke@gmail.com.